Vizcaya

Penn Studies in Landscape Architecture
John Dixon Hunt, Series Editor

This series is dedicated to the study and promotion of a
wide variety of approaches to landscape architecture, with
special emphasis on connections between theory and practice.
It includes monographs on key topics in history and theory,
descriptions of projects by both established and rising designers,
translations of major foreign-language texts, anthologies of
theoretical and historical writings on classic issues, and critical
writing by members of the profession of landscape architecture.

Vizcaya

AN AMERICAN VILLA
AND ITS MAKERS

Witold Rybczynski AND Laurie Olin

WITH PHOTOGRAPHS BY
Steven Brooke

PENN

UNIVERSITY OF PENNSYLVANIA PRESS
PHILADELPHIA

Publication of this volume was assisted by grants from
The Vizcayans and The Getty Foundation.

Printed in Canada on acid-free paper

10 9 8 7 6 5 4 3 2

Published by
University of Pennsylvania Press
Philadelphia, Pennsylvania 19104-4112

Library of Congress Cataloging-in-Publication Data

Rybczynski, Witold.
Vizcaya : an American villa and its makers/Witold Rybczynski and Laurie Olin ;
with photographs by Steven Brooke.
p. cm. (Penn studies in landscape architecture)
Includes bibliographical references (p.) and index.
ISBN-13: 978-0-8122-3951-5
ISBN-10: 0-8122-3951-2 (cloth: alk. paper)
1. Vizcaya Museum and Gardens (Miami, Fla.). 2. Gardens—Florida—Miami.
I. Olin, Laurie.
SB466.U7 V53 2003
2006041847

CONTENTS

MAPS AND ILLUSTRATIONS

AMP   Personal collection of Arva Moore Parks, Miami, Florida
AR   *Architectural Review*
MEH   Photograph by Mattie Edwards Hewitt
SB   Photograph by Steven Brooke
VMGA   Vizcaya Museum and Gardens Archive, Miami, Florida

MAPS

ILLUSTRATIONS

CHRONOLOGY

1859   James Deering is born in South Paris, Maine.

1874   Paul Chalfin is born in New York City.

1880   James Deering joins his father, William, and half-brother, Charles, in Evanston, Illinois, to found what will become the Deering Manufacturing Company.

1882   F. Burrall Hoffman, Jr., is born in New Orleans.

1888   Diego Suarez is born in Bogotá, Colombia.

c. 1890   William Deering and his wife start wintering in St. Augustine, Florida. They later move to Coconut Grove, where Charles and James visit, frequently staying at Brickell Point.

1893   The Deering Manufacturing Company has a major exhibit in the Hall of Industry of the World's Columbian Exposition in Chicago.

1900   James Deering arranges a prize-winning exhibit of Deering farm equipment at the Paris International Exposition.

1901   William Deering retires.

1902   The House of Morgan arranges a merger between competing McCormick and Deering companies to form the International Harvester Company.

1903–7   Hoffman studies architecture at the École des Beaux-Arts in Paris. During this period he also goes on a world tour with his brother, William.

1904–5   After studying painting at the École des Beaux-Arts, Chalfin works as curator at the Boston Museum of Fine Arts. He is a frequent guest of Isabella Stewart Gardner at Fenway Court.

1906–9   Chalfin travels in Europe on a Lazarus Fellowship in mural painting and stays at the American Academy in Rome.

c. 1906	Diego Suarez accompanies his widowed mother to her native Florence, where he enrolls at the Accademia di Belli Arti to study architecture.
c. 1908	James Deering retires.
	Charles Deering purchases land at Buena Vista and commissions O. C. Simonds to lay out a large garden. He adds Frank M. Button to the landscaping team and meets the plant explorer and botanist David Fairchild.
1909	Following an apprenticeship with Carrère & Hastings, Hoffman opens an architectural practice in New York City.
1910	James Deering meets Chalfin and engages him as artistic adviser.
	Charles Deering hires Clinton Mackenzie to design a Spanish-style villa at Buena Vista.
Summer 1910	James Deering and Chalfin travel in Europe, buying antiquities and planning a villa in Florida.
Winter 1910–11	Deering and Chalfin work on villa designs.
Spring 1911	Deering and Chalfin tour Italy, visiting Villa Rezzonico in Bassano del Grappa.
1912	Deering and Chalfin select Hoffman to be the architect of Vizcaya.
	Deering's purchases of antiquities continue.
December 1912	Deering buys 130 acres of land on Brickell Point in Coconut Grove with frontage on Biscayne Bay.
Winter 1912–13	Hoffman visits the site for the first time and begins work on design of the villa and overall site development.
1913	Charles Deering starts to buy land at Cutler, eventually assembling 200 acres. Two years later, he moves his winter home.
Summer 1913	Hoffman travels in the Veneto and visits villas there.
Fall 1913	Construction begins on the house at Vizcaya. Leases are obtained and quarries opened to supply building materials. A stone yard is established on the site.
1914	James Deering forms a committee to manage the project. Chalfin maneuvers to further limit the role of Hoffman and takes control of the Village and outbuildings while Hoffman continues to design them.
Spring 1914	Deering and Chalfin visit Florence and stay at Arthur Acton's villa, La Pietra. They are introduced to a young Colombian architect, Diego Suarez, who shows them around Florentine gardens and villas.

Fall 1914	Suarez accompanies Lady Sibyl Cutting to America and, with the outbreak of World War I, becomes stranded in New York City. He meets Chalfin, who hires him to work on garden design at Vizcaya.
1914	Deering purchases additional property to the south, and Chalfin proposes a lagoon with islands for this land.
	The north-south canal on the old South Miami Avenue right-of-way is completed, with a natural rock bridge at the entry drive. Barges begin to arrive with mature trees for planting.
	Deering commissions the boats *Nepenthe* and *Psyche*.
January 1915	Suarez visits the construction site and revises the landscape plan. Construction of engineering works, siteworks, and architectural work is in full swing. Chalfin begins work on the interior décor of the house.
Summer 1915	The exterior of the house is effectively finished, except for the troublesome east façade.
1915	Suarez is demoted to employee status but continues design development of garden and landscape elements in Chalfin's office. The *Blue Dog* houseboat is built. Suarez designs the Barge, and A. Stirling Calder is engaged to execute sculpture for the Barge. Construction of new South Miami Avenue, the farm buildings, gate lodges, and boathouse continues.
	Chalfin finishes the interior of the house.
1916	Suarez leaves the project.
Christmas Day 1916	Deering moves into Vizcaya.
1917	Deering announces that the estate must be finished within the next two years. The eastern gardens and parterres are completed; work continues on the Village and the Casino interior. Pumps for the garden waterworks are installed.
March–April 1917	John Singer Sargent stays with Charles Deering at Brickell Point and makes a series of watercolors at Vizcaya.
June 1917	Hoffman's contract is effectively terminated. He enlists in the army and goes to France to serve with the Corps of Engineers.
1917	*Architectural Review* devotes its entire July issue to Vizcaya. Articles also appear in *Vogue* and *Harper's Bazaar*.
1918	Chalfin produces a final plan for the south lagoon gardens. Work continues on the causeway between the piazza and the Casba. Work continues on the grottos, terraces, southern lake, the marine garden

and bridge, and the walkways. Gaston Lachaise is commissioned to make peacocks for the bridge.

Marion Davies and her mother are houseguests at Vizcaya. Davies meets William Randolph Hearst in Palm Beach.

1919   The Peacock Bridge is completed.

1920   The Village and parts of the gardens are opened to the public on weekends. Work continues on bridges, planting, and the lagoon gardens. Palms are transplanted from the abandoned Cape Florida project to the lagoon area. David Fairchild advises James Deering that he can have excess trees from the plantations at his brother Charles's estate at Cutler.

1921   Construction work on the Vizcaya gardens is finished.

March 1923   Deering's old friend, the painter Gari Melchers, and his wife, Corinne, visit Vizcaya.

1925   Charles Deering sells the Buena Vista property.

September 1925   James Deering dies on board the SS *City of Paris* returning from Europe.

1926   The Great Miami Hurricane. All Deering's boats are wrecked; the garden, and many outdoor sculptures and garden furnishings, are badly smashed up. The gardens are generally put back together, but with some significant losses of oaks. The hedges of the sea arms are ruined and not replaced. There are changes in the arrangement of sculpture and garden furnishing. Much of the native plants and palms survive, especially in the south lagoon area.

1927   Charles Deering dies in Miami.

1934–36   Chauncey McCormick invites Chalfin to oversee extensive repairs in the gardens, arrange the house, and write a guidebook.

1935   The estate is opened to the public on an occasional basis. Vizcaya is hit by two hurricanes, in September and November.

1945   The archdiocese of Miami purchases 130 acres of the Vizcaya estate, fills in the lagoon, and builds a hospital, a school, and a housing development.

1951   Dade County purchases the house and the remaining estate from the Deering nieces, who donate the interior furnishings of the house.

1952   Vizcaya is opened to the public as a museum.

1954   The *New York Times* publishes an interview with Chalfin in which he disparages Hoffman's contribution to Vizcaya. A retraction follows.

1956   Chalfin is made an honorary member of the American Institute of Decorators; the Florida South chapter of the American Institute of Architects gives him an award for Vizcaya.

1959   Paul Chalfin dies in Montclair, New Jersey.

1970   Tree planters on the barge are removed and concreted over.

1974   Diego Suarez dies in New York City.

1978   Replanting of hedge maze and portions of the garden by the landscape architect John Riordan.

1980   F. Burrall Hoffman, Jr., dies in Hobe Sound, Florida.

1986   Completion of project to enclose courtyard with glass.

1992   Hurricane Andrew. The mangrove areas are flattened, the Barge is smashed up, railings and terraces are damaged. Trees are broken up and stripped, especially the oaks. Further changes and loss of richness in planting as result of reconstruction. The house survives intact.

2005   Hurricanes Katrina and Wilma. The house suffers water intrusion and damage to the interior. Serious damage to the Barge and the yacht landing. The garden and tree canopy sustain extensive destruction.

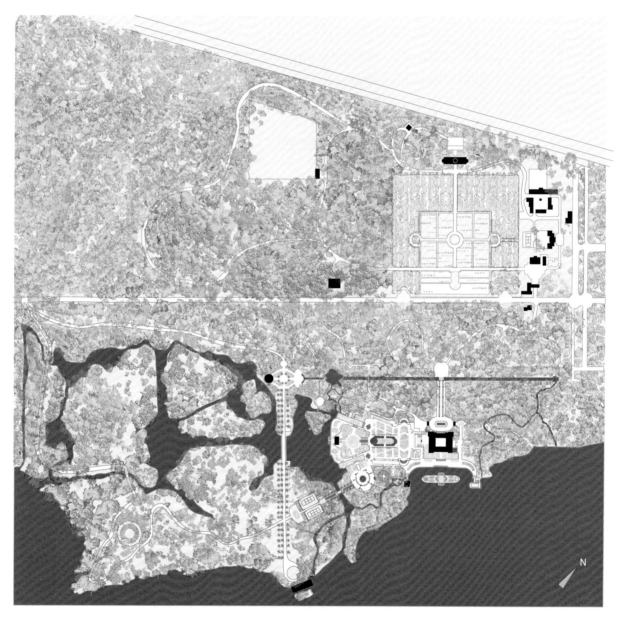

The Vizcaya Estate, 1921.

PART I
House

Witold Rybczynski

Prosperity is a condition of great achievements;
it is not their cause.

—GEOFFREY SCOTT, *The Architecture of Humanism*

chapter 1

AMERICAN RENAISSANCE

Vizcaya lies at the midpoint of a remarkable period in American architecture, when multimillionaires built palatial country retreats in fanciful emulation of the European past. Two celebrated houses serve as hefty bookends to this relatively brief episode: George Washington Vanderbilt's Biltmore, constructed in the mid-1890s, and William Randolph Hearst's San Simeon, which was substantially complete in 1925. The intervening three decades produced some of the most striking examples of conspicuous architectural consumption that the United States has ever seen—or is likely to see.

There were several reasons for this extravagance. During the last quarter of the nineteenth century, as a result of industrialization, population growth, and urbanization, the gross national product of the country surged dramatically. The new wealth was highly concentrated. Shipping, railroads, oil, steel, heavy industry, and manufacturing were controlled by powerful industrial trusts, which in turn produced vast family fortunes: Vanderbilt, Carnegie, Rockefeller, Morgan, and many more.

For the first time, wealthy Americans were among the richest people in the world. Uneasily aware of their parvenu status in comparison to titled Europeans, they appropriated many of the trappings and social customs of the Old World: horseback riding and foxhunting, shooting, yachting, art collecting, entertaining on a grand scale. As ever, great wealth found expression in great architecture. This meant not only opulent city mansions, but also palatial country estates—summer houses on Long Island, "cottages" in Newport, mansions along the Hudson and in the Berkshires, and winter places in the Carolinas and Florida. These homes were generally not country houses in the British sense but more like European villas—seasonal retreats occupied for relatively brief periods of time.

The Gilded Age was not merely attracted to Europe, it was obsessed with a specific period of European history—the Renaissance. The art historian and critic Bernard Berenson, who advised many aspiring Yankee Medicis on art collecting, wrote in 1894: "The spirit which

5

animates us was anticipated by the spirit of the Renaissance, and more than anticipated . . . . That spirit seems like the small rough model after which ours is being fashioned."[1] In 1922 Werner Hegemann and Elbert Peets, the authors of an important architectural and planning manual pointedly titled *The American Vitruvius*, wrote of a "modern revival of civic art," referring specifically to Renaissance classicism.[2] Harry W. Desmond and Herbert Croly, the authors of *Stately Homes in America*, an influential book published in 1903, were unapologetic about the palatial character of what they called the "modern American residence." They explicitly compared self-made American industrialists and businessmen to self-made Quattrocento Florentine merchants and bankers, describing Renaissance Italy—with some exaggeration—as "a rough democracy, in which any man who had the necessary luck, brains, and will, might struggle to the top and fight for the privilege of staying there."[3] Thus when American multimillionaires looked to the architectural legacy of Europe, they did so not merely as admirers or imitators, but rather as self-styled successors. It was this belief that gave them the self-confidence—some would call it sheer gall—that produced country estates such as Vizcaya.

Some contemporary observers found the spectacle of a fabulously wealthy elite creating latter-day palaces in the midst of a democratic republic unsettling, or at least bizarre. Henry James, who lived in Newport, Rhode Island, as a teenager, characterized its marble mansions as "white elephants." "They look queer and conscious and lumpish—some of them, as with an air of the brandished proboscis, really grotesque," he wrote, "[a] reminder to those concerned of the prohibited degrees of witlessness, and of the peculiarly awkward vengeances of affronted proportion and discretion."[4] Later critics were even more damning. "The essential character of all these culture seekers was that their heart lay in one age, and their life in another," wrote Lewis Mumford in high dudgeon. "They wanted, finally, to cover up the bleakness of their American heritage; and they did that, not by cultivating more intensively what they had, in fertile contact with present and past, but by looting from Europe the finished objects which they lacked."[5]

Mumford's protestations to the contrary, importing foreign ideas—and foreign architectural forms—had always been a part of being American. Even before Monticello and Mount Vernon, eighteenth-century American builders drew from the deep well of European architectural traditions, translating Palladio and Wren into wood and brick plantation houses. The nineteenth century looked farther afield. In 1832–35, on the shore of the Delaware, Thomas Ustick Walter built a house for Philadelphia banker Nicholas Biddle modeled on the Parthenon; in 1864 Alexander Jackson Davis rebuilt the Hudson valley country house of industrialist George Merritt to resemble a medieval English monastery. Even H. H. Richardson, whom Mumford admired, photographed Romanesque details during his frequent European travels and incorporated them into his burly designs.

Yet these early architectural imitations pale beside the country houses of the American Renaissance, which were larger, more sumptuous, and more fantastic in every respect. The unprecedented scale and architectural ambition of the great houses built between 1890 and 1925 give descriptions of them a Ripley's Believe-It-Or-Not quality: so many thousands of square feet of hand-rubbed mahogany, so many tons of Tennessee marble, so many alabaster columns, so many Venetian glass chandeliers. Such vulgar statistics detract from the considerable architectural achievements of the country-house builders, many of whom, like Richard Morris Hunt, Charles McKim, Thomas Hastings, and Horace Trumbauer, were the leading architects of the day. Their skills were many and varied: adapting European models to settings and landscapes that differed considerably from the original; integrating portions of antique architectural fabric—wall panels, portals, fireplaces—imported from Europe; incorporating twentieth-century conveniences such as central heating, elevators, and electric lighting; and using the latest building materials and techniques such as reinforced concrete and structural steel.

The country-house architects were masters at integrating the house with its gardens. Never before—or since—has American domestic architecture and landscape design been in such felicitous harmony. Here, too, the Renaissance offered useful lessons. "[The garden-lover] should observe, for instance, that the old Italian garden was meant to be lived in," advised Edith Wharton, "a use to which, at least in America, the modern garden is seldom put. He should note that, to this end, the grounds were as carefully and conveniently planned as the house, with broad paths (in which two or more could go abreast) leading from one division to another; with shade easily accessible from the house, as well as a sunny sheltered walk for winter; and with effective transitions from the dusk of wooded alleys to open flowery spaces or to the level sward of the bowling-green."[6]

The great country houses were works of intense collaboration, not only between architects and garden designers, but also between architects, decorators, and small armies of skilled craftsmen—plasterers, stonemasons, ironworkers, sculptors, cabinetmakers, upholsterers—for this was an age when building construction still involved considerable individual artistry. Not the least important of these collaborators were enlightened, informed clients, who had the taste to recognize what was good and beautiful, and who made this broad creative partnership possible.

Our infatuation with novelty makes it easy to denigrate the derivative architecture of the American Renaissance. James Marston Fitch expressed a near-universal view in 1973 when he dismissed the period as an "aesthetic wasteland" and its architecture as a "reactionary application of eclecticism . . . [that] ultimately smothered all traces of originality."[7] Eclectic this architecture certainly was, but originality was hardly smothered. These architects delicately trod a tightrope, balancing an admiration for the past with a desire not merely to copy but to explore and advance a particular architectural heritage. That is, to look both backward and forward. This sounds contradictory, but the test of a first-rate intelligence, as F. Scott Fitzgerald wrote, is the ability to hold two opposed ideas in the mind at the same time and still retain the ability to function. He was not referring to the country-house architects, but he might as well have been. Their complex works, too long ignored, bear closer, serious examination, and Vizcaya serves as the beau ideal of their peculiar but lasting achievement.[8]

chapter 2

DEERING'S TIME

Vizcaya is unusual, if not unique, among the great American country houses in one important respect. In general, the architects of these large and extremely expensive projects were old pros, seasoned practitioners of the first rank. They produced buildings that are best understood by studying their designers' oeuvre. For example, Biltmore reflects Hunt's intense preoccupation with the French Renaissance; The Elms, in Newport, is part of Trumbauer's lifelong exploration of French Neoclassicism; and Highlawn, in Lenox, Massachusetts, shows William Adams Delano's characteristic delicacy and his mastery of the Georgian Revival. Vizcaya, by contrast, is sui generis. It is the work of three neophytes: a failed painter and art scholar, whose creative legacy is chiefly this one great project; a young architect, who never built anything of similar consequence—before or after; and a twenty-five-year-old gardening dilettante who became involved in the project more or less by accident. Vizcaya is the serendipitous product of several imaginations, a true meeting of artistic minds. To understand its creation, it is first necessary to introduce the curious cast of characters that assembled and worked together at the dawn of the twentieth century on the palmy shore of Biscayne Bay.

The client first. James Edward Deering (1859–1925) was born in South Paris, a small inland town in southern Maine. He was the youngest son of William Deering, a successful wool merchant turned real estate developer and entrepreneur. In 1870 the father moved to Illinois to oversee an investment in a factory that produced farm machinery. Less than a decade later, he put all his capital—one million dollars—into an automatic hay-baling machine invented by John F. Appleby. Conventional baling machines used wire, whose discarded metal ends were ingested by grazing cattle with disastrous results. The novelty of Appleby's device lay in its use of sisal twine, which was harmless to cattle. William Deering took a big gamble and built three thousand machines in time for the 1880 harvest—and the orders came pouring in.[1] Overwhelmed, he called on his sons for help. James quit college and returned to Evanston.

His older half-brother, Charles, who had graduated from Annapolis and served twelve years in the navy in Europe and the Far East, resigned his commission. Together they founded what became the Deering Manufacturing Company.

The Deerings were not inventors, but businessmen—ambitious, aggressive, and hard driving. Their company grew by leaps and bounds.[2] By 1900 they employed nine thousand workers making binders, reapers, mowers, tractors, rakes, and corn harvesters—more than three hundred thousand machines a year—in a huge complex of buildings that covered 80 acres (fig. 1). Deering became one of the largest farm equipment manufacturers in the United States, almost as big as its chief competitor, the mighty McCormick Harvesting Machine Company, which had been in business for more than fifty years. "I knew William Deering, and Charles, and James quite well, in business and otherwise," recalled a Chicago competitor, John J. Glessner (the same Glessner who commissioned a famous house from H. H. Richardson in 1885). He called them "enterprising, broad-minded, and courageous men," and also described them as "punctilious and honorable in every way."[3] The last statement must be taken with a grain of salt, for the rough-and-tumble business world of the late nineteenth century was characterized by industrial espionage, cut-throat competition, and dirty tricks, at all of which the "punctilious" Deerings excelled. At one point, James Deering received secret reports from a spy in the McCormick organization. "We have had many opportunities to verify Mr. Daniel's statements, and have found them always absolutely truthful," Deering coolly assured his sales manager.[4]

Although old William Deering ran the company with an iron hand, his sons were active partners; Charles was secretary, James treasurer. According to Charles, James had "a thorough knowledge of the manufacturing side of the business . . . he was keenly interested in the experimental side of farm implement manufacture."[5] He was also involved in marketing, visiting sales agencies, and exchanging coded telegrams with far-flung company representatives in Paris, Odessa, and Buenos Aires. It was James who convinced his reluctant father and brother that in order to raise its international image the firm should participate in the 1900 Paris Universal Exposition, and it was he who made sure that the Deering exhibit outshone that of the rival McCormicks.

FIGURE 1. The Deering Works, Chicago, 1901. Nine thousand workers made binders, reapers, mowers, tractors, rakes, and corn harvesters in this vast factory. (Vizcaya Museum and Gardens Archive)

In 1901, at seventy-five, an ailing William Deering retired, leaving the company in the hands of his two (by now impatient) sons and his son-in-law, Richard Howe. The trio integrated the enterprise vertically, acquiring steel mills, iron mines, and coal fields. By this time Deering was engaged in an all-out "Harvester War" with its arch-rival, McCormick. It was a war without a winner, however, for the ruthless price-cutting threatened the financial health of both companies. Since neither side would retreat, the obvious solution was a merger, but several attempts fell through, since the two competitors distrusted each other. In 1902 the three sons of the late Cyrus McCormick asked George W. Perkins, a newly minted partner of J. P. Morgan & Company, to negotiate a merger with the Deerings. Perkins successfully consolidated McCormick, Deering, and three smaller harvester manufacturers. At the time of the merger, McCormick was valued at $37.7 million, and Deering at $31.6 million.

The so-called combination was a creature of the House of Morgan, which had already engineered such industrial trusts as U.S. Steel and General Electric. "The new company is to be organized by us," Perkins boasted to his boss, "its name chosen by us; the State in which it shall be incorporated is left to us; the Board of Directors, the Officers, and the whole outfit left to us."[6] The "outfit," which Perkins christened International Harvester, was capitalized at $120 million (almost $2.5 billion in modern dollars), controlled 85 percent of the American market, and operated internationally.[7] Among American corporations, only U.S. Steel, Standard Oil of New Jersey, and the American Tobacco Company were larger.[8] International Harvester was run as an industrial trust, overseen by Cyrus H. McCormick, Jr., as president, Charles Deering as chairman of the board, and Perkins. James Deering was first-ranking vice president, responsible for the three vast Chicago-area plants; the other vice presidents included Glessner and Harold F. McCormick, Cyrus's younger brother. Howe was secretary and treasurer.

The Deerings were no bluff midwestern industrialists. For one thing, they were unusually interested in the arts. When Bernard Berenson made his 1903–4 tour of the eastern United States, seeking out wealthy potential patrons, two of the prominent Chicagoans he met during a private dinner were Daniel Burnham and William Deering.[9] Charles Deering was a close friend of John Singer Sargent and Augustus Saint-Gaudens. In 1893, encouraged by Sargent, he took a leave of absence and spent a year painting in Paris. He also became friends with the famous Swedish painter Anders Zorn while the latter was in Chicago during the World's Columbian Exposition.

Zorn, who was commissioned to paint Charles Deering, also produced a full-length portrait of James, then forty-four. It depicts a debonair man-about-town, small, fastidiously dressed, his hands casually in his pockets, his demeanor radiating forceful self-assurance (fig. 2). James Deering was an important public figure. He played a major role in shepherding a Franco-American trade treaty through Congress, testifying before Senate committees and meeting with President McKinley.[10] When Philippe Bunau-Varilla toured the country in 1901, to urge the United States to take over construction of the Panama Canal, his host in Chicago was James Deering.[11] The energetic businessman also acted as public spokesman for the Agricultural Implements Association and took a leading role in the National Association of Agricultural Implement and Vehicle Manufacturers, which lobbied for reduction in trade tariffs.[12]

FIGURE 2. Anders Zorn, *James Deering*, c. 1903. The celebrated painter portrayed a dashing man-about-town. The portrait later hung in Deering's bedroom in Vizcaya. (Private collection)

James worked too hard to be called a playboy, but he was active socially. When the "Three Hundred," Chicago's social register, was published in 1897, he was prominently listed among the forty-odd "patriarchs" (his father and brother were not included).[13] James had some of the reticence of the self-made man. He had spent only two years at college (one at Northwestern, one at MIT) and was largely self-educated, teaching himself to read German, Italian, and French. He was an ardent Francophile and was later awarded the Légion d'Honneur. Exceptionally well traveled, he toured South America as a young man, and later Japan, representing the company in its far-flung operations. There is evidence that he was generally uninterested in the cultural life of the places he visited.[14] Unlike Charles, he was neither an artist nor a connoisseur. Yet he did have links to the arts: one of his best friends was a painter.* Gari Melchers (1860–1932), though little remembered today, was a prominent American artist, then living mainly in Paris and Holland.[15] In the spring of 1902, Deering and Melchers went on a two-month trip through Italy and a walking tour in Switzerland (fig. 3). "We both want to do the same thing, which is to make foot trips and live in the open air," wrote Deering.[16] A few years later, Charles joined them on a seven-week automobile trip in Spain, a form of touring made famous by Edith Wharton. Melchers remembered the adventure as "a continuous and long period of unalloyed bliss—no day like the other, everything we saw, everything that happened was even better than it had been on the day before."[17]

The picture that emerges of James Deering is complex. He was described by his family and friends as exceptionally warm, generous, and affectionate. His nephews and nieces particularly loved their Uncle Jim. Yet many later firsthand accounts, particularly those of women, referred to him differently: "austere, not at all approachable," "an astringent little man," "he didn't seem to enjoy life the way ordinary people do."[18] James Deering had spent his entire working life in the rough world of men, dealing with factory workers, farmers, and traveling salesmen. In male company, he could be indelicate—"about as handsome as a brick privy" was a favorite expression.[19] Among women of his own class he was scrupulously polite but probably somewhat ill at ease, and he may have appeared remote.

The McCormick-Deering merger did not go smoothly. The former competitors mistrusted each other and continued to operate independently as separate "divisions." For example, instructing a sales manager who was leaving for a posting in Australia, James Deering made it very clear that "your first duty will be to do and see done everything possible to serve the interests of the Deering Harvester Company."[20] There was much wasteful duplication, and profits stagnated. In 1906 Perkins summoned the McCormicks and the Deerings to New York to bang heads. He forced them to accept a company reorganization and brought in his own managers. The strategy proved effective, and two years later the profits of International Harvester doubled. The stock went up, healthy dividends were paid, and the company declared a

---

* Charles was a large-scale collector of Spanish art. James's collection was modest: four Tiepolos, a Manet, and works by Melchers and Walter MacEwen (1860–1943), another painter-friend.

FIGURE 3. SS *Aller*, April 1902. James Deering (*left*) and the painter Gari Melchers (*far right*), on board ship en route to Genoa and an Italian walking tour. The young woman is Corinne Lawton Mackall, an art student who would become Melchers's wife. (Courtesy of Belmont, The Gari Melchers Estate and Memorial Gallery)

$20 million bonus dividend.[21] The Deerings, whose share of the original issue amounted to more than $40 million ($800 million in today's dollars), were suddenly very rich, indeed.[22]

About 1908, James Deering ceased to be actively involved in the day-to-day affairs of International Harvester. Perkins had a low opinion of his abilities, and Perkins's biographer has suggested that Deering was forced out of the company.[23] That seems doubtful. Perkins had every reason to install his own people at International Harvester, but there is no evidence that James Deering was anything but an exceptionally able executive. A more likely reason for his departure was poor health. A few years earlier, he had suffered a bout of "nervous prostration" from overwork that kept him out of the office for a full year.[24] Sometime after 1902, he started to feel generally tired, which was the reason for the Spanish car tour.[25] He was eventually diagnosed with pernicious anemia, a deficiency of the red blood cells. Although he remained International Harvester's vice president until 1919, and a company director for the rest of his life, shortly after the reorganization James Deering essentially retired.

For the first time in his life, the forty-nine-year-old businessman found himself with time on his hands. Moreover, thanks to International Harvester's success, he also had a great deal of money. James Deering had always lived comfortably, with an apartment in Chicago and a country place in Wheaton, Illinois. But while old William Deering, who was described as a "Puritan in spirit and life," had been in charge, his junior partners (his sons and son-in-law) had been strictly limited as to how much money they could withdraw from the business.[26] "My father has always very justly believed, as it seems to me, that an unlimited pocket-book is not good for a young man," reflected James. "This has sometimes not been agreeable to me, but I have nevertheless recognized its wisdom."[27] It was not until his father retired that James Deering began to live like the multimillionaire he had become. One has the sense that after thirty years of hard work, overseen by a strict and somewhat starchy father, he was kicking over the traces. He summered annually in France, Germany, Spain, and Italy. He threw large parties, and his name appeared regularly in the society pages of Chicago and New York newspapers. Though a gregarious person, Deering never married. "You and I are not likely to have children of our own, I fear," he wrote to a friend, though only thirty-eight at the time.[28] "I am a bachelor, with no thought or expectation of marriage," he explained to a Parisian friend.*[29] One should resist the urge to psychoanalyze. To paraphrase Freud, sometimes a bachelor is only a bachelor.

About this time, Deering bought a house on Lake Shore Drive, Chicago's Gold Coast. To arrange the interior of his new home he hired the celebrated New York decorator, Elsie de Wolfe. De Wolfe (1865–1950) had taken up decorating—until then strictly a man's profession—only five years earlier. She was a New York socialite who claimed to have been raised in England (though it appears more likely that she grew up in New York), and pursued a modest career as an actress. She gave up the stage at the age of forty. Though no beauty, she had a glamorous sense of style, considerable wit, as well as a flair for self-promotion. Her friend Stanford White invited her to decorate the interior of the Colony Club, a women's club that he was building. It was her first job. "Give it to Elsie, and let the girl alone," White told his doubtful clients. "She knows more than any of us."[30] Her décor—uncluttered, eclectic, sophisticated, and vaguely French—was a great success. She introduced Americans to treillage, or decorative trelliswork, and to chintz. "The Colony Club started me on my way," she recalled. "I can think of my business as a small snowball suddenly achieving the stature and shape of a giant snowman."[31]

By the time that Deering engaged her, de Wolfe had become widely known as an arbiter of taste for the well-to-do. Her considerable client list included the Crockers of San Francisco, the Armours of Chicago, the Weyerhausers of Minneapolis, and Henry C. Frick, whose new mansion on Fifth Avenue was the talk of New York. She was so busy, in fact, that she did not spend as much time on Deering's project as he wished. When he complained, she sent one of her assistants, Paul Chalfin, to Chicago. Chalfin immediately made himself useful by identifying the two complete sets of Adam and Empire antique furniture that Deering had bought from Marshall Field as fakes and obliging the store to take them all back.[32] Deering, impressed with the young man's knowledge, invited him to come to Europe with him that summer as a sort of artistic guide and adviser.

Paul Chalfin (1874–1959) was in his mid-thirties, very self-confident, something of a dandy, affected in manner and speech, and openly homosexual (fig. 4). He came from a well-to-do New York family and had solid artistic credentials. After two years at Harvard, he had

* It is possible that Deering had gonorrhea as a young man, a common enough disease at that time, which might explain his reluctance to marry.

enrolled at the Art Students League in New York and then attended the École des Beaux-Arts in Paris, where he studied painting with Jean-Léon Gérôme, a historic genre painter who also taught Thomas Eakins. In Paris, Chalfin enrolled in the private academy of the flamboyant James McNeill Whistler. After returning to New York, he studied some more, worked for a year as a curator at Boston's Museum of Fine Arts, then won a prestigious painting scholarship (given by the Metropolitan Museum and the American Academy in Rome) that took him to Paris, Venice, Florence, and Rome. However, when he returned to New York, artistic commissions eluded him. He stopped painting altogether (he claimed to have developed an allergy to oil paint). He hung around the edges of the New York art scene, writing criticism and working for de Wolfe. When he met Deering, Chalfin was in danger of becoming one of those brilliant young men who, in Virginia Woolf's words, "remain 'brilliant' and young well into the 4oties and never do anything to prove it." The offer to spend a summer as an artistic consultant to a multimillionaire could not have come at a more opportune time.

Deering and Chalfin set off together for Europe in the summer of 1910. They spent time in Paris, where Deering had an apartment, and also in Italy. Like most wealthy Americans,

FIGURE 4. Paul Chalfin, c. 1912. James Deering's flamboyant artistic adviser was photographed at Vizcaya by Alice Woods. (Courtesy of Arva Moore Parks Collection)

Deering traveled in luxury, motoring from one grand hotel to another, but isolated from the world around him. Chalfin, in an attempt to broaden his horizons, took him to art museums and other cultural sites. One has the sense that he earned his salary; Chalfin later described traveling with Deering as "like taking around a child who knew very little and got tired easily."[33]

It was during this trip, according to Chalfin, that Deering revealed his plan to build a winter home in Florida. Today pernicious anemia is easily treated by injections of vitamin B12, but at that time little was known about the disease, and the doctors advised Deering to move to a warmer climate during the winter. Since he usually spent the spring in France, where he planned to buy a house, he considered the Riviera, as well as southern Italy, Egypt, and North Africa, but settled on south Florida instead.[34] Palm Beach—then called the "Newport of the South"—had become the premier winter destination for the swells of New York, Philadelphia, and Chicago, and a place that Deering knew well. The Royal Poinciana was the largest resort hotel in the world, the newer Breakers was even grander. But he did not settle in what Henry James called "the hotel-world" of Palm Beach. His parents had wintered in Florida for a number of years, and owned a modest house in Coconut Grove, just south of Miami, then a small town of about ten thousand; his brother, Charles, owned a two-hundred-acre estate in Buena Vista, about six miles up the coast. Although Coconut Grove, with its beautiful setting on Biscayne Bay, attracted a small number of well-to-do wintering northerners (including William Jennings Bryan), in Floridian terms it was the frontier. Yet this is where James Deering decided to build his winter house. He was once asked why he chose such an out-of-the-way spot. He answered that he had been everywhere and that this was the place he felt most comfortable.[35] Which was no answer at all.

A multimillionaire country house builder such as Deering had a number of well-known architectural precedents to draw on. The first generation of Gilded Age leisure homes had been built in Newport, Rhode Island, in the 1880s and 1890s. These extravagant mansions were euphemistically called "cottages," but their urban location, lined up along Bellevue Avenue, barely qualified them as country houses. The first truly grand American country house was George Washington Vanderbilt's winter home in Asheville, North Carolina. Although it had been completed fifteen years before Deering began his project, Biltmore (1889–95) remained a benchmark for country-house builders. Not only was it big—at 255 rooms, the largest private residence in the country—but its design and execution were of exceptional quality. The house was the last work of Richard Morris Hunt (1827–95), at the time the dean of American architects; the grounds were laid out by the great Frederick Law Olmsted (1822–1903).

Biltmore resembled a French château of the period of François I. Hunt, who had built four of the largest Neoclassical Newport mansions—The Breakers, Marble House, Ochre Court, and Belcourt Castle—here reverted to the French Renaissance style of his youth. He incorporated many references to specific historic buildings: the stair tower was based on the Château de Blois, the entrance tower on the fifteenth-century Palais Jacques Coeur in Bourges, and the animated massing of spires and chimneys recalled the Château de Chambord. Yet Biltmore was not a replica; there was no attempt to artificially age the materials, for example, or to give the illusion of age. Even today, more than a century after it was laid, the carved Indiana limestone looks crisp and sharp. Nor was the house a historical pastiche; Hunt was not copying the French Renaissance, he was *performing* it.[36] Not everyone found the performance convincing. Henry James, who was a solitary guest at Biltmore for an unseasonably frigid week in February 1905, described it in a letter to his friend Edith Wharton as a "strange, colossal heartbreaking house." "It's *in effect*, like a gorgeous practical joke—but at one's own expense, after all, if one has to live in solitude in these league-long marble halls and sit in alternate Gothic and Palladian cathedrals, as it were—where now only the temperature stalks about—with the 'regrets' sighing along the wind of those who have declined."[37] James was particularly irritable that week, having suffered an attack of gout.

"Gothic and Palladian cathedrals" elliptically alluded to the historical décor, which varied from room to room. The interiors, designed by Hunt's office, incorporated historical fragments that had been brought—"looted" in Mumford's phrase—from Europe: the painted ceiling in the library was from an eighteenth-century Venetian palazzo; the major decorative features in the banquet hall were five sixteenth-century Flemish tapestries; furniture and furnishings came from around the world. The fashion for decorating rooms in a variety of historical styles had been introduced to Americans by Hunt in an earlier house, the William K. Vanderbilt mansion (1878–82) on Fifth Avenue. Vanderbilt's wife, the irrepressible Alva Smith Vanderbilt, worked with the architect to make each room—the parlor, the salon, the dining hall, the library—a perfect historical set-piece.* The visitor experienced Louis XV, Henry II, and French Renaissance, before arriving at the Moorish billiard room. This startling mélange set New York high society on its ear. That discerning architecture critic Mariana Van Rensselaer called the Vanderbilt mansion "the most beautiful house in New York."[38]

Hunt's clients craved Flemish *boiseries*, but they expected their houses to be up to date as far as domestic conveniences were concerned. Biltmore included generators that powered electric lights, two passenger elevators, a forced-air central heating system, and mechanical refrigerators. The forty-three bathrooms had hot and cold running water; and the house was served by synchronized electric clocks. Hunt was as pragmatic about the use of modern building materials—the roof structure was steel—as he was about his architectural design, which was direct and unfussy. He was not finicky about historical accuracy; the chief purpose of his design was to give pleasure to its occupants.

Hunt once boasted about Biltmore that "The mountains are just the right size and scale for the château!"[39] He might have added "and for the gardens." Under Olmsted's guidance, Vanderbilt eventually acquired more than a hundred thousand acres, and the estate included a managed forest, and a farm, as well as gardens. In the vicinity of the house, the design of the landscape was French and geometrical: a *tapis vert* in front of the entrance, a viewing terrace, and a rectangular *parterre* containing water gardens. Farther away, Olmsted created a more

---

* Alva was a great patron of Hunt and commissioned him to build two Newport cottages: Marble House and, after her divorce and remarriage, Belcourt Castle.

characteristic picturesque landscape that merged into an artfully designed forest setting that led to a manmade bass pond. Below the house was a pastoral English deer park that sloped down to a lagoon and the French Broad River. The Shingle Style country houses designed by Stanford White in the 1880s, for example, had landscaped grounds, but they lacked the structure and intensity of Olmsted's landscape. His design at Biltmore—an impressive approach road, regular gardens near the house, and a more naturalistic treatment elsewhere—became the model for many later country estates, including James Deering's.[40]

Herbert Croly, the founding editor of the *New Republic* and editor of *Architectural Record*, wrote in *Stately Homes in America* that Biltmore differed radically from Newport villas and Long Island estates because it was the product not merely of money, but also of leisure. The estate was not designed for a busy businessman who could only spare a few days away from the city, but was intended for "a cultivated gentleman who has the use of his own time, who wants to build up an all-round country place, and who has all the time and money he needs in which to do it."[41] Which was precisely James Deering's situation.

Deering might have felt some bond with Vanderbilt, a bachelor when he began his house, who also sought a southern winter home for health reasons. However, by 1910, some things about Biltmore were distinctly old fashioned. As Mark Hewitt has pointed out, although Hunt used a French château style at Biltmore, he planned the house like an 1880s Shingle Style cottage, "with an openness and informality that belied his Beaux-Arts training."[42] Where a château might have had an interior *cour*, Hunt located a glass-roofed, palm-filled winter garden open to the entrance hall and surrounding spaces. The subtle house plan, with carefully shifted axes, rooms opening into each other, and long unobstructed interior views, somewhat undercut, as Hunt no doubt intended, the monumentality of the architecture. But monumentality was precisely what Deering's generation wanted. While a few country-house architects, such as Philadelphia's Wilson Eyre, continued to use informal plans influenced by the British Arts and Crafts movement, the taste of most American architects—and of their clients—shifted to a more stately grandeur.

The exterior of Biltmore was likewise somewhat démodé, although the château style persisted. In 1902 Stanford White built one of the grandest houses of the period, Harbor Hill, at Roslyn, Long Island, and as late as 1914, William Adams Delano was still exploring the Norman style at Oheka, in Cold Spring Harbor, New York. But, elsewhere, tall roofs and picturesque massing gave way to Neoclassicism. Hunt himself had started this fashion in the palatial Marble House, built in 1892 in Newport for Alva Vanderbilt. Following the 1893 World's Columbian Exposition in Chicago, where Hunt and McKim built great classical pavilions (and Olmsted devised the plan), Neoclassicism was firmly established as the preferred architectural style.

McKim, Mead & White, with McKim as designer, built a beautiful Neoclassical house for yet another Vanderbilt brother. The Frederick W. Vanderbilt mansion at Hyde Park, New York (1896–99), overlooked the Hudson River. Like many of the best architects of his generation, Charles Follen McKim (1847–1909), known to his friends as "Bramante," was an avowed classicist. He had studied at the École des Beaux-Arts in Paris, and the masterful design of the

Hyde Park house exhibits the geometrical rigor characteristic of that school. The plan was loosely based on Palladio's four-sided Villa Rotonda. The four porticos were not identical: a dramatic semicircular portico faced the spectacular view of the Hudson; slightly less grand porticos, supported by six giant Corinthian columns, extended the house to the north and south; while the smallest portico sheltered the entrance. As the house was rectangular rather than square, the two-story, central hall, the informal living space of the house, was oval rather than circular. Like Palladio's original (the Villa Rotonda is 80 feet square, the Vanderbilt mansion is 50 by 150 feet), the plan was both highly ordered and eminently livable.

By 1910 McKim's academic classicism had been overtaken by the more expressive Modern French style (also called Contemporary Parisian, and today often referred to simply as Beaux-Arts). Among the leading exponents was the firm of Carrère & Hastings. John M. Carrère (1858–1911) and Thomas Hastings (1860–1929), both Beaux-Arts graduates, met while working in McKim, Mead & White's office and went on to establish one of the most successful architectural practices in the country. They launched the firm on the strength of a large project in Florida for Henry M. Flagler, a friend of Hastings' father. Flagler had been a founding partner, with John D. Rockefeller, of Standard Oil. Advised to spend the winters in Florida for his first wife's health, he invested his fortune in real estate. Charmed by the old Spanish colonial town of St. Augustine, he commissioned Carrère & Hastings to design a grand resort hotel. Hastings decided that "the logical expression of the semi-tropical climate and historical background was in some form of Spanish-Renaissance style."[43] The Hotel Ponce de León (1885–87) was a fantasy version of Salamanca and Moorish Granada, a theme that Hastings continued in the adjoining Hotel Alcazar (1887–88), which housed an enormous indoor swimming pool. The sprawling hotels charmed even the demanding Henry James. In *The American Scene*, he described the Ponce de León as "near producing, all by itself, the illusion of romance as a highly modern, a most cleverly-constructed and smoothly administered great modern caravansary can come; it is largely 'in the Moorish style' (as the cities of Spain preserve the record of that manner); it breaks out, on every pretext, into circular arches and embroidered screens, into courts and cloisters, arcades and fountains, fantastic projections and lordly towers, and is, in all sorts of ways and in the highest sense of the word, the most 'amusing' of hotels."[44]

After one particularly cold winter in St. Augustine, Flagler decided to shift his operation farther south. He acquired a local railroad and extended the line as far as Lake Worth, where he founded the resort town of Palm Beach. There he built the Hotel Royal Poinciana (1893–94), pushed the railroad to Miami where he built the Royal Palm Hotel (1897), and a few years later added the luxurious Breakers (1900) in Palm Beach.[45] All three hotels were Colonial-style wooden structures, designed by Flagler's contractors, James McGuire and Joseph A. McDonald, two ex-ship builders from Nova Scotia. In 1901 Flagler commissioned Carrère & Hastings to build a fifty-five-room mansion in Palm Beach as a wedding present for his new bride. The architects had previously built a house for Flagler in St. Augustine; Kirkside (1893) was a Colonial mansion with a central court. The new house, Whitehall (1901–3), also had a court, or rather a patio, for its style was Spanish (fig. 5). The construction drawings were complete when the architects received a letter from their willful client. "Gentlemen:—This afternoon

I have noticed, for the first time, the elevation (as shown on plan #12) of the gables of my house here. I don't like them. I much prefer something more on the Colonial order, and less of the Spanish. I wish you to send me a sketch modifying the present idea."[46] Hastings, the firm's lead designer (and married to Flagler's daughter's sister-in-law), wished to please, but he was loathe to revise the design entirely. Instead, he added both a Classical porch facing Lake Worth and a giant Doric portico on the entrance side, but kept most of the Spanish features: the red-tile roofs, the patio, the bracketed wood balconies—and the offending gables. The opulent interiors were designed by the fashionable New York firm of Pottier & Stymus.[47] Chalfin, who visited the house in February 1914, was not impressed. He found it "all intolerably tasteless, expensive, gaudy, immense and insincere. On the whole one of the most shallow and repugnant houses I have encountered."[48] Whitehall is one of James's white elephants—with palm trees.

James Deering, who had fallen in love with Seville during his automobile tour of Spain, decided that the style of his house would be Spanish.[49] He was undoubtedly familiar with Whitehall, which was the only really large country house in south Florida. Deering also knew the Hotel Ponce de León, since he had frequently visited St. Augustine where his parents had owned a winter home before moving to Coconut Grove.[50] But probably the most important influence on his stylistic choice was the example of his brother, Charles. About 1910, Charles Deering commissioned designs for a villa, gate lodge, and water tower for his estate at Buena Vista, north of the mouth of the Miami River. He was an enthusiastic Hispanist who, a few years later, purchased and restored several old houses and a medieval castle in Spain.[51] His architect for

FIGURE 5. Whitehall, Palm Beach (1901–3), Carrère & Hastings, architects. The Spanish-style patio of Henry M. Flagler's palatial winter home, which was the largest house in southern Florida. (Courtesy of Florida State Archives)

FIGURE 6. Charles Deering House, Buena Vista (c. 1910), Clinton Mackenzie, architect. This watercolor view shows the terrace beside the dining room of this Spanish-style villa. (Historical Museum of Southern Florida)

Buena Vista was Clinton Mackenzie (1872–1940), a New Yorker, who had built a Spanish Mission Revival–style country house for himself on Oyster Bay in Long Island. Mackenzie's delightful watercolor sketches for Buena Vista show a Spanish house, more Renaissance than Mission, with stucco walls, tile roofs, picturesque arched loggias, and landscaped patios (fig. 6).*[52]

"We spent one entire winter making plans for various types of Spanish houses," Chalfin, who by now was working for Deering full time, recalled, "but one night, with his characteristic abruptness in making decisions [Deering] swept them all aside and we came to the determination that the building should be of the Italian villa type."[53] The plans of the "Spanish houses" have not survived, nor was any explanation given for this volte-face. It may be that Deering remembered his Italian trip from Naples to Lake Como with Melchers. Or, it may

---

* Only a picturesque water tower was built. In 1916 Charles bought land at Cutler, about ten miles south of Coconut Grove, where he built a Spanish-style villa that still stands. He sold his Buena Vista holdings in 1925.

have been Chalfin's doing. He was familiar with Italy, and later recalled saying to Deering "it should not be a castle in Spain . . . suppose we try Italian," although at the time he could not imagine what kind of Italian house would be suitable for Florida.[54]

Americans' interest in Italian villas had been piqued by Edith Wharton, whose *Italian Villas and Their Gardens*, a survey of historic villas in Tuscany, Rome, and Lombardy, with illustrations by Maxfield Parrish, was published in 1904. Wharton was following in the footsteps of Charles A. Platt (1861–1933), an American landscape painter, whose *Italian Gardens* of 1894 was the first book in English on Italian villas and gardens. *Italian Gardens* was profusely illustrated with Platt's own photographs of famous villas, including the Villa Lante, the Villa Borghese, and the Villa d'Este.* In 1890, inspired by his Italian travels, Platt had redesigned his own house and garden at Cornish, New Hampshire, in a Classical style, with an ample, open loggia. Several commissions from his Cornish neighbors (who included Saint-Gaudens and Herbert Croly, for whom he built a house) led him to architecture, and he became one of the most influential country-house architects and garden designers of the day.

Platt's largest residential project was Villa Turicum (1908–18) in Lake Forest, Michigan. Platt had described the Villa d'Este on Lake Como as "an enormous structure of perfect simplicity of design . . . the only decoration of its exterior is the doorway and staircases leading to it," which is how he designed the Villa Turicum, with interior courts and an arcaded loggia overlooking a series of garden terraces stepping down to Lake Michigan.[55] The house, which no longer exists, was lavish—the richly decorated drawing room was more than sixty feet long—but its wide eaves and plastered walls recalled a comfortable Tuscan villa. The client was Harold F. McCormick of International Harvester.†[56] Despite their families' rivalry, McCormick and Deering were friends (Deering always called him "Mr. Harold") so it is likely that Deering would have known the house, which was largely complete by 1911.[57]

In the spring of 1911, Deering and Chalfin returned to Italy to look at houses. They visited the papal villas in Rome, the Medici villas in Florence, the dramatic island villas of Lake Maggiore, and the Villa d'Este, whose gardens Wharton called "one of the most enchanting bits of sylvan gardening in Italy."[58] They also went to Venice. In the early 1900s, that city's quirky mix of ornate late Gothic, exuberant baroque, and gilded Byzantine buildings had little influence on American architects, who tended to look to Rome and Paris. But upper-class Americans who were artistically inclined were drawn to Venice, thanks to John Ruskin's *The Stones of Venice*, the writings of Charles Eliot Norton (who studied under Ruskin), the paintings of Sargent and Whistler, James's Venetian novels, and above all the example of that great devotee of Venetian art and architecture, Isabella Gardner.

Isabella Stewart Gardner (1840–1924) was the grande dame of American arts, a singular woman whom Berenson once described as a "pre-Hollywood star."[59] A New Yorker, she had married John Gardner, a Boston shipping magnate. On the death of their only son, she turned

---

* Chalfin bought both Platt's and Wharton's books for Deering's library.
† McCormick's first choice as architect was Frank Lloyd Wright, but McCormick's wife, Edith, the daughter of John D. Rockefeller, disliked Wright's design and opted for Platt.

her considerable energy to world travel, society, and the arts. She befriended Berenson while he was still a Harvard student, and likewise took Sargent under her wing. Henry James, another friend, thought her "a great little personage."[60] Mrs. Jack, as she was popularly called, was an enthusiastic Italophile; only a year after Platt's *Italian Gardens* was published, she created an Italian garden on her Brookline estate. She first visited Italy when she was eighteen, and returned as an adult in the mid-1880s. She was enthralled by Venice. Between 1890 and 1897, she and her husband regularly rented the Palazzo Barbaro on the Grand Canal. There they—or rather she—entertained artistic friends such as Berenson, Sargent, Zorn, the Parisian essayist Paul Bourget, the New England painter Joseph Lindon Smith, and, of course, Henry James. James wrote part of *The Wings of the Dove* while staying with the Gardners and modeled the fictitious Palazzo Leporelli on their Venetian house, a photograph of which provided the frontispiece for the 1908 Scribner edition.[61]

It was not unusual at the time for wealthy Americans to develop an attachment for Venice, but Isabella Gardner carried her enthusiasm farther than most. In 1891, using a modest inheritance, and with the aid of Berenson and the scholar Charles Eliot Norton, she began to amass what became a formidable art collection. In 1897 she decided to create a museum for her paintings. She conceived the building from the inside out. She bought Venetian architectural fragments—columns, ironwork, fireplaces, choir stalls, paneling, whole façades—and had them arranged in a Boston warehouse to form simulated rooms.[62] She first planned to build an extension to her house on Beacon Street, but as her collection grew more space was needed, and shortly after her husband's death she bought a large lot on the Fenway, a park recently laid out by Frederick Law Olmsted.[63] Her architect was Willard T. Sears (1837–1920), a seasoned Boston practitioner who had built the Roosevelt summer house on Campobello Island in Canada and had done work on the Gardners' summer house in Maine. Though she was in her sixties when construction began, Isabella was involved in every detail of what became known as Fenway Court (1899–1903), personally participating in painting and plastering, for example. While it is an exaggeration to call her the building's architect, as one historian has done, it is certainly true that the indefatigable Mrs. Jack exerted a great influence on the design, particularly on its decorative aspects.[64]

Henry James admiringly called Fenway Court a "*palais-musée.*"[65] The design was simplicity itself: a four-story, rectangular structure with the rooms arranged around a central court (fig. 7). As a concession to the Boston climate, the court was covered with a glass roof supported on delicate steel arches. A frieze of crenellations, modeled on the Doges' Palace, softened the impact of the advanced (for its time) engineering structure. The glass roof turned the court into a lush palm-filled sculpture garden. Here is a 1927 description:

> The center of the court is occupied by a mosaic pavement trodden for centuries by Roman feet, but so perfectly preserved that it gives the impression of having been made expressly for its present place. At the end of the court, opposite the entrance, is a Venetian fountain. . . . In the cloisters, which are paved with ancient-looking flaggings and arcaded with columns of precious Italian marble, are many sculptures bearing the incomparable hue of age. . . . From the Venetian windows

which look upon the court hang the eight beautiful balconies from the famous palace on the grand canal, the Ca d'Oro. . . . At every step we come upon some fascinating piece of artistic workmanship, a bit of iron grillwork from Spain, a Gothic stone altar, a fragment of arab sculpture, delicate as lacework, from the mosque of Bokhara.[66]

The eight projecting stone balconies in the court were from the Ca' d'Oro, but they actually date from the nineteenth century, not from the fifteenth as Gardner was led to believe.[67] Most of the columns, capitals, and window frames were old, purchased en masse and individually from Venetian art dealers. The inconsistent result—the arcade is supported by an unorthodox

FIGURE 7. Fenway Court, Boston (1899–1903), Willard T. Sears, architect. Isabella Stewart Gardner's Venetian palazzo in Boston was a major influence on Paul Chalfin, who was her frequent guest as a young man. Thomas E. Marr took this photograph shortly after the building was completed. (*American Magazine of Art*)

mixture of single and paired columns—is part of the charm of the court, which even today exerts an almost mesmerizing effect on visitors. Although the arcade was referred to as a "cloister," there is nothing religious about the space. This is an exercise in sensuality and aestheticism, pure and simple. Carved medallions and decorative reliefs enliven the walls; the other-worldly atmosphere is enhanced by the sound of trickling fountains.

The rooms, on whose walls hang Botticelli, Giorgone, and Vermeer, are equally fabulous. Gardner made no distinction between art and décor. It is likely that she was influenced by the Italian dealer and collector Stefano Bardini, who lived in Florence.[68] In 1883 Bardini installed his antiquarian collection of ancient architectural fragments in the thirteenth-century Palazzo Mozzi and incorporated altars, portals, stairs, columns, and ceilings into the actual fabric of the building.* Gardner's similarly eclectic technique of displaying art, later emulated by Duncan Phillips and Albert C. Barnes, consisted of mixing paintings of different periods and juxtaposing them with furniture and other precious objects. The rooms were more or less thematic, but the décor was intended to capture the spirit of a period rather than literally re-create an epoch. Sargent's depiction of flamenco dancers, *El Jaleo*, was displayed in a Spanish cloister (added to the house in 1914), with Moorish arches and old Mexican ceramic tiles; Veronese hung on a gilded leather wall; Rembrandt, Rubens, Van Dyck, and other old masters were in a room with a painted wooden ceiling and brocaded wall hangings. But the décor was intensely varied. Titian's *Rape of Europa*, considered by many the most important painting of the Renaissance, was displayed next to a sixteenth-century Persian carpet (recommended to Gardner by Sargent), two eighteenth-century Venetian consoles, and a length of silk fabric that had originally been her Charles Frederick Worth dinner gown.

Although it was primarily a museum (Gardner occupied an apartment on the top floor), the influence of Fenway Court on early nineteenth-century American domestic design was considerable. While country houses such as Biltmore were visited by a select few, Fenway Court was open to the general public, albeit for only two weeks a year during Gardner's lifetime. The scale and furnishings made the interiors appear uncontrovertibly domestic. Mumford, for example, clearly thought of Fenway Court as a residence: "As a home, it became a pattern for the homes of rich people in America for a whole generation, and so, at tenth hand, it became a pattern for the poorest suburban villa, with its standardized reproductions of dressers and tables and carpets."[69] He saw nothing to admire in "Mrs. Jack Gardner's palace." Neither did a later critic, the historian Henry-Russell Hitchcock. "Except for the incorporated fragments of Italian detail, mostly in the court," he wrote in a Boston architectural guidebook, "its architectural interest is negligible."[70]

What disturbed Mumford and Hitchcock was not merely Gardner's historicism, but the fact that she did not think like an architect. The unprepossessing brick exterior, which resembles a well-built high school, belies the rich Venetian Gothic court within. Sears used an exposed steel structure to support the glass roof, anticipating Otto Wagner's glass-vaulted hall

---

* Deering and Chalfin bought furniture and architectural fragments from the Florentine collector and knew the Palazzo Mozzi-Bardini.

in the Post Office Savings Bank in Vienna by five years, but Gardner insisted that the rest of the building be constructed with traditional load-bearing masonry vaults and heavy wooden beams, just like a Renaissance palazzo. She incorporated American handcrafted products—Mercer floor tiles and Koralewski ironwork—but combined arts and crafts simplicity with theatrical lighting effects. Finally, she blended old and new building elements (as Renaissance Venetian builders had always done), which offended the Modernists' purist notion of architecture as a self-contained work of art.

Isabella Gardner was anything but a purist. The court, for example, is a complete fabrication, since Venetian palazzos did not have central courts, but it is realized with such aplomb that few question the illusion. To achieve the battered and slightly shabby appearance that she admired in old Venetian stuccowork, she had the roughly plastered walls of the courtyard sponged with pink and white paint. She used real historic artifacts, but when these were unavailable, she did not hesitate to have replicas made. To light the stairwell, she unceremoniously cut apertures into the wall, into which she inserted antique wooden screens. Her eclectic approach to décor was quite different from the stiff period interiors of Hunt's grand houses. She was more interested in creating an overall mood than in producing historical verisimilitude—her rooms were imaginative, and sometimes even imaginary. Practicing a kind of architectural fusion, although she would never have called it that, she combined Cinquecento Venice, contemporary American Arts and Crafts, Ruskinian Gothic, and Orientalism (a Buddhist temple room honored her friend, a Japanese poet).[71] The result, as architecture critic Aline Saarinen observed, was "a masterpiece of its kind . . . not architecture, in the sense of J. P. Morgan's Library [designed by McKim, Mead & White], which was begun the year Fenway Court was finished, but a delightful ensemble."[72] What held the ensemble together—just barely—was not an intellectual theory but the connoisseurship and taste of a remarkable, strong-willed woman whose museum's motto, inscribed over the front door on a seal of her own design, was *C'est mon plaisir.*

Gardner's museum belongs in any catalogue of the great Gilded Age houses, although in a special category. "Every detail of Fenway Court was personal, in contrast to the glaring impersonality of other palatial American houses," wrote Harold Acton, who visited Boston in 1932. "Among the iron eagles, green velvet copes, red velvet baldaquins, carved chests and Gothic credences, one is aware that each of these objects reflects the taste of this ambitious despotic woman."[73]

Charles Deering met Isabella Gardner through Sargent, and they became fast friends. There is no evidence that James Deering knew her, but Paul Chalfin did. While he lived in Boston, he was a frequent guest at Fenway Court, including a memorable 1904 Christmas Eve dinner to which Mrs. Gardner invited seven "waifs and strays who don't have families here."[74] His regard for the person that some called the "Isabella d'Este of Boston" is evident in an effusive thank-you note that he wrote after another visit: "I can recall writing many times without hesitation to thank people who had shown me, after dinner, the collection of tea-cups their grandmother had, or the fragment they stole from the Forum in such and such a year,—but to be thanking you for an encounter with the beauty of which you are captain, seems, Madam, utterly preposterous. I should as readily think of thanking heaven for the horizon."[75] Well! Gardner's sublimation of architectural novelty, her flair, her dramatic historicism, her sense of freedom, and her literal celebration of Venice appealed to Chalfin's artistic temperament. So did her elevation of aestheticism to almost a religion. Above all, he appreciated the triumph of a dilettante's personal sensibility over professionalism and academic convention. He would learn the decorating business from Elsie de Wolfe, but his taste was formed by Mrs. Jack.

chapter 3

HOFFMAN'S PLAN

In December 1912, James Deering closed on the purchase of a shoreline property called Brickell Point, on Biscayne Bay, at the north end of Coconut Grove. He paid a steep $1,000 an acre for 130 acres (later adding 50 acres more). His collection of architectural artifacts now included a massive stone fountain, a 20-foot-tall sixteenth-century chimneypiece, as well as a pair of huge bronze and wrought-iron gates. Clearly his winter home promised to be a large undertaking. Chalfin had his own ideas about architecture—as about everything else—but he had no technical expertise in construction, so they needed an architect. Deering could afford the best. The obvious candidate would have been Thomas Hastings, a leading designer of country houses with extensive Florida experience (Carrère had died in 1911), or Charles Platt, the recognized expert in Italian villas and gardens. Established practitioners such as McKim, Mead & White or the Philadelphian Horace Trumbauer would have been safe choices. Or an up-and-coming younger firm such as Delano & Aldrich, which had just completed an impressive country house in Lenox, Massachusetts, for the great-granddaughter of Commodore Cornelius Vanderbilt. As far as is known, none of these men was approached.

Like many wealthy clients, Deering did not want a celebrated architect. Barbara Deering Danielson, Deering's niece, recalled her uncle saying that "if some famous architect were his architect that architect would build what he wanted and not what Uncle Jim and Chalfin wanted." What her uncle desired, as she remembered it, was "a young, unknown architect who would do what he and Chalfin told him to do."[1] Deering was used to getting his own way, and he definitely wanted to be a client who had, as Isabella Gardner once put it, "the fun of doing it himself."[2]

Putting what promised to be a complicated and expensive project in the hands of a novice would be taking a big chance, but that is what they decided. In 1912, with his client's authorization, Chalfin offered the job to Francis Burrall Hoffman, Jr. (1882–1980), "a wealthy young man who had an excellent office staff" (fig. 8).[3] Hoffman was known to Richard Howe, Deering's brother-in-law, and he was recommended to Chalfin by Ethel Barrymore.[4] Chalfin himself had met Hoffman two years earlier. At Elsie de Wolfe's request, Chalfin had been organizing an architectural lecture series at the Colony Club and had invited William Adams Delano to be a speaker. Delano became ill and suggested Hoffman as a substitute. The personable thirty-year-old architect was a New York City blue blood from an established family. Like Chalfin, he had attended Harvard and the École des Beaux-Arts. In Paris he had studied in the atelier of Henri-Adolphe-Auguste Deglane, a leading architect and one of the designers of the Grand Palais at the Universal Exposition of 1900.

Despite taking time off from his studies to make a round-the-world tour with his brother William, Hoffman graduated from the École with honors. He returned to New York to serve a two-year apprenticeship with Carrère & Hastings, who had designed his parents' townhouse and for whom he had worked after graduating from Harvard. In 1909 Hoffman opened an office in New York City, sharing space with another young architect, Harry Creighton Ingalls. They were not partners, but helped each other on projects. Hoffman was young but not without experience. While still a Harvard student, he had built a country house for a friend in Southampton.[5] His first project in New York City was a handsome mausoleum in the Bronx's Woodlawn Cemetery for Edmund Walstein Davis, a wealthy sportsman (fig. 9).[6] With Ingalls,

FIGURE 8. F. Burrall Hoffman, Jr., c. 1915. The dapper young architect, an École des Beaux-Arts graduate, trained with Carrère & Hastings. (Photograph by Alice Woods, courtesy of Arva Moore Parks Collection)

he had built a small theater on West 44th Street. Like most architects of that time, Hoffman was an eclectic. While at Carrère & Hastings, he had worked on Arden House, the Norman-châteauesque estate of financier E. H. Harriman, and on his own he had just finished a Colonial Revival country house for a Harvard classmate.[7] Shortly after being hired by Deering, he was commissioned to build a substantial Georgian Revival mansion on Long Island (fig. 10).[8]

"Mr. Chalfin asked [me] if [I] would make plans for his client Mr. Deering in such a way that use should be made of the many treasures of antiquity that had been acquired," Hoffman later recalled.[9] Naturally he accepted. The commission was a great opportunity for the young architect, but he was obliged to work under several constraints, not the least of which was having, in effect, two clients. He got on well with Deering. "Deering was not what you'd call intellectual," Hoffman later recalled. "He had taste and the desire to do things well."[10] This desire manifested itself in an intense interest in the most detailed aspects of his future home. While the house was being designed, Deering, who was in Chicago, peppered Hoffman with correspondence. In one two-day period in September 1913, he sent a telegram expressing concern about getting started with construction, a long five-page letter recapping an earlier conversation about various requirements ("I should like my bath tub piped for cold salt water"), another letter responding to a basement plan he had just received ("I would put the Billiard table near the Swimming pool"), and a follow-up letter containing more details about the location of the billiard table.[11] Two days later Deering sent a note to Ingalls, who was assisting Hoffman on the project: "Will you not at your leisure write us something about plumbing?"[12] Clearly the retired executive, used to directing a large enterprise, had time on his hands.

Deering "managed" the design of his new house much the way he had managed his factories: he studied the problem, he involved himself in every detail, he made his wishes known,

FIGURE 9. Edmund Walstein Davis Mausoleum, Woodlawn Cemetery, New York City (c. 1908), F. Burrall Hoffman, Jr., architect. This handsome structure is Hoffman's first documented architectural commission. (Vizcaya Museum and Gardens Archive)

FIGURE 10. Ballyshear, Southampton, Long Island (c. 1915), F. Burrall Hoffman, Jr., architect. An elegant Georgian Revival residence designed for Charles B. Macdonald, a golf course designer. (Vizcaya Museum and Gardens Archive)

and he expected his employees to deliver.* He knew what he wanted, and he usually got it. He insisted on certain technical features, such as proper ventilation in the rooms, and extensive fire protection measures, and in his polite way he made specific design demands. "Here is an idea which possibly is worth considering," he once wrote to Hoffman, "if only for rejection." His diffident proposal was to have a sort of walled outdoor beach, next to the pool, "in which people could roll and sun themselves."[13] The so-called Sand Pit, filled with three feet of beach sand, was built opposite the swimming pool.

The mercurial Chalfin, on the other hand, was a different matter. Although he was not an architect, he knew a lot about architectural history, he had a good eye, he could sketch, and he had definite ideas about aesthetics. Moreover, he was not shy about giving the architect orders. "There must be times like this," he once warned Hoffman, "like that for the island, and like that which I eternally regret for the fore court, when we come to a dead issue, and where I have to ask you to conform even against your instinct and your artistic conscience, to my preconceptions."[14] (The reference to the fore court was to a surrounding parapet wall that Hoffman had convinced Chalfin to approve.)[15] The same letter contained sketches of precisely how Chalfin wanted the swimming pool steps to be designed. He could be devious with the young architect and was not above going behind his back. "I don't want to write anything to Hoffman, or to Mr. Deering, before seeing you," Chalfin once wrote to Ingalls,

---

* Deering also insisted on records. He was old enough to distrust the telephone, and even telegraph messages were followed up by a letter. Consequently, the archives at Vizcaya are a treasure trove of correspondence, invoices, receipts, payrolls, even stenographers' notebooks.

"since I am sure that with you I can get a sympathetic point of view on the changes before discussing them."[16]

Hoffman's freedom was further constrained since his design had to incorporate Deering's "many treasures of antiquity." Chalfin and Deering had accumulated a vast haul from such leading Florentine art dealers as Elia Volpi and Giuseppe Salvadori, as well as Stefano Bardini. The artifacts and architectural fragments occupied several floors of the midtown Manhattan warehouse of P. W. French & Company, which thanks to Deering's patronage would become one of the premier art dealers in the city. Following Isabella Gardner's example, Chalfin created individual room settings in the warehouse, with temporary walls and ceilings supporting the paneling, door frames, tapestries, paintings, and so on. Hoffman's daunting task was to integrate these predetermined tableaux into his design, without losing an overall sense of coherence.

On top of everything else, Hoffman was not starting with a blank slate. Deering and Chalfin had decided that the house should be an Italian villa, and they had a specific model in mind. At one point during their 1911 Italian tour, they had headed off the beaten track into the Veneto, the seldom-visited Venetian hinterland. Starting in the sixteenth century, wealthy Venetians built inland summer retreats throughout this region, along the banks of the Brenta River, on the fertile plain of the Po valley, and in the foothills of the Dolomitic Alps. The most famous villa architect was Andrea Palladio, but while Palladio's villas greatly influenced British architects in the eighteenth century, as well as American Colonial house builders, their chaste severity did not appeal to Americans of Deering's time. Edith Wharton, for example, admired Palladio's churches and palazzos, but thought his villas "a little cold" and expressed the commonly held view that "neither in the Rotonda nor in his other villas did Palladio hit on a style half as appropriate or pleasing as the typical manner of the Roman villa-architects."[17]

Deering and Chalfin's model was the Villa Rezzonico (c. 1670) in Bassano del Grappa, an out-of-the-way foothills town famous for its white asparagus and its fiery liquor (fig. 11). They had been taken around the villa by an old countess with whom they were staying. The obscure house was built in the late seventeenth century.*[18] Its castlelike appearance (Chalfin actually thought that it was originally a military installation), with a squat turret at each corner, was intended to evoke a medieval fortified Italian country house, or *castello*. Cosimo de' Medici the Elder began this quaint custom in the fifteenth century when he instructed his architect, Michelozzi di Bartolomeo, to build him a villa at Trebbio in the style of a feudal fortress. He liked it so much that he built a second larger one at Cafaggiolo.[19] Turrets also appeared in the Veneto, in the fifteenth-century Villa Grimani near Verona, in Palladio's Villa Pisani in Bagnolo, and in seventeenth-century country houses such as the Villa Benzi and the Villa Castello di Colloredo Mels.[20]

Like many baroque villas, the Villa Rezzonico was severe on the exterior, with undecorated windows and plain plaster walls unrelieved by loggias or porticos, but extremely richly decorated

---

* The Villa Rezzonico was illustrated in *Baroque Architecture and Sculpture in Italy*, a popular American book on Italian baroque architecture published in 1912, which Deering had in his library.

FIGURE 11. Villa Rezzonico, Bassano del Grappa (c. 1670), Baldassare Longhena, architect. This Veneto villa was the inspiration for Vizcaya. This photograph was contained in *Baroque Architecture and Sculpture in Italy*, a popular book that was in Deering's library.

on the inside. The architect is now thought to have been Baldassare Longhena (1598–1682), the Venetian baroque master who built the beautiful Santa Maria della Salute.*[21] His masterful touch is evident in a vast, beautifully decorated two-story central *sala* ornamented with dramatic plaster reliefs on the ceilings and vaults and flanked by two monumental staircases. The Villa Rezzonico was a distinctly odd choice for Deering and Chalfin: it was not situated on water but in the mountains; it did not have an outstanding garden; and the plan was rather unrefined—all eight rooms are identical in size and shape. Yet they "recognized [it] immediately as what was needed."[22] The relationship of the simple turreted building to its natural surroundings may have appealed to them. Or they may have liked the contrast between the exterior and the interior; from the outside, the house gave no hint of the riches within.

Hoffman spent the winter of 1912–13 in Coconut Grove familiarizing himself with the site. Brickell Point consisted of low-lying hammock—swampy mangrove jungle—near the water,

* It was not until the 1950s that the Villa Rezzonico was identified as a late work of Longhena.

rising to an elevated ridge several hundred feet inland (fig. 12). The ridge was covered by a dense hardwood forest. The conventional solution would have been to locate the house on the ridge and lay out the garden as a series of terraces stepping down to the water's edge. But Deering—who, like his brother, was a dedicated naturalist—wanted to preserve the hardwood forest. He decided that his house should be right on the water. This complicated the construction, since the building—and the grounds around it, including the garden—would have to be raised several feet to be above the level of high tide. But despite Hoffman's and the contractor's protests, Deering stood firm.

In hindsight, it is obvious that Deering's instincts were sound. Vizcaya's best landscape feature is its intimate relationship to Biscayne Bay. "There are some outlooks that stir the blood like the sound of trumpets," observed the garden historian Sir George Sitwell, "and others that lull the senses to dreamy and indolent repose."[23] The sparkling prospect of the lagoonlike bay, which is curiously Venetian with the bluish coastline of Key Biscayne on the horizon, definitely belongs to the latter category. It is important to underline the originality of Deering's decision. The ancient Romans built some famous seaside villas, but there were no historical precedents among Renaissance villas, which were generally inland, and even when situated on lakes or rivers, were not immediately on the water. The same was true of American country houses. Mansions at Newport, for example, looked to the sea over vast expanses of lawns; country houses on Long Island were likewise pulled well back from the shore. A rare exception was Gwinn (1906–12), a house that Charles A. Platt designed on the shore of Lake Erie for William Gwinn Mather, a Cleveland industrialist. Platt sited the house as close to the water as possible, with a curved Neoclassical portico and a terrace overlooking a curved seawall with a pavilion at either end. "The effect which I tried for from the start," he said, "is

FIGURE 12. Brickell Point, c. 1917. The swampy mangrove hammock did not appear an auspicious site for an Italian villa. (Photograph by Mattie Edwards Hewitt, Vizcaya Museum and Gardens Archive, vol. 17, 74)

to make the house appear to be directly on the lake."[24] While the overall impression of the house is slightly odd—a sort of maritime White House—Gwinn and its beautiful gardens were admired and widely published in both professional and popular journals, and its unusual water-side location was much commented on.[25] It is likely that Deering would have known of it.

Deering's decision created a challenge for Hoffman and Chalfin. Most country houses of the period were designed in the form of a narrow rectangle, with one long side facing an arrival area and the other facing a garden. But since Deering wanted his house close to the water, the only logical place for the garden was on the side. Thus the house faced four directions: the arrival area (west), the bay (east), the garden (south), and the jungle landscape of the hammock (north).* Chalfin appreciated the unusual nature of this arrangement. When he visited the Villa Corsi, a Florentine Renaissance house with a seventeenth-century garden on the side, he wrote Hoffman: "It coincides with *our problem* [emphasis added] in two important particulars—It has an outlook east and south over artificial flat spaces—terrace east and pasture and separate garden south. While to the north there is a forest in just our relation to the house. In front of the villa there are fields where we have sea—with a wall between where we have a sea wall."[26]

The simplest way to make a four-sided house is to make it roughly square. The precise origin of the hollow square plan that Hoffman adopted is unknown, as no preliminary sketches have come to light.[27] However, since Chalfin and Deering spent almost two years working on the project *before* Hoffman came on the scene, it is likely that they had already arrived at the general concept of a square house with a central court. The Villa Rezzonico does not have a court, but there were many other precedents. Chalfin would have known the villas of Florence and would certainly have been familiar with the great Medici Villa La Petraia, which has a splendid central *cortile*. L'Ambrogiana was a Medici hunting lodge designed in the 1580s by Bernardo Buontalenti in the form of a hollow square with four corner towers. In the early 1900s, when Chalfin was in Italy, the Villa Ambrogiana was a mental hospital—and much changed—but he may have seen Giusto Utens' famous representation in the lunette of the *sala* of the Medici villa at Artimino.[28] There were also American country houses with courts, such as Whitehall, the Villa Turicum, and Gwinn. Or, the idea may have come from Clinton Mackenzie's preliminary design for Charles Deering's house (fig. 13). The site at Buena Vista, only a few miles up the coast, was remarkably similar to Brickell Point: a view to Biscayne Bay on the east, arrival from the west, and a garden on the south. Mackenzie's solution was a roughly square house with a central patio surrounded on all sides by an arcade, with an open-air gallery on the second floor leading to the bedrooms. Chalfin and Deering could have simply transformed the Spanish patio into an Italian *cortile*.

Hoffman would have appreciated the merits of Mackenzie's plan, for both were "Paris men," as École graduates were then called.[29] The École des Beaux-Arts, which was officially founded in 1816, although it had its roots in Louis XIV's royal academy of architecture, exerted

---

* The house is actually oriented at 45 degrees to the north-south axis, but to simplify communications during the construction, Deering instructed that the garden side should be referred to as south, the bay as east, and so on.

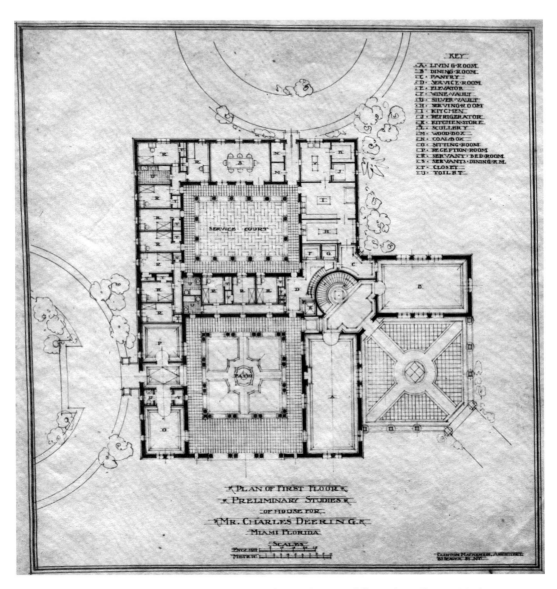

FIGURE 13. Charles Deering House, Buena Vista (c. 1910), ground floor plan, Clinton Mackenzie, architect. The courtyard influenced Deering's and Chalfin's concept for the house. (Historical Museum of Southern Florida)

a huge influence on the course of late nineteenth- and early twentieth-century American architecture. After 1855, when Richard Morris Hunt (the first American to attend the École) returned from Paris, it became the custom for talented American architects to round off their educations by studying in Paris. This included most of the best country-house architects: McKim, Carrère, Hastings, Delano, Chester Aldrich, Ernest Flagg, Grosvenor Atterbury, Julia Morgan (the first woman to graduate from the École), George Howe, and John Russell Pope. The leading firms where young architects apprenticed, such as McKim, Mead & White, and Carrère & Hastings, were consciously organized along École lines. For those who could not go to France, the Beaux-Arts Institute of Design in New York City (where Clinton Mackenzie taught), which started in 1894, coordinated study programs in various parts of the country.

John F. Harbeson, who headed the architecture department of the University of Pennsylvania, in 1927 published a widely used American guide to the Beaux-Arts teaching method. He listed the key features of the École: the division of the school into *ateliers*, or studios, each under the leadership of a *patron*; the use of practicing architects as teachers; an emphasis on design from the beginning of the program; the tradition of older students helping the younger (and vice versa); and the system of the *esquisse*.[30] The *esquisse*, or preliminary sketch, was the first stage of the Beaux-Arts design method. Students, working alone *en loge* (in a cubicle), without the aid of books or outside assistance, were given nine hours to translate the programmatic requirements of an assigned problem into a sketch design. Over the subsequent weeks, this design was refined and elaborated, but it could not be substantially altered.

The Beaux-Arts method emphasized the study of precedents. Students were expected to be familiar not only with the great buildings of the past, but also with the exemplary buildings of modern times. "In studying any problem, look for solutions of similar programs," wrote Harbeson, "find wherein the program of these previous examples differs from the program being studied. That is the point to attack, the part of the problem that requires a new solution."[31] The heart of the *esquisse* was the *parti*, or the central organizing idea of the design. According to Paul Philippe Cret, who established a celebrated Beaux-Arts curriculum at the University of Pennsylvania in 1903, "selecting a parti for a problem is to take an attitude toward a solution in the hope that a building developed on the lines indicated by it will give the best solution of the problem."[32] As Cret's description made clear, the *parti* was derived from the client's programmatic requirements. Hoffman's *parti* was a house organized around a central outdoor space, which was the heart of the design.

Composition was the foundation of the Beaux-Art method, and the key to composition was a well-designed plan. "In an architectural drawing, you must proceed by the axes," taught Harbeson.[33] An axis was a compositional line on the plan. It was seen in the mind's eye, but it was not an abstraction. In the completed building, axes corresponded to sight lines, or lines of movement, and determined the location of doors, windows, loggias, porticos, and stairs. A Beaux-Art plan generally had a hierarchy of axes: major and minor, more important and less important. In a courtyard plan, for example, it was the usual practice to create two axes intersecting in the center of the court. That is what Mackenzie had done at Buena Vista, and this is also what Hoffman did in his plan. The major east-west axis corresponded to the movement from the entrance, across the court, and to the waterside terrace with its splendid view of the bay. The minor north-south axis represented a secondary line of movement to the garden. Hoffman made the court itself a perfect square, 60 by 60 feet. However, unlike Mackenzie, who made the Buena Vista patio symmetrical, Hoffman placed arcades on only two sides—north and south—which accentuated the major axis. He located a different architectural "event" on each side of the courtyard: on the west side, the entrance loggia; opposite, overlooking the blue waters of Biscayne Bay, the cool and breezy open east loggia; on the south side, an enclosed loggia facing the garden; and on the north side, a wide open-air staircase (fig. 14).

Hoffman's plan does not exhibit the precise symmetry characteristic of a Beaux-Arts design. The living room, for example, is not perfectly balanced by the dining room, nor does the music room have a corresponding space on the other side of the east loggia. The size and proportions of the major public rooms—the reception room, living room, dining room, library, and music room—were in large measure determined by the room settings that Chalfin had assembled in New York. Hoffman ingeniously adjusted his plan to meet these requirements, with the four architectural "events"—the loggias and the open stair—functioning as architectural anchors. Together with the court itself, they create a strong architectural framework for the different-sized rooms.

Beaux-Arts planning was axial and regular, but it also stressed functionality. Hoffman laid out the public rooms in a U-shape to form the sequence that guests would follow on social occasions: loggia, entrance hall, reception room, living room, dining room. The living and dining rooms occupy corresponding corner positions on the bay side of the house, which gives them direct access to the waterside terrace. The doorways between the living and dining rooms are arranged *en filade*—lined up—so that guests could move processionally to dinner.

Hoffman's planning ability is particularly evident on the upper floors, which housed Deering's suite, five guestrooms, all with their own bathrooms, and three additional guestrooms in the two towers (figs. 15, 16). Deering's bedroom and sitting room, and the two primary guestrooms, face east, which not only gives them views of the bay, but also the morning sun. At the center of the east façade, on the main axis, is Deering's private balcony. A loggia on the south side, looking down the length of the garden, served as a small dining room. The pantry and kitchen are next door. This unusual location—kitchens were usually on the first floor—was intended to prevent smells from being drawn into the court. The kitchen was in a service block that overlooked the entrance drive and arrival area, and contained fourteen servants' rooms as well as the servants' hall. This part of the house followed the common Renaissance practice of inserting extra floors for servants' use by creating low-ceilinged *ammezzati*, or mezzanines. At Deering's insistence, the outdoor passage that linked the two sides of the service wing was carefully screened from public view.

As in a Renaissance villa, Vizcaya's basement is at ground level, in this case slightly above mean high tide. This is not readily apparent from the exterior, since the ground on three sides of the house was raised to create an artificial platform. On the north side, the grade was left at its natural level, which allows the basement to open directly to the garden. This part of the

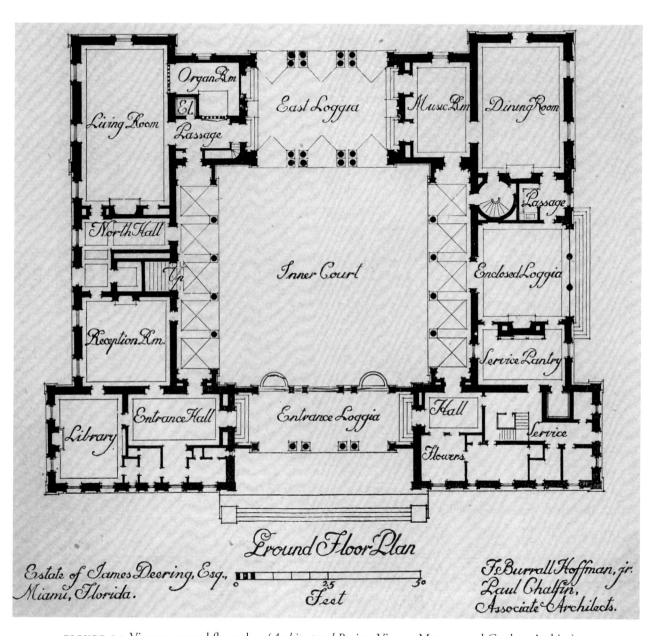

Living Room

Organ Rm

El.

Passage

East Loggia

Music Rm

Dining Room

North Hall

Inner Court

Passage

Enclosed Loggia

Reception Rm.

Up

Service Pantry

Library

Entrance Hall

Entrance Loggia

Hall

Service

Flowers

Ground Floor Plan

Estate of James Deering, Esq.,
Miami, Florida.

F. Burrall Hoffman, jr.
Paul Chalfin,
Associate Architects.

0   25   30
Feet

FIGURE 14. Vizcaya, ground floor plan. (*Architectural Review*, Vizcaya Museum and Gardens Archive)

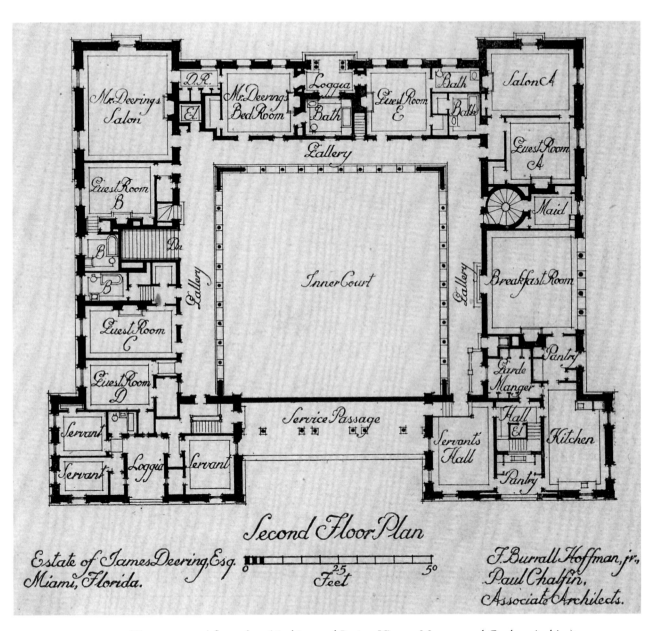

FIGURE 15. Vizcaya, second floor plan. (*Architectural Review*, Vizcaya Museum and Gardens Archive)

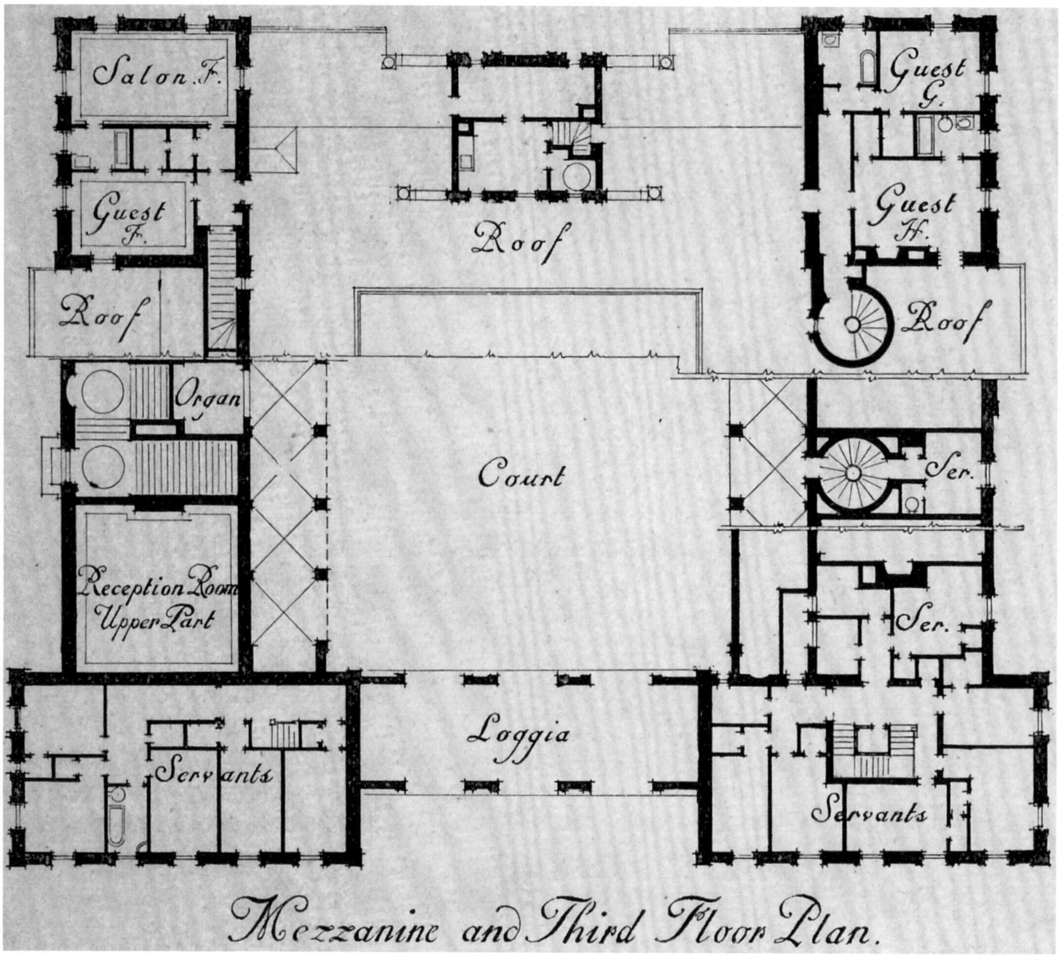
Salon F.
Guest G.
Guest F.
Roof
Guest H.
Roof
Roof
Organ
Court
Ser.
Reception Room
Upper Part
Ser.
Loggia
Servants
Servants
Mezzanine and Third Floor Plan.

FIGURE 16. Vizcaya, third floor and mezzanine plan. (*Architectural Review*, Vizcaya Museum and Gardens Archive)

basement contained what Deering called a "sports room," the indoor/outdoor swimming pool with changing rooms, a billiard room, and a bowling alley. He had also wanted a shooting gallery, but this could not be accommodated. Deering was very concerned about the welfare of his guests. "Though I personally get no fun out of it," he advised Hoffman, "I think I am likely to have a roulette table in the establishment. If so, a little partition should be put in the billiard room behind which this can either be operated or at least stored out of sight, for in a community like Miami it would be easy to get an undeserved reputation as a gambler."[34] In the same spirit, he recommended that Hoffman include a concealed bar. "It could be opened for the ungodly and closed for the godly," he added, with a rare show of humor.[35] This area also contained a smoking room. In this traditional male preserve, Deering insisted—to Chalfin's chagrin—on displaying his collection of mounted hunting trophies: the heads of deer, mountain sheep, and bison. He also had pieces of Samurai armor acquired during his Japanese trip. Chalfin held his nose, and decorated the walls with old cartoons for tapestries.

Chalfin may have been an aesthete of the first order, but he had an unexpectedly practical side. For example, he was very concerned that the house should withstand the rigors of a tropical climate. That was one of the things that he did not like about Flagler's Whitehall. "The plan provides nothing for keeping specially cool, nothing for currents of air, nothing for outdoor life," he explained to Hoffman, "and shows no devices for resisting dampness, heat, insects, torrential rains or hurricane tides, uneven temperatures or any other of those special conditions which have made the development of our plans so complicated and lengthy."[36] (That was Chalfin being crabby—actually, Whitehall had an open first-floor loggia and a glazed second-story arcade that could be completely opened and shaded with Bermuda shutters.) Hoffman, who was born in New Orleans, his mother's hometown, shared Chalfin's concern. His plan provided a variety of outdoor rooms: the shaded arcades, several loggias with varying degrees of enclosure, above all, the court itself (fig. 17). Thanks to the arcades, in case of showers guests could walk under cover from the entrance loggia to the living and dining rooms.

Such intimacy with the out-of-doors makes Hoffman's design more truly Mediterranean than almost any other American country house. There are no interior corridors; instead the guestrooms are reached by means of a roofed outdoor gallery (as in Mackenzie's design). The unorthodox (for America) open-air circulation concerned Deering. "This is something that only experience can tell the disadvantage of," he complained, but did not insist on a change.[37] At his request, Chalfin installed canvas curtains on the upper galleries to provide protection from sun and rain; awnings and curtains performed the same function for the east and west loggias.[38] There were mosquitoes, but Deering resisted the idea of screen doors. Chalfin suggested curtains woven out of silk with weighted bottoms instead, but it is unclear if they were ever installed.[39] The windows were protected from sun by external Venetian blinds that were raised into concealed pockets. When lowered and closed tight, the blinds acted as hurricane shutters; they could also be tilted open for shade and ventilation, like Bermuda shutters.

FIGURE 17. View of completed inner court, looking toward east loggia, c. 1917. Deering used the court for dining, lounging, and watching movies. (Photograph by Mattie Edwards Hewitt, Florida Historical Society)

Thanks to the interior court, the house is deceptively intimate; in fact, the gross floor area, not including the basement, exceeds 30,000 square feet—large, but hardly the largest house of the day. Oheka (1914–17), designed by Delano & Aldrich for the industrialist Otto H. Kahn, enclosed 50,000 square feet. Both were dwarfed by Whitemarsh Hall (1916–19), a 100,000-square-foot behemoth outside Philadelphia, designed by Horace Trumbauer for Edward Stotesbury, a Philadelphia banker.

During the winter season, which lasted from mid-December to mid-April, Deering had a household staff of about thirty, which included a housekeeper, a French chef, a Swedish cook, a butler, two footmen, a valet, and six housemaids (later there would be one or two nurses).* Even during the summer, when the house was empty, a large staff was required. The furnace had to be regularly turned on (to counteract humidity). Rooms had to be cleaned and aired to combat mold and mildew. Every summer the books in the library were individually

---

* The outside staff, which included gardeners, groundsmen, farmworkers, mechanics, boatmen, and a chauffeur, numbered as many as a hundred.

wrapped in newspaper to guard them against the ravages of silverfish. Special precautions had to be taken to protect curtains and drapes from cockroaches, and stored linens had to be regularly washed to prevent fungus. Even the fifty-nine clocks had to be kept wound in order to prevent corrosion.[40]

A large house that depended on domestic help required not only extensive living accommodations, but also a carefully designed "back-of-the-house." Service stairs and dumbwaiters delivered meals to pantries and *garde-mangers*. Valeting and sewing rooms were scattered about the house. A service area on the first floor contained a room for cutting and arranging flowers, a valeting and boot room, a linen and china room, and a rouge room, named after the jeweler's rouge, or fine buffing powder, that was used to polish gold and silver plate. The labyrinthine basement housed cellars for food and wine, as well as a secret liquor store that was added during Prohibition. There was a vault for valuables, a coal storage bin, a boiler room, and a mechanical room that contained the fans that circulated heated air. The laundry, which was located in a freestanding pavilion on the south side of the house, had a 10,000-gallon tank for collecting rainwater. Water for the house was supplied from a deep well. There were two electrically operated pumps and a standby gas-powered engine, in case of power failures. Deering was particularly concerned about fire safety. Ingalls tried to convinced him that sprinklers would be a good idea. Chalfin, who found the idea "grotesque," was able to defeat it when he remembered that such systems would require annual testing. Deering instead insisted on having fire hoses and hydrants installed in concealed wall cabinets on every floor of the house. He also demanded that the estate have a fire engine, which was parked in a garage next to the laundry.

American country-house owners of the period expected domestic convenience, but Deering, with his background in engineering and industry, was especially interested in new technology. As early as 1911, he had adventurously—only eight years after Kitty Hawk—flown in a French biplane around Paris "for over half an hour, covering 25 miles," according to an admiring *New York Times* correspondent.[41] At a time when telephone switchboards were the norm, the house was served by an automatic electric telephone exchange, which provided callers with privacy since it eliminated the operator. There was a central vacuum system with outlets on every floor to which 80-foot-long hoses could be attached, a burglar alarm system, and a synchronized electric clock system. An "annunciator" allowed Deering to call servants with the minimum exertion, should he become bedridden. The issue of his likely future ill-health weighed heavily on him. As early as 1915, he asked Chalfin to make sure that the house and gardens would accommodate a wheelchair, although he admitted that "this sounds somewhat ridiculous and is not very cheerful for a man my age."[42] He had an Otis elevator located next to his bedroom, so he could descend directly to the swimming pool in the basement. Like his bath, the swimming pool could be filled with fresh or sea water. There was a central brine refrigeration system and coal-fired central hot-air heating. He requested a weather vane and an anemometer to measure wind direction and speed, and he wanted the dials mounted in the east loggia. Chalfin convinced him that they should be located in the court instead. He did not share Deering's enthusiasm for gadgets. "The house is already awfully overorganized," he complained to Hoffman. "I dislike master clocks intensely."[43]

Chalfin spent more time on the construction site than anyone else.*[44] He was not stand-offish with the workers. According to one of the contractors, "Chalfin talked the language of the workmen, whom he knew by name. He made sure that they took a personal interest in their work."[45] In 1915 Chalfin commissioned a Miami boatyard (at Deering's expense) to build a luxurious houseboat, *The Blue Dog*, which could be moored at the building site and serve as his temporary home. The 74-foot-long barge had three staterooms, a salon with a stone fireplace, servants' quarters, and a large canopied upper deck furnished with comfortable rattan furniture.†[46] Chalfin, whose responsibilities at the time included decorating and furnishing Deering's house in Chicago as well as his apartment in New York, was paid a princely monthly salary of about $1,000, in addition to his living expenses in Florida.[47] "I felt very rich," he later recalled.[48] Although Deering maintained strict control over every detail of his Florida house, he formally authorized Chalfin to make purchases on his behalf. Chalfin was intimately involved in all aspects of design and construction. He received copies of correspondence between Deering, who was often in Chicago, and Hoffman. When he was not traveling with his employer, he often met Hoffman and Ingalls in their East 40th Street office.

By this time Chalfin was functioning as much more than merely artistic adviser. Initially he borrowed Hoffman and Ingalls' office staff to prepare details for the house. Later he established his own design studio and workshop in New York, which at its height, in 1916, employed eighty-five people, architects and draftsmen, as well as painters, carpenters, and upholsterers. It was understood that, eventually, Chalfin would strike out on his own as an architect and decorator (Deering even agreed to lend him money to launch his business). In the meantime, the studio had only one client, and the payroll, rent, and overheads, which amounted to as much as $15,000 a month, were paid by Deering.[49]

Although Deering supported Chalfin, that did not mean—as in the case of the master clocks—that Chalfin's opinion always prevailed. There was the matter of the organ, for example. Deering was intent on having a large organ, manufactured by Welte & Söhne of Freibourg. Chalfin thought that the console should be in the music room rather than in the living room, where it intruded on the décor. The console ended up in the living room, where Deering wanted it. On purely aesthetic matters, however, Deering often deferred to Chalfin. He once instructed Hoffman that the upper walls of the smoking room were for "miscellaneous pictures of a kind that Mr. Chalfin is not willing to see put in other rooms as being out of character with the decoration of the furniture."[50]

In the same letter, Deering mentioned "what we have called the Village." This referred to a complex of buildings, some distance from the main house, designed in a charming picturesque style that recalled the rustic architecture of a small Veneto town. Closest to the house were a gatehouse (fig. 18) and nearby living quarters for the chauffeur. These are the most architecturally ambitious buildings in the group, with giant Ionic pilasters and a monumental

---

* While Deering's house was under construction, Hoffman was involved in several other projects, including two churches and a large country house on Long Island.

† There was also a second, more modest houseboat, the *Singerie*, where Chalfin's staff often stayed.

gate leading to a courtyard. Alongside the courtyard were a garage and a machine shop. There were many vehicles at Vizcaya; in 1918 the roster of passenger cars included two Packards, two Fords, a Dodge, and a Fiat, as well as a Harley-Davidson motorcycle and two Indiana trucks (fig. 19).[51] The Village contained buildings for the superintendent, the estate workers, and workshops, as well as a number of farm buildings including a dairy, stable, carriage shed, poultry house, and greenhouses. Like its Renaissance antecedents, Deering's estate included a working farm and extensive citrus groves. Partly this was a matter of convenience, providing necessities for the house, but it also served to reinforce the *villeggiatura* experience.

The beginning of construction was inauspicious. The builders were unable to locate solid load-bearing soil near the surface, which meant that expensive pilings might have to be used. Deering bridled at the extra cost. The alternative was to move the house inland, something the architects—now convinced of the wisdom of Deering's choice—were loath to do. On October 1, 1913, Hoffman telegraphed Deering: "Have consulted with Ingalls and Chalfin and agree best to keep house on present site."[52] Finally, soil of sufficient bearing capacity was located at a shallow depth, so the house could rest on simple footings.

Hoffman and Ingalls finished the working drawings in February 1914, and construction began that spring. It was a mammoth project. The superintendent was Joseph A. McDonald, Flagler's builder. The first general contractor was George Sykes, a New Yorker who had worked with Hoffman, but when he proved unequal to the task, he was replaced by Fred T. Ley & Company, a large New York builder (later responsible for the Chrysler Building). The technical challenges of the remote site were daunting. A railroad spur for delivering building

FIGURE 18. The gate lodge, c. 1917. The main entrance, off South Miami Avenue, signaled the Italian theme. (Photograph by Mattie Edwards Hewitt, Vizcaya Museum and Gardens Archive, vol. 8, 44)

materials had to be built from Flagler's Florida East Coast Railway, which ran next to the northwest boundary of the site. A long channel—now called the Deering Channel—and a harbor were dredged in the shallow bay to allow ships to berth and discharge building materials and art shipments. A stationary steam engine pulled wagons on narrow-gauge tracks that snaked over the site. At the height of construction, as many as a thousand workers were employed on the house and gardens.

The work is documented in a series of photographs, which were made for Deering so that he could monitor the progress of the project while he was in Chicago and elsewhere. Many of the images were made by Mattie Edwards Hewitt (c. 1870–1956), who specialized in location photography for architects, landscape architects, and designers.[53] She had worked for Carrère & Hastings, so perhaps it was Hoffman who recommended her. Deering had the construction photographs bound into thick, leather-covered volumes. There would eventually be twelve, containing several thousand images. The first photographs show surveying, excavation, footings being poured, and land for the future terraces and garden being built up to the required level. South Miami Avenue originally ran too close to the house for Deering's taste. Chalfin arranged with the City of Miami to have the road moved several hundred feet inland and had a canal blasted out of the coral along the old right-of-way. The rubble provided material for garden and terrace landfill. Tall viewing towers were built to test the vistas from the upper floors of the house. By July the foundations were being poured.

The main building material of the house is concrete: solid, largely unreinforced concrete walls and reinforced concrete floors carried on steel I-beams. This technique, with which Joseph McDonald was intimately familiar, was developed by Carrère & Hastings for the Ponce de León and the Alcazar, which were the first large public buildings in the United States

FIGURE 19. The garage court, c. 1917. Two of the many estate vehicles, with the machine shop in the background. (Photograph by Mattie Edwards Hewitt, Vizcaya Museum and Gardens Archive, vol. 8, 49)

to be built entirely of concrete.[54] It was also used at Whitehall. Resistant to termites, decay, hurricanes, and fire, concrete was an ideal material for south Florida. Vizcaya's massive exterior walls are 22 inches thick, the interior walls 18 inches. The simple construction technique— the concrete was poured between movable wooden forms—made for fast progress. By August the walls were up to the level of the first floor; by October they were almost up to the second. In the photographs, the tramway tracks, carrying fresh concrete to the top of the formwork, resemble a roller coaster (fig. 20). Ingalls, who seems to have overseen technical issues, wanted to use concrete throughout, but Chalfin insisted on stone for lintels and trim and on covering the concrete roof with clay tiles. In October the tiles, which Chalfin found in Cuba, arrived, and a test section of roofing was built to finalize the details at eaves, valleys, and ridges.

When he was in Florida, Deering visited the site every day. He was popular with the workers, who called him "Mr. Jimmy." At the time there were about four hundred men engaged in the project. "There was the feeling of a family," recalled Joe Orr, one of the contractors. "The workmen were organized into teams for tennis, cricket and soccer. Deering . . . awarded medals."[55] By March 1915, a year into the construction, the walls had reached their full height and work began on the roof structure: massive cypress beams, 3 by 8 inches, placed 16 inches apart. The exterior of the house was shrouded with scaffolding as masons added stone trim and plasterers began finishing the walls (fig. 21). The columns of the loggias made their appearance. Except for the antiquarian architectural elements imported from Italy, the stone trim was carved on the site. The window frames and column trim were limestone from Cuba; lesser details were local Florida keystone. Work on the south and west façades proceeded smoothly, but then

FIGURE 20. The construction site, February 1915. A steam-powered system of tramways delivered concrete to the upper levels of the building. (Photograph by Mattie Edwards Hewitt, Vizcaya Museum and Gardens Archive, vol. 2, 35)

things started to slow down. There were problems with the north side of the house. When the foundations for the exterior stairs were poured, Chalfin realized that the curved flights would block too much light from the billiard room. Hoffman redesigned the stairs to be straight, and the foundations were demolished and recast. Deering went along with the change, but wrote to the architect: "I have no comment to make, except to say that it is evident that there will be more light, and it seems to me to be equally evident that the entrance will not be as attractive as it was at first planned to be."[56] When the stairs were changed, someone, probably Chalfin, redesigned the entrance door, adding two massive, attached rusticated columns.

There were also problems with the east façade. Deering, in Chicago, examined photographs of the finished work and wrote to Hoffman: "I am, as you conjecture, particularly interested in the front façade. There, it seems to me, lies the question of the chief artistic success or failure of the house."[57] He also telegraphed Chalfin, asking if he was satisfied. Chalfin's answer was curt: "Not satisfied with east façade. Will write you."[58] In the letter, Chalfin explained that he was disturbed by the overhanging eaves, which had been a bone of contention during the design phase (fig. 23). Deering and Hoffman wanted deep overhangs, while Chalfin thought that eaves were superfluous. But that was not his current objection. "I am now opposed to them because they cast a shadow at certain times of the day down to the ground, leaving the part of the façade under the middle motif free of shadow, and thus dividing the whole façade into five parts."[59] The simple solution, as Chalfin saw it, was to eliminate the eaves. Deering, unconvinced, instructed him to do nothing until he, Deering, saw the situation for himself during his next visit to Florida. Nevertheless, Hoffman took it upon himself to cut back part of the eave on the left side of the house in order to test the effect (fig. 24). When he saw the photographs, Deering was upset and ordered the work stopped. For the next few months, while construction of the rest of the house continued at a brisk pace, the east façade stood untouched.

FIGURE 21. The construction site, July 1915. The roof was complete and plastering of the west façade was well under way. (Photograph by Mattie Edwards Hewitt, Vizcaya Museum and Gardens Archive, vol. 3, 36)

Deering had been promised a house in eighteen months. That was a reasonable estimate. Trumbauer took only ten months to build Whitemarsh Hall; admittedly, the suburban site was less challenging, but the 145-room house was considerably larger.[60] By the end of the second year it was evident that Vizcaya was nowhere near completion. Deering wanted to move in, even if the decoration of the rooms was incomplete, but Chalfin would not be hurried. He blamed Hoffman for the delay; Hoffman blamed the contractor. It was an uneasy time. Finally, after forming a committee to coordinate the complex construction process, Deering decided that the project needed one person in charge. "Should be glad to have you take this final authority in all matters," he instructed Chalfin in January 1916.[61]

That winter, with Deering and Chalfin on the site, work resumed on the east façade. The truth was that even cut back the eaves looked awkward; this important façade called for a more considered treatment. A second test was made. A photograph shows the eaves on the left side entirely concealed by a low parapet (fig. 25). Hoffman wrote Deering that "the revised scheme and detail of central gable third story east front as restudied by Chalfin and me" would cost

FIGURE 22. The construction site, July 1916. More than a thousand workers were employed at Vizcaya at the height of construction, including these black laborers, many of whom came from the Bahamas. Note the anemometer and wind direction indicator on the courtyard wall. (Photograph by Mattie Edwards Hewitt, Vizcaya Museum and Gardens Archive, vol. 6, 28)

$1,950.[62] Deering agreed to the parapet solution. Yet for several months, nothing happened. Taking advantage of the change, Chalfin decided to redo the entire façade. He did not like the shape of the volutes that Hoffman had designed, and he thought the central loggia was too plain. Since they were rebuilding the eaves, Chalfin took the opportunity to correct these shortcomings. His changes turned Hoffman's rather simple Renaissance design into a full-fledged seventeenth-century baroque composition (fig. 26). Chalfin added the parapet walls, as well as four finials and two statues. He reshaped the offensive volutes, giving them more of a flourish, replaced the columns on Deering's private loggia (Hoffman had short columns on pedestals), added elaborate plaster carving and a *mascherone*, or grotesque mask, to the keystone of the *serliana*, and modified the upper-story windows with decorative pediments and rocaille panels. He sent eight full-size drawings of details to Ley. The change cost $6,000 in all.[63]

FIGURE 23. The east façade, August 1915. Although the work was complete, Chalfin did not like the deep shadows cast by the eaves. (Photograph by Mattie Edwards Hewitt, Vizcaya Museum and Gardens Archive, vol. 3, 53)

FIGURE 24. The east façade, September 1915. Note that the eaves on the left section have been cut back. (Photograph by Mattie Edwards Hewitt, Vizcaya Museum and Gardens Archive, vol. 4, 11)

Chalfin did not get his way on one issue: the windows of the tower rooms. There were three windows on the north and west sides, but only two on the east sides, which in his opinion created an unbalanced effect when the towers were seen at an angle. Chalfin wanted to add a false window to each tower, arguing that it would be cheaper to get this done while the east façade was being altered. Deering, concerned that this would further delay completion, vetoed the proposal. He was not convinced it was necessary, he told Chalfin, but if it had to be done, it would have to be done later, even if it cost more.[64]

By then, work was well under way on the interiors. The court was complete, and except for the east façade, which would not be finished until the fall, the exterior of the house was done. From then on, the site photographs are chiefly of the rooms that Chalfin was building

FIGURE 25. The east façade, August 1916. Chalfin and Hoffman experimented with a parapet wall on the left side. (Photograph by Mattie Edwards Hewitt, Vizcaya Museum and Gardens Archive, vol. 5, 25)

FIGURE 26. The east façade, December 1916. The façade has been significantly altered: note the prominent volutes, the more elaborate window frames, and the richly ornamented *serliana*. The false windows in the towers have not yet been installed. (Photograph by Mattie Edwards Hewitt, Vizcaya Museum and Gardens Archive)

inside Hoffman's concrete shell. One by one the rooms took shape: the library, the entrance hall, the living room, the dining room. Finally, in the fall of 1916, the interior was substantially complete. Deering moved in on Christmas Day, arriving ceremoniously by boat. Chalfin organized festivities that included cannons firing a salute and a masquerade ball.

That April, after Deering returned to Chicago, work continued on the surroundings of the house and, of course, the garden. Chalfin had the false windows, complete with shutters, added to the towers. There were many details to attend to. During his stay, Deering had compiled extensive "to do" lists, which he sent to Chalfin over the next few months.[65] They reveal that the demanding employer expected no less than perfection. "Need hook to hang binoculars in my loggia also in open loggia." "Give me memo of explanation of names of bedrooms." "No bedroom should have a ticking clock. Every bedroom should have a bedside clock. (Why was I requested to buy none in Paris?)" "Dressing Room: Men's room has small place to hang raiment—women's none at all—must rearrange this." "Electric push buttons needed in Court." And on, and on.

Deering came up with the name for the house.[66] It was indicative of his interest in Florida that he eschewed an Italian name and chose Vizcaya, the name of the Spanish Basque province after which Biscayne Bay is said to have been named (the Castilian "v" being pronounced "b"). He said he liked the way it sounded. Characteristically, Deering and Chalfin batted the idea around for a year before coming to a final decision. At one point Deering favored Viscaino, the name of Ponce de León's ship's master. Chalfin objected that Viscaino simply meant a native of Vizcaya. "Supposing that Viscaino's name had been Genovese, meaning an inhabitant of Genoa, it would have been obviously more proper to call your villa Genoa than to call your villa Genovese," he argued.[67] Deering relented, and Vizcaya it stayed.

In July 1917 the *Architectural Review* devoted an entire issue to Vizcaya, copiously illustrated by Mattie Edwards Hewitt's photographs. Though unattributed, the text appears to have been written by Chalfin.[68] He explained that the house was intended to look as if it had been modified and added to over a long time. The corner towers and the court had the feeling of the fifteenth century, he wrote, "the garden front shows early sixteenth-century details, while the north front is influenced by the types of Longhena, and the eastern [sic] façade by the work of Juvarra and Piedmontese, and the bold rolling volutes and the Gallicized upper loggia to the east derive from the eighteenth century."[69] Years later, in one of a series of articles that he wrote for the *Miami Herald*, he described the fronts differently: "One might say, then, looking a little beyond the 16th century, that at Vizcaya the architecture of the days of Columbus looks toward the sea; that of Michelangelo looks northward (the 16th); that of Louis XIV toward the garden (the 17th), and that of Madame de Pompadour greets you as you approach through the park."[70]

Although inconsistent, these frequently quoted descriptions give the impression that each façade of Vizcaya was designed to represent a different historical period.[71] This is misleading. Designing each façade in a different historical style would not give the impression of old age, merely of eccentricity. Chalfin's fanciful—and somewhat garbled—descriptions reflected only his general intention: that the exterior, like the décor and furnishings of the house, should reflect a span of several hundred years. Vizcaya was to be a house "where no uniform style is worn by the sweet and human objects within," he wrote, "but where a garment of beauty is spread over the things of centuries."[72]

When architects such as Hunt or McKim looked to history, they usually found inspiration in a single period—François I or Italian Renaissance—and aimed for stylistic consistency. Chalfin's goal was different. He once observed about the villas that he and Deering had visited that "Italian prototypes are often the growth, outwardly, of several centuries."[73] An unattributed 1917 *Vogue* article on Vizcaya, which was either written by Chalfin or based on his comments, explained this phenomenon: "Comparatively few Italian houses have a continuity covering centuries, but those which have show clearly a progress from the day that the house was a man's fortress, down to the ostentation of the later sixteenth century and the period of Versailles, through the lawlessness of Italian rococo, the charm and enterprise of the Pompeian period, the frigid doctrinaire emotion of a Napoleonic period, the Risorgimento with its incredible Victorianism, and even an hysterical return to artistry in Italian art nouveau."[74] One of the Italian villas that Chalfin and Deering visited several times during their travels fits this description. La Pietra, outside Florence, was the home of the Anglo-Italian art collector and dealer Arthur Mario Acton (1879–1952) and his wife, Hortense Mitchell, a Chicago socialite and banking heiress whose family Deering would have known. Their son, Harold Acton, who would become a noted writer and historian, was born and raised at La Pietra and called the house an "architectural palimpsest," referring to a parchment that has been written on more than once, with the earlier writing still visible.[75] The original structure was a fortified farmhouse of the fourteenth century, which had been transformed in 1460 into a typical Quattrocento villa, a hollow square with a central court. In the seventeenth century, a new owner, a cardinal, remodeled the exterior, adding pediments to the fifteenth-century lintels and frescoes inside and modifying the court into an open-air rotunda. In the 1800s the rotunda was roofed over with a glass skylight, and the narrow medieval stair was replaced by a circular Neoclassical version.[76] Arthur Acton added a central Mannerist fountain.

Little is known of Arthur Acton's forebears (some said he was born illegitimate), except that his mother was Neapolitan and his father a descendant of an English adventurer who had settled in Naples.[77] Before his marriage, Arthur worked as an agent for Stanford White, furnishing the interiors of several large houses. He did the same for Chalfin, with whom he carried on a warm correspondence—"my dear Chalfin"—and to whom he sold several paintings and objets d'art, both for Deering and for himself. Chalfin liked what Acton had done at La Pietra. The house contained a large and eclectic collection of (mostly lackluster) paintings, as well as furniture, architectural fragments, bibelots, and bric-a-brac. The *salone* was decorated with Cinquecento tapestries, Oriental vases, and eighteenth-century chairs. The walls of the vaulted dining room were adorned with Renaissance sculptures and Italian primitives. The sitting room contained a mixture of rococo furniture and assorted chinoiseries. The ambiance was of an ancestral home in which objects had accumulated over generations. In fact, Acton had bought and refurbished the villa with his wife's fortune and had lived in La Pietra for less than a decade when Chalfin saw it.

In 1921 Berenson, writing to Isabella Gardner from Florence, introduced his neighbor Arthur Acton in less than flattering terms: "He is a 'bounder,' but he has a flair for good things, and would appreciate yours, if there were a chance of his getting to see them."[78] This could just as well serve as a thumbnail description of Chalfin, who must have appreciated the high degree of artifice that colored the mock-aristocratic life at La Pietra. He once confessed to Acton that Vizcaya was "almost imposing as the Palazzo Pitti, if you [can imagine the] Pitti standing on a lagoon in Africa."[79] It is a remarkably candid admission. Chalfin was aware that what he was trying to do in Florida could be construed as faintly ridiculous. In that regard, he was struggling with the same problem that confronted all the historicizing country-house builders of the Gilded Age. "At the core of the American Renaissance was a conflicted idea which tried to come out as serene idealism," writes Robert Hughes.[80] The conflict was between wealthy Americans' belief in their own superiority (manifested in the economic might of corporations such as International Harvester) and their real cultural insecurity. The solution, promoted by Berenson and others, was to seek artistic sanction in the past by idealizing an older civilization such as the Renaissance, and in that same spirit of idealism, boldly laying claim to it. That was what Augustus Saint-Gaudens had meant when, in 1891, he famously said to Daniel Burnham, during a meeting of the architects planning the World's Columbian Exposition in Chicago: "Look here, old fellow, do you realize that this is the greatest meeting of artists since the fifteenth century!"[81] Chalfin's ambition, influenced no doubt by Fenway Court and La Pietra, was to go one step further. At Vizcaya, he would not merely capture a historical moment, but do something more subtle and more complicated. He would re-create the sweep of history.

Vizcaya has a hollow square plan, but unlike Mackenzie's Buena Vista house, the individual wings are clearly articulated: a long block with towers facing the bay; two short wings on the north and south sides; and a lower and longer wing closing the court across the west side. This articulation intentionally disrupts the architectural unity of the composition. The short south wing, with its delicate loggias, and the north wing, with its rather heavier stairway and entrance, are distinct from the more massive and more richly decorated towered block. The low service wing, which overlaps the house by about fifteen feet, gives the impression of having been added later.

The east façade—the only elevation that is symmetrical—is, as Deering wrote, the key to the composition (fig. 27). The best view of Vizcaya is not from the land, but from a boat on Biscayne Bay, which is exactly how Deering saw it first, that Christmas Day in 1916. The long, straight channel forms a maritime allée, marked by buoys rather than poplars, perfectly aligned with the center of the house. The distant view of the house from the water explains why Chalfin and Deering were attracted to the Villa Rezzonico: the distinctive silhouette with its two towers is clearly recognizable from several thousand feet away (fig. 28).

The 1917 *Vogue* article stated that the house "seems to break out into a smile with its voluted gable, its statues and vases, subordinated to a great mass."[82] The gable centerpiece, with a sundial and a Latin inscription, is surmounted by a curved broken pediment with a finial supporting a weathervane. More finials and statues decorate the parapet walls. Below the sundial is Deering's private loggia in the form of a *serliana*. The arch displays the rich ornamentation and plaster carvings of Chalfin's last-minute modifications. The arches of the tripartite open loggia below are supported by quadruple Doric columns, which John Singer Sargent, who visited Vizcaya, considered the house's "finest architectural effect." Sargent pointed out to Deering that the canvas curtains, which bisected the column cluster, somewhat spoiled the effect.[83] Chalfin agreed, but was unable to find an alternative solution.[84]

For all its richness, Vizcaya's architecture is remarkably rustic. The walls are roughly plastered stucco and the roofs are irregular red-clay tiles, just like an Italian Renaissance villa. Chalfin, no doubt influenced by Isabella Gardner, took a good deal of trouble to make the exterior appear handmade. He had the walls painted pink—like Fenway Court—using a lime-based wash to give a variegated appearance; the roof tiles were naturally weathered, having been removed from hundred-year-old buildings in Cuba.[85] The local oolitic limestone, some quarried on the site, with its irregular porous surface appeared weathered almost at once.

The simplicity of Vizcaya's exterior is not often remarked upon, but it was unusual among the ornate country houses of the Gilded Age. Even Platt's simple villas have a more polished appearance. Vizcaya was no Jamesian white elephant. The rough-and-ready exterior architecture was a matter of taste, not economy. Deering never divulged the total cost of Vizcaya, but according to Hoffman, the house alone, not including the interior décor, while originally

FIGURE 27. The east façade. Deering considered this side of the house "the key to the composition."

FIGURE 28. The east façade, view from Biscayne Bay. The most dramatic view of the house and its rich baroque motifs is from a boat, which is how Deering and his guests saw it after a day on the water.

estimated at $229,000, may have cost as much as $3 million (about $60 million in today's dollars).*[86] Deering bridled at the excessive cost, but soldiered on. In July 1916, as the house was nearing completion, he wrote Chalfin that "however innocently I got into it, I am in the game and feel that I should play it through to the point of getting a complete house . . . . Fortunately for me, my partners are very considerate and permit me to withdraw the capital that I need for these expenditures."[87] Deering is said to have "sputtered and fussed quite properly about Mr. Chalfin's lack of business or any sense of economy," and he was fastidious about accounting for even minor expenses.[88] Like all house builders, Deering experienced moments of anxiety. In 1919, when the lagoon gardens were being planned, he instructed Chalfin: "We want nothing shabby or indecent, but aside from this principle everything should be made as cheap as it can be made," and he confessed about Vizcaya that "I have made an investment here which I should not have made."[89] Yet he was never strapped for money. While he was building Vizcaya, he redecorated his home in Chicago, bought himself a house in Neuilly,

---

* A rough calculation suggests that the construction cost of the Vizcaya house was about $4/cubic foot, at a time when an *expensive* country house cost $1/cubic foot.

gave a million dollars to a Chicago hospital, and donated generously to French war relief. He was the richest man in Florida. In 1925 he was reported to have paid the highest personal income tax in the state—almost $180,000 (Charles Deering was ranked number three).[90] In his will James Deering bequeathed $500,000 to his nephew, $175,000 to his brother, more than $350,000 to sundry relatives and friends, as well as $1.5 million to charity.[91]

The garden façade on the south side is composed of three separate sections: the tall tower on the right, a central block, and the narrow end of the low west wing on the left (fig. 30). The central block, with a tripartite arched loggia surmounted by a second loggia, supported by delicate Ionic columns, is the most arresting part of the composition. After the verticality of the waterside façade, the house here is surprisingly horizontal. It is also unexpectedly casual, not exactly picturesque, but markedly unsymmetrical, like many sixteenth-century Tuscan villas. This unusual irregularity was intentional—the first version of the design had a tower at each corner, like the Villa Rezzonico, but Hoffman and Chalfin decided to eliminate the two towers on the west side.[92] As on the east side, the terraces were mainly grass. The broad stair leading to the garden was originally designed as two flights at right angles to the terrace and was altered to a single straight flight during construction.

The west façade, facing an oval entrance court, is long and low (fig. 31). The entrance loggia is formed of the same tripartite arches as on the other façades, but here supported by paired columns. By reducing the height of the central bay (the service passage is recessed), Hoffman subtly reproduced the *castello* effect, though with more squat proportions. The "towers" have loggias on the upper floors, and because the mezzanine servants' rooms have lower ceilings, there are three floors in the space of two, further reducing the scale of this distinctly ungrand entrance. The overall effect is notably informal and low key, because of the small scale, partly because the window placement is not symmetrical. The undramatic entrance heightens the experience of arriving at the open loggia and its stunning view of the bay.

The north façade appears considerably taller than the rest of the house, since the land was not artificially raised (fig. 32). The battered basement wall is finished in dressed stone rather than plaster. On the left, the swimming pool emerges dramatically from beneath the house between vaulted arches, giving the appearance of a canalside Venetian palazzo. The monumental double staircase leads up to the entrance. (Deering was right, a curved stair would have been prettier.) There is no tripartite loggia; instead, the heavy doorway is flanked by attached rusticated Doric columns surmounted by curved brackets supporting a balcony. The house overlooked a small *tapis vert* surrounded by a natural landscape of mangrove woods and wild hammock. A path through the woods terminated at a boat landing on a canal. In Deering's day, a small footbridge led to a rustic sitting area overlooking the bay.

The architecture critic Brendan Gill described Vizcaya as "far more than a mere adaptation—it was a work of considerable originality, successfully pretending to be centuries old and managing against high odds to bring into harmony scores of architectural elements unrelated

FIGURE 29. The east terrace, c. 1917. This view from James Deering's loggia shows the large expanses of grass originally on the terrace. (Photograph by Mattie Edwards Hewitt, Vizcaya Museum and Gardens Archive, vol. 7, 72)

FIGURE 30. The south façade. The informal tripartite composition, facing the garden, appears to have been built over several different periods.

in time, style and place of origin."[93] This achievement was the result of the peculiar nature of Chalfin and Hoffman's collaboration. Chalfin wanted to create the illusion that the house had been extended over time; Hoffman could not resist the architect's urge toward unity. He used the same quoins, the same window frames, and the same materials throughout. He made the details of the three arched loggias identical. The red-tiled roof also provides a strong sense of visual continuity, as does a horizontal masonry stringcourse that starts on the south façade, continues across the west façade (as a parapet), and turns the corner. Thus, thanks to Chalfin's and Hoffman's dissimilar approaches, the difference between the "parts" of the house is sometimes blurred and sometimes emphasized. The result is neither entirely painterly nor conventionally architectural, but always interesting.

Vizcaya is distinguished from its Renaissance predecessors by the full-blown architectural treatment given to each of its four façades. Hoffman and Chalfin deserve much credit for this architectural tour-de-force. What accounts for their success is a high degree of stylistic consistency: they both favored the richly expressive architecture of the seventeenth century, popularly called baroque. Hoffman made a field trip to northern Italy the year after starting work on the design, and he later recalled, in an interview with the author James Maher, being impressed by the scale of the Veneto villas and adjusting his plans accordingly. "What was really

FIGURE 31. The west façade. The entrance is distinctly ungrand.

important was not a particular villa," he emphasized, "it was discovering the baroque."[94] Chalfin was temperamentally drawn to the baroque, like his contemporary Geoffrey Scott, whose little masterpiece on the subject, *The Architecture of Humanism*, was published in 1914. Scott had been part of Berenson's circle in Florence, knew Arthur Acton, and was a friend of both Edith Wharton and Elsie de Wolfe. Although there is no evidence of direct contact between Chalfin and Scott, they represent a similar aesthetic sensibility. Scott was attracted to the Italian baroque because it was an architecture that was based not on theory but on direct experience. "The baroque is in the highest degree interesting," he wrote, "because of its purely psychological approach to the problem of design, its freedom from mechanical and academic 'taboos,' for its use of scale, its search for Movement, its preoccupation with Mass composition and Spatial values."[95] This view would have appealed to Chalfin who, like Scott, was an aesthete and an architectural dilettante. Of Vizcaya Chalfin wrote: "It is thus fundamentally by its simplicity that the house proclaims its inspiration as *Baroque.*"[96]

The Villa Rezzonico was the model for the twin towers on the east side.[97] Longhena's monumental stair clearly inspired the open stair at Vizcaya, and Chalfin incorporated the rusticated columns of Rezzonico's eighteenth-century *barchessa*, or outbuilding, into Vizcaya's north entrance.[98] Vizcaya's quoins, simple cornices, tile roofs, and plainly plastered walls also echo Longhena's severe design. But the Villa Rezzonico was not the only inspiration. Like Hunt at Biltmore, Hoffman and Chalfin introduced several other architectural "quotations."

FIGURE 32. The north façade. The chief features are the Mannerist entrance and the double staircase.

Chalfin identified the Roman eighteenth-century Villa Albani as a precedent for the open loggia facing the bay, although Hoffman's claim that he based it on the mid-sixteenth-century Villa Pliniana is more compelling.[99] The loggia of Pliniana, which overlooks Lake Como, has three arches supported by paired columns. Deering's balcony is in the form of a *serliana*, a device popularized by Palladio, but with Chalfin's rich modeling and the paired columns, it, too, has the flavor of the eighteenth century. The striking centerpiece of Vizcaya's east front is not based on a specific villa. Its overall shape—a broken curved pediment flanked by volutes—resembles the extraordinary centerpiece of the Palazzo Carignano in Turin, designed by Guarino Guarini in 1679. However, according to Chalfin, the inspiration was another Piedmont architect, the great Filippo Juvarra. In that case, it was probably his ornate altarpieces, such as the ones in Santa Teresa or in the Church of the Visitation in Turin, that serve as models for Vizcaya's centerpiece.[100]

One of the most original devices in Vizcaya is the hierarchical design of the three loggias: single columns on the garden side, paired columns on the entrance side, and quadruple columns on the bay side. Paired columns were common in Renaissance architecture ever since Bramante's famous House of Raphael (c. 1510), but quadruple columns were exceedingly rare. Clusters of four columns appear in the eighteenth century, but only in drawings—in Piranesi engravings and in sketches by the famous Bolognese stage-designer family, the Galli-Bibienis. The most obvious built precedent is more modern: Charles Garnier's Nouvel Opéra de Paris (1861–74), whose grand stair hall has two sets of quadruple columns supporting an arcade. Both Hoffman and Chalfin spent several years in Paris and would have known this prototypical Beaux-Arts building well, although the use of such a theatrical device bears Chalfin's imprint.

Some of Hoffman's watercolor travel sketches have survived.[101] Although quite conventional, they show a sensitive hand and a discerning eye. Nevertheless, the picturesque qualities of Vizcaya's composition are at odds with his training as an École rationalist. Rather, they reflect Chalfin's painterly touch. The creative relationship between the two men was complicated for it was not simply that of architect and client's representative. "I like to keep a close watch over the young men," Chalfin once wrote to Deering, "I mean by these both Hoffman and Sturrock [who was supervising the planting of the gardens], for fear that ideas which are good in themselves and which originate with them should not be in harmony with the awful long sighted scheme I have for the whole."[102] One could say, using a cinematic analogy, that if Hoffman was Vizcaya's director, Chalfin was its executive producer—an active, involved producer in the mold of Cecil B. De Mille (fig. 33). "Ninety percent of the beauty of Vizcaya is due to Paul Chalfin," James Deering used to say.[103] "Ninety percent" may be a little high, but there is no doubt that Chalfin, the virtuoso connoisseur, took the lead in this creative partnership, obsessively driving the project for more than a decade. He was fortunate to have at hand as skillful an architect as Hoffman to interpret his ideas and give them buildable form, and as sympathetic a client as Deering to share—and, of course, pay for—his vision.

The result of this fortuitous collaboration is a curious blend of architecture and theatricality, which may explain why Vizcaya has not been taken seriously by most architectural historians. But it should be. Vizcaya is a sincere and informed attempt to work within a historic

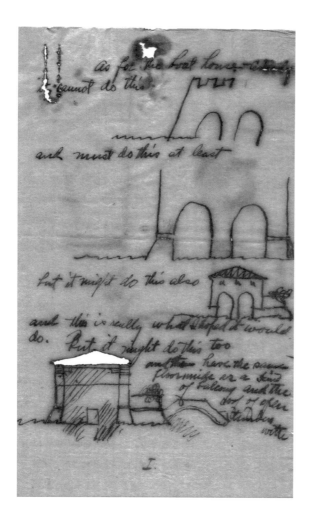

FIGURE 33. Chalfin's sketch, July 10, 1914. "I like to keep a close watch over the young men," Chalfin told Deering. This is a sketch that Chalfin sent to Hoffman illustrating his ideas for the boathouse. (Vizcaya Museum and Gardens Archive)

tradition. This sets it apart from the frankly scenographic designs of Addison Mizner, who created charming but fluffy historical pastiches in Palm Beach a decade later. Nor is Vizcaya simply an attempt to capture a historical moment, like the romantic western ranch houses of John Byers, or to manufacture a dreamy stage set, as Mellor, Meigs & Howe did in many of their Philadelphia country houses. Ultimately, Chalfin's subtle fusion of history, historicism, and historical memory defies intellectual analysis. "What we feel as 'beauty' in architecture is not a matter for logical demonstration," wrote Scott in *The Architecture of Humanism.* "It is experienced, consciously, as a direct and simple intuition, which has its ground in that subconscious region where our physical memories are stored."[104] This sentiment is echoed in the Latin inscription on the centerpiece of Vizcaya's chief façade: DONA· PRAESENTIS· CAPE· LAETUS· HORAE· ACLINQUE· SEVERE.* "Accept the gift of pleasure when it is given. Put serious things aside."[105] It is Horace, but it sounds like Chalfin admonishing his patron: Enjoy.

* The last word of the inscription should be "SEVERA."

chapter 4

CHALFIN'S ROOMS

In the summer of 1914, while Vizcaya was still under construction, Deering and Chalfin made a final shopping expedition to Europe. This time they were looking for specific objects to complete the house. As usual, they did not travel together. Deering stayed in Paris while Chalfin scouted antique dealers in Florence and Rome. Deering joined him in Rome, and they traveled together to Florence and Munich.[1] While Deering returned to Paris and London, Chalfin went to Venice, then stopped in Paris en route to New York. In July he wrote Hoffman from Paris with an unmistakable air of triumph: "The house is finished: The feature rooms almost all have this feature. All the mantels but one are bought, and door frames, etc., are established facts. And my head is cram full of ideas."[2] Chalfin had sole responsibility for the interiors. Hoffman's architectural drawings show the rooms as unfinished concrete boxes. Inside these boxes Chalfin, with the aid of his large design office and workshop, installed an inner architectural layer. The common practice in domestic decoration, following Alva Vanderbilt's lead, was to create a sort of historic sampler. Décor was sometimes linked to a room's function—a glittering Louis XV ballroom, or a manly Georgian study—but rarely was there any attempt to relate one room to another. At Whitehall, for example, the delicate Louis XIV music room is next door to a rustic "Swiss" billiard room, and the François I dining room adjoins an Elizabethan breakfast room.[3] Chalfin's goal at Vizcaya was more nuanced. He did not want merely to decorate the rooms, he wanted to orchestrate them. As one walked through the house, one would move from geographic locale to geographic locale, from century to century, from mood to mood. In this, he was again influenced by Isabella Stewart Gardner, but Vizcaya was not Fenway Court. "I would not have the house a museum," instructed Deering.[4] Vizcaya was definitely a home, a home in which, to the usual three dimensions, a fourth had been added: time.

The visitor arriving by car from Miami entered by the west loggia. "Only the sense of the infinite outdoors, deftly shut away, brings one into the house—so gradual is the transit within through the iron grilles and open arcades of the first loggia," Chalfin wrote. "The luxurious green from out-of-doors forms curtains at the arches, through which sunlight falls upon many flowers grouped on a marble pavement."[5] Brightly painted canvas awnings and curtains— yellow, blue, and white, the original colors of the Venetian republic—lend a festive air to the noble loggia. The dramatic geometrically patterned floor of red, black, and white Veronese marble recalls a seventeenth-century palazzo; so does the tall vaulted ceiling of plain white plaster. Facing the visitor is the focal point of the space, a fountain made from an ancient Roman bath (fig. 34).*[6] The yellowed marble, dating from the second century A.D., is carved in bas-relief. Narrow jets of water emerging from a pair of sea monsters restrained by cherubic putti splash into the basin. The putti flank a Roman statue of Bacchus, the god of wine. According to Chalfin, "Deering always had in one hand a tiny glass of whisky, and in the other a cigarette, sipping first from the one and puffing from the other."[7] Chalfin bought the statue from the Galleria Simonetti in Rome in 1912. It was characteristic of him to pick a statue that was not a faultless antique but rather a sixteenth-century work that had been—quite obviously—repaired in the eighteenth century. The loggia is full of such antiquarian curios: Adam wall brackets carrying Venetian lamps; two large urns of Egyptian granite on marble pedestals; two richly embellished Italian doors that Chalfin had bought from Bernheimer in Munich (he later claimed that they were from the Hôtel de Beauharnais in Paris) (fig. 35). This eclectic décor forms a sort of overture, as if Chalfin wanted to prepare the visitor for what was to come. There are rules here, the room declares, but they will be broken; there are precious objects, but no preciousness; there is history, there is connoisseurship, but above all, there is pleasure.

The loggia does not give a view into the court. Hoffman's construction drawing shows an 8-foot screen wall the length of the loggia, but that was never built. Instead, Chalfin installed iron grillwork on each side of the fountain and blocked the view with planting. The door on the left leads into the entrance hall, with adjacent ladies' and gentlemen's coat rooms. This is in every way a cool space, reticent, disciplined, Neoclassical, as if Chalfin wanted to underline that Vizcaya had many facets (fig. 36). The geometrical rigor of the black and creamy white marble floor reflects the grid of the flat coffered ceiling. Pilasters subdivide the wall, which is covered in gray on emerald-green printed wallpaper, an extremely rare grisaille made in the early nineteenth century by a Parisian master, Joseph Dufour (fig. 37). Over the doors, gilded classical motifs stand out against the black background. The style is Directoire, named after the Directory that ruled France in 1795–99, immediately after the Revolution. Directoire, which formed a transition between Louis XVI and the Empire, was created in Paris by Charles Percier in 1798. Chalfin's interpretation of Percier's linear and severely angular style is tempered by an Italian richness of materials and details, black and gold furniture, and gilded decorative motifs.

The library is at the far end of the entrance hall (fig. 38). This bright, well-lit corner room is the reverse of the hall: warm yellows and oranges rather than cool grays and greens, English

---

* The entrance hall in Deering's Chicago house also had a wall fountain, illustrated in Elsie de Wolfe's *The House in Good Taste.*

FIGURE 34. The entrance loggia. Two putti flanked a heavily restored Roman statue of Bacchus, the god of wine. The marble basin was second century A.D. (Photograph by Mattie Edwards Hewitt, Vizcaya Museum and Gardens Archive)

FIGURE 35. The entrance loggia. A richly embellished Italian door enhances the eclectic décor.

FIGURE 36. The entrance hall. The geometrical rigor of the black and creamy white marble floor reflected the grid of the flat coffered ceiling. (Photograph by Mattie Edwards Hewitt, Vizcaya Museum and Gardens Archive)

FIGURE 37. The entrance hall. The wallpaper is an extremely rare grisaille made in the early nineteenth century by a Parisian master, Joseph Dufour.

intimacy rather than French splendor. Most of the floors in Vizcaya are marble or Venetian terrazzo; here the floor is mahogany. The English gentleman's study was a well-established tradition in American country houses, but Chalfin made Deering's library Adamesque rather than Georgian. Robert Adam, the great Scottish architect and decorator, began his London practice, with his brother James, in 1759. The Adams' delicately designed interiors were all-of-a-piece, unified ceilings, fireplace surrounds, sconces, doors, carpets, and wall coverings. Chalfin copied Adam designs for the molded plaster ceiling, the cornice, and the wall decorations, but in the process lightened them so that the room became Italianate. The delicate Adamesque fireplace mantel is carved wood surmounted by a mid-nineteenth-century Italian mosaic of an ancient Roman urn. Chalfin installed a mixture of furniture: eighteenth-century Italian side chairs, said to have belonged to Maria Paulina Borghese (and supplied by Stefano Bardini); comfortable seating furniture in the English style; and a built-in mahogany bookcase attributed to Sheraton. Deering's eighteenth-century desk, purchased in Paris just before the outbreak of World War I, was originally a shop counter, to which Empire decorative pieces, both inlaid and painted, were added (fig. 39). Chalfin later said that he was not completely happy with the décor, which he thought too busy. The library was the first room he designed, he said, and he had been seduced by the draftsman's skillful drawings. In the rest of the house, he did not make the same mistake, and allowed himself to be "freer."[8]

Robert Adam often set paintings into fixed frames in the wall, making them an integral part the décor. Chalfin installed a large genre painting of a pair of children (Deering was particularly fond of children) as a panel between the library doors. He identified the painter as John Singleton Copley, although the painting is today attributed to Richard Livesay, a lesser eighteenth-century contemporary. This was not merely slapdash research on Chalfin's part—although he did sometimes exaggerate the provenance of his finds. Unlike Isabella Gardner, he was not interested in paintings; he was as likely to use replicas as the real thing. Gardner created rooms that would set off a painting; Chalfin never allowed art to usurp the décor. It was a painting's contribution to the overall mood of a room that concerned him.

The library is an intimate space (18 by 24 feet) where Deering could see visitors informally. On formal occasions, guests were shown from the hall directly into a space that Chalfin called the Marie Antoinette Salon, but is really a reception room (fig. 40). By the early 1900s, British country houses generally combined the twin functions of public and private entertaining in a so-called drawing room, but American country houses tended to follow the practice recommended by Edith Wharton and Ogden Codman, Jr., in their influential *The Decoration of Houses*: an informal *salon de famille*, or living room, for everyday use, and a *salon de compagnie*, or reception room, for formal entertaining.[9]

Deering's reception room is about 25 feet square, with a tall ceiling. The décor is French, but French as if a mid-eighteenth-century Italian aristocrat had been to Paris and brought back furniture in the latest fashion. According to Chalfin, such rococo interiors were found in Turin and Palermo during the reign of the house of Savoy. Deering's prize possession here was the mid-eighteenth-century molded and painted plaster ceiling, which was brought from the Palazzo Rossi in Venice. Chalfin added an iron and glass chandelier, as well as large mirrors

FIGURE 38. The library. Chalfin created an Adamesque room in the Italian manner. (Photograph by Mattie Edwards Hewitt, Vizcaya Museum and Gardens Archive)

FIGURE 39. The library. Deering's desk, an eighteenth-century French Empire pastiche, forms the centerpiece of his study.

with murky glass and ornamental porcelain frames, all Venetian. The carved, gilded, and painted *boiseries*, on the other hand, are intended to recall the Italian Piemonte. He covered the wood parquet floor with a Portuguese needlework rug, likewise mid-eighteenth century. The rest of the décor is French: an eighteenth-century mantel, Louis XV *fauteils*, cabriole-legged tables. The sofa and some of the chairs have cane backs that wittily pick up the theme of the striking silk wall covering, which depicts exotic birds and butterflies flitting between tall palm trees. Thus Chalfin introduced a hint of the Florida subtropics. The silk wall covering (replaced in 1966) was originally bought from Dino Barozzi in Venice. It is sometimes attributed to Philippe de Lasalle, a celebrated eighteenth-century Lyon weaver, but is almost certainly Italian (fig. 41).

Chalfin's approach to decoration was both obsessive and remarkably clear headed. It is best summarized in a response he gave to a journalist who was writing a series of articles on the subject for *Architectural Review*: "In my practice of the profession I have striven to draw houses and interiors throughout myself—but not to draw the furnishings. I like to design curtains and the manners of upholstering originating with the classic styles. I like to execute them solely and entirely in my shops, and under the strictest personal supervision, also always in the presence of documents—documents for a brass-headed nail, a key scutcheon, the lining of a chair back, or the trappings of a princely bed. But I have avoided designing and executing furniture, lest the whole, coming from one mentality should prove too homogeneous to live, should lack humanness and scope, and the good that comes with reconciling the variety and cross purposes of life at large."[10]

From the reception room, one passes into the north hall. The door on the left leads to the north terrace; on the right is a private telephone cabinet. Straight ahead, a fantastically carved

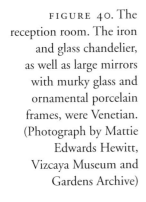

FIGURE 40. The reception room. The iron and glass chandelier, as well as large mirrors with murky glass and ornamental porcelain frames, were Venetian. (Photograph by Mattie Edwards Hewitt, Vizcaya Museum and Gardens Archive)

FIGURE 41. The reception room. The striking silk wall covering is a reproduction of a design by an eighteenth-century Italian weaver.

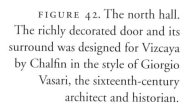

FIGURE 42. The north hall. The richly decorated door and its surround was designed for Vizcaya by Chalfin in the style of Giorgio Vasari, the sixteenth-century architect and historian.

door opens into the living room (fig. 42). This, the largest room in the house—20 feet high and 25 by 50 feet in plan, roughly a double-cube, following Classical rules of proportioning—is Chalfin's meditation on the Renaissance (fig. 43). "In the true Italian habit of the 16th century, the walls are plain, the floors rich, the ceiling magnificent," he wrote.[*11] He enlarged the heavy beamed ceiling, parts of which date from the late sixteenth century and were originally in a Venetian palazzo, to fit the room. The dark floor is gleaming Venetian terrazzo that was partly covered by a rare Hispano-Moresque carpet woven for a fifteenth-century Spanish admiral. A mid-sixteenth-century Ferrara tapestry, depicting the labors of Hercules, was the only adornment on the white walls. The sixteenth- and seventeenth-century furniture includes a Neapolitan trestle table and a wooden stool bought from Arthur Acton. The focus of the room is a massive French Renaissance chimneypiece of Caen stone, said to have come from the Château de Régneville (fig. 44). The ceiling height of the first floor at Vizcaya was set at twenty feet in order to accommodate this huge chimneypiece, which was the most expensive single object at Vizcaya, bought for $12,900 from C. J. Charles in New York. At the other end of the room is the Welte pipe organ, its console incompletely camouflaged as an altarpiece. Chalfin made the organ doors from a seventeenth-century Neapolitan painting that he unceremoniously cut in two.

Chalfin conjured up a romantic image of the living room: "Through an eastern window that faces the sea you hear waves lapping softly, lazily, ceaselessly, on the long stone steps of the lower terrace."[12] However, the room itself is rather solemn. The Renaissance did not place much store in comfort, and Chalfin's attempt to create modern sitting arrangements while at the same time preserving a sixteenth-century atmosphere is not completely successful, even though comfortable modern sofas were originally included. The antique Roman columns carrying electric candelabra in the shape of fruit trees are distinctly un-Renaissance. It all adds up to a fin-de-siècle version of a Renaissance room, with a feeling of what Mario Praz once described as "overfullness."[13]

Guests proceeding from the living room to the dining room first came into a hallway with a ceiling that Chalfin purchaced from Arthur Acton and subsequently entered the open east loggia (fig. 45). Here, for the first time, they had a clear view of the sparkling waters of Biscayne Bay. The loggia recalls the entrance loggia, but it is richer and more accommodating, a placc to linger rather than pass through. The geometrically patterned colored marble floor is based on a seventeenth-century original. The vaulted ceiling is decorated with relief medallions of Apollo and the nine muses. A five-foot model of a Spanish caravel hangs from the ceiling. The room was originally furnished with casual wicker furniture fitted with brightly colored cushions and functioned as the house's outdoor living room.

The loggia features four beautiful late eighteenth-century cedar doors with sculptured bronze decoration and marble surrounds, from the Palazzo Torlonia in Rome (fig. 46). Chalfin bought them from the New York dealer Eugene Glaenzer for the vast sum of $10,000. Through

---

[*] The walls of sixteenth-century Veneto villas were often frescoed, but frescoes were one Renaissance decorative technique that Chalfin did not use in the house, though he included frescoes in some of the garden structures.

FIGURE 43. The living room. Chalfin extended the late sixteenth-century heavy beamed ceiling, taken from a Venetian palazzo, to fit the room. (Photograph by Mattie Edwards Hewitt, Vizcaya Museum and Gardens Archive)

FIGURE 44. The living room. The massive French Renaissance chimneypiece of Caen stone is the focus of the room.

FIGURE 45. The east loggia. This outdoor living room, facing Biscayne Bay, was furnished with casual wicker furniture fitted with brightly colored cushions. (Photograph by Mattie Edwards Hewitt, Vizcaya Museum and Gardens Archive)

FIGURE 46. The east loggia. The late eighteenth-century cedar doors, with sculpted bronze decoration and marble surrounds, are from the Palazzo Torlonia in Rome.

one of the doors, guests proceeded to the dining room. But first they came into the small but exquisite music room (fig. 47). The space originally contained an Adam harp, a seventeenth-century Italian spinet, and a gilded Italian zither, but it was really an excuse for Chalfin to introduce some frivolity to balance the Renaissance solemnity of the two main rooms. The style he chose was the exuberant rococo of Milan and Genoa of the mid-eighteenth century. "Some one seems to lurk here, wearing old creamy satin," he gushed, "looking into dim mirrors at strings of pearls and corals upon a narrow and corseted bosom, ready with facile musical sighs."[14] Ornate painted canvas panels line the walls and ceiling (fig. 48). A delicate gilt arm-chair—also from Arthur Acton—complements the decoration of shells, coral, and contorted garlands and the gilt foliage and glass flowers of an eighteenth-century Venetian chandelier. In rococo, more is more.

The music room serves as a lighthearted anteroom to the dining room, which Chalfin insisted on calling a banquet hall, to emphasize its impressive sixteenth-century décor (fig. 49). Here hang the rare sixteenth-century tapestries that are Vizcaya's treasures: a delicate Flemish mille-fleurs from Tournai and two Ferrara tapestries from Robert Browning's house in Asolo. The marble and terrazzo floor is covered by a large seventeenth-century embroidered rug. The ceiling is a reproduction of one in the sixteenth-century Palazzo Gonzaga in Mantua, but the furniture is authentic: a mid-sixteenth-century Bolognese walnut refectory table that sat twelve, seventeenth-century Florentine chairs, a late fifteenth-century sacristy cupboard. A stone-topped side table is supported by a pair of ancient Roman carved marble lion-griffins, said to be from Pompeii or Herculaneum. The fireplace mantel was copied from a Florentine original (fig. 50). Eight ancient *broccatello* marble columns support bronze mortars filled with candelabra in the form of iron branches. The overall effect is as solemn and ponderous as the living room. In fact the dining room was rarely used. Deering entertained chiefly at midday, and since the groups usually numbered as many as thirty, lunches were usually served al fresco in the court.[15]

Beyond the dining room is the enclosed loggia, entered from the court through another of Deering's treasures: wrought-iron gates from the Palazzo Pisani in Venice (fig. 51). The gilded gates, with a rich grill that includes a representation of a doge's cap, have original arched surrounds of red Verona marble. Chalfin called the enclosed loggia an "enchanted room" and made it the grand finale of the public room sequence. The stunning space is almost a cube, with floor, walls, and ceiling richly decorated in the Italian Neoclassical style of the late eighteenth century. The richly patterned marble floor was made in sections in New York. A fireplace with a red Nubian mantel occupies the center of one wall. Four painted canvas panels depicting imaginary cityscapes are built into the walls. Though they are sometimes credited to Chalfin, they are late eighteenth-century Neapolitan scenery paintings from the New York dealer C. J. Charles (fig. 52). Chalfin intended the room to capture a period when "the learning of Antiquarians and the Italian tradition of scene-painting joined hands to produce a fictitious world of extravagant magnificence."[16] The sunny space, known as the tea room, originally had furniture "frail and white and gold, and covered with faint gay old stripes,—yellow, black, blue, rose."[17] The spaces between the loggia columns on the garden side are filled with stained

FIGURE 47. The music room. This intimate sitting room contained an Adam harp, a seventeenth-century Italian spinet, and a gilded Italian zither. (Photograph by Mattie Edwards Hewitt, Vizcaya Museum and Gardens Archive)

FIGURE 48. The music room. The ornate painted canvas panels that line the walls and ceiling are mid-eighteenth-century Milanese.

FIGURE 49. The dining room. Seventeenth-century Florentine chairs surrounded a mid-sixteenth-century Bolognese walnut refectory table. (Photograph by Mattie Edwards Hewitt, Vizcaya Museum and Gardens Archive)

FIGURE 50. The dining room. Behind the Venetian—or is it Florentine?—bust is a sixteenth-century Flemish tapestry woven at Tournai.

glass, the semicircular panels under the arches incorporating images of a caravel and seahorses. The choice of an emblem for Vizcaya was another issue over which Deering and Chalfin disagreed; Deering wanted a Spanish caravel as a symbol of Viscaino, the sailor, while Chalfin favored a seahorse, "a charming reference to the fact that the old gentleman was as you say a sea horse."[18] This time, Chalfin had the last word. He included a caravel motif in the tea room and hung the ship's model in the open loggia, but he decorated the rest of the house with a multitude of seahorses, including one atop the forecourt gateways and another as the centerpiece of the weathervane. Deering had to be satisfied with a caravel on his stationery.

To pass upstairs one crosses the court, or patio, as Chalfin called it, paved with locally quarried coral blocks. The border was originally native moss, "which forms beautiful grey green lines or patterns against the grey of the coral," he wrote.[19] Palms and thick foliage were planted in the four corners. The sixteenth-century Italian dolphin fountain dribbled water into a basin, just enough to create a gentle burble. The court was the great outdoor living room of the house, and it was also used for dining and as an outdoor screening room in the evening.* Deering and Chalfin considered stretching a roof, of "pink or rose silk," over the space to create shade.[20] Chalfin wanted interchangeable fabrics, less or more opaque, depending on the light conditions. This device was abandoned as too costly, but a 1917 *Vogue* article on the house mentions that "canvas stretched over the tiles transforms this court to a ballroom," so a temporary roof may have been used for special occasions.[21]

The broad open-air staircase, inspired by the Villa Rezzonico, leads to the second floor, where an open-air gallery on three sides of the court provides direct access to the bedrooms. Across from the stair is yet another loggia. It is entered through sixteenth-century Milanese gilded iron gates set in a carved stone arch. A pair of porcelain Ch'ien Lung Foo dogs guards the entrance, and announces the theme of the room: an Italian vision of the Orient. The lacquer and gilt furniture is Venetian (fig. 53). The eighteenth-century fireplace mantel is black and gold with lacquer inlays, and a pair of large eighteenth-century French Oriental figures and two Ming porcelain bowls continue the theme. Chalfin introduced an unexpected complement to the assorted chinoiserie: a set of eighteenth-century French mural paintings with marine scenes (fig. 54). He attributed the murals to Claude Joseph Vernet, although they are more accurately described as "in the manner of Vernet."

The loggia, which overlooks the garden, was a wonderfully breezy place to have breakfast and is sometimes called the breakfast room. Deering had originally wanted an outdoor loggia, which would have restricted the room's use on cool evenings. Instead, Chalfin devised a solution that he had seen at Fenway Court, where three of the balconies can be closed by glazed panels that slide out of wall-pockets. With similar sliding panels, the breakfast room could be converted from an open-air loggia into a fully enclosed room. In the evening, curtains of old

---

* The heavy glass roof that was installed in 1986 has turned the outdoor court into an indoor atrium, significantly altering the experience of the house.

FIGURE 51. The tea room. The décor is Neapolitan of the late Directoire period. The beautiful wrought-iron gates, one of Deering's treasures, were from the Palazzo Pisani in Venice. (Photograph by Mattie Edwards Hewitt, Vizcaya Museum and Gardens Archive)

FIGURE 52. The tea room. The late eighteenth-century Neapolitan scenery paintings depict imaginary cityscapes.

FIGURE 53. The breakfast room. This small loggia overlooking the garden was an Italian vision of the Orient. It was used for informal dining. (Photograph by Mattie Edwards Hewitt, Vizcaya Museum and Gardens Archive)

FIGURE 54. The breakfast room. The eighteenth-century French mural paintings are an unexpected complement to the assorted chinoiserie.

Genoese plush were drawn over the panels as well as over the mural paintings, transforming the room into a cozy velvet cocoon. The presence of a second, intimate dining room on the upper floor is a measure of how Hoffman and Chalfin provided Deering and his guests with a variety of choices. They could assemble formally in the reception room, hide away in the library, meet for intimate tête-à-têtes in the music room, or, on languid afternoons, lounge in the east loggia.

Deering's own suite takes up fully half of the wing facing the bay and includes a sitting room, a bedroom, a dressing room, and a bath. In the sitting room, which occupies the northeast corner of the house, Chalfin pulled out all the stops and produced what many consider to be Vizcaya's finest room (fig. 55).[22] Showing off, he once described it as Italian Directoire in the manner of the late eighteenth-century architect Giocondo Albertolli, who worked on the Royal Palace of Milan for the Hapsburg governor of Lombardy. Whatever its provenance, the effect of the room is beautiful, with yellow silk panels, white and gold woodwork, and mahogany furniture (fig. 56). The carved marble mantel was designed by Robert Adam for Rathfarnham Castle in Dublin. Characteristically, Chalfin combined this British piece with French Empire furniture, a rare oval Savonnerie carpet, Louis XVI embroidered silk wall panels, and Italian painted *boiseries*. As the centerpiece of what he called a "robin's egg gray" ceiling, he cheekily included a bas-relief of a seahorse.

The Neoclassical theme continues in Deering's bedroom, but as Empire. As usual, Chalfin was ahead of his time—Directoire and Empire would not become fashionable until the 1930s. Pale green silk, based on eighteenth-century patterns, covers the walls, which have a delicate Neoclassical cornice and frieze; the carpet is an eighteenth-century Aubusson. The eighteenth-century fireplace is Adamesque. According to Chalfin, the bed *à la Polonaise*, that is, with an extremely small canopy, belonged to Maria Louisa, Napoleon's second wife, and was from the Château de Malmaison (fig. 57). The opulent bathroom next door is paneled in black, white, and gray marble. Chalfin designed an ingenious shaving stand, piped for water. "Even the foot of this stand has been so arranged that you can get both your feet close to it," he explained to Deering. "I do not use bay rum or other things myself when I shave, but I like plenty of hot water and something solid."[23] The tented ceiling, draped in embroidered linen, reprises a popular European fashion of 1800 (fig. 58). The gold-plated bath faucets (there are four of them, providing sea and fresh water) are in the shapes of swans.

Large glazed doors open onto a private loggia. Every great building has a place that is its true "center," the spot where the power of the architecture is focused. Sometimes it is a grand space, a porch, or a special room. At Vizcaya, it is not the court, as one might expect, but this little balcony. From here, one looks down on the terrace, the quay, the stone Barge, and straight down the long axis of the Deering Channel, far out into the bay. The view is framed by the arch of the *serliana*, which is supported on pairs of antique Roman columns of delicately veined Seravezzo marble with exquisitely carved white marble capitals. The space is vaulted and in Deering's time contained a chaise longue and a side table. One can imagine the master of Vizcaya here in the evenings, looking out over the placid lagoon, smoking the last of the half-cigarettes that he allowed himself despite his doctor's orders.[24]

Chalfin gave the guestrooms colorful names. The salon of the large suite that was for special guests is Galleon, and its bedroom, Caravel. Galleon is decorated in the eighteenth-century style of Pisa, a mixture of French, English, and Italian, all rather imposing with Louis XV furniture and faux-marble wall panels (figs. 59, 60). The décor of Goyesca, a guestroom of another suite, in the south tower, is Neoclassical with canvas wall panels painted with Roman-inspired grotesques. Across, in the north tower, is Lady Hamilton, decorated in gray and violet grisaille wallpaper and containing a late eighteenth-century Neapolitan bed that is supposed to have belonged to Horatio Nelson's mistress, the notorious Emma Hamilton. The three rooms on the north side of the court are Pantaloon, Manin, and Cathay. Pantaloon (which was occupied by Deering's housekeeper) has gaily painted Venetian furniture of the mid-eighteenth century. Cathay, as might be expected, is another study in whimsical chinoiserie, described by Chalfin as "a dream of a Chinese couch as Venice saw it, all parasols and bells and lattice work, carved and lacquered and draped over coralline red, lined with golden yellow, from ostrich plumes of another faded red" (figs. 61, 62).[25] Manin, named after the president of the last, short-lived, Venetian republic, contains the most modern decorative period represented at Vizcaya, Biedermeier, the Austro-Germanic variant of the late Empire style.

For Espagnolette, Chalfin created an eighteenth-century Venetian interpretation of French rococo décor, with carved and gilded wood furniture, panels painted in the style of Watteau, a silk Tabriz rug, and a gray marble fireplace of the period (fig. 63). This exquisitely feminine room is distinguished by its favored location, facing the bay, immediately next to Deering's suite. It has an unusual feature, a door panel that provides a discreet connection to Deering's private balcony. According to Chalfin, "There was always a flutter of scandal about Deering and his women."[26] He was said to have had a mistress of long duration with whom he traveled and who was a frequent visitor to Vizcaya.[27] The suspicion that Espagnolette was intended to serve as a love nest is reinforced by the Pompadourlike décor, the fantastically contorted canopied bed, and the saucy name: an *espagnolette* is an eighteenth-century French decorating motif depicting a young décolletée woman, usually in bronze and said to be inspired by Watteau.

Deering was circumspect and restrained in affairs of the heart, as in most things. "He always wore beautiful clothes but in inconspicuous good taste," recalled Chalfin, summing up his employer in a phrase.[28] James Deering was neither a flamboyant connoisseur like Isabella Gardner, nor a voracious collector like William Randolph Hearst. The first time that Chalfin took his employer around his newly completed house, Deering told him: "Mr. Chalfin, there are two things, both of them the work of a single man, which excite my admiration. One of them is Webster's Dictionary and the other is this house."[29] This odd tribute speaks volumes about Deering's fastidious and ordered notion of beauty. Yet he was proud of his house, and there is no doubt that he was deeply involved in its creation.[30] He seems to have genuinely shared Chalfin's infectious and obsessive search for *l'objet juste*, in the same way that many art patrons enjoy participating in—or, at least, observing at close quarters—the creative process. The flamboyant Chalfin obviously tapped a deeply buried romantic strain in Deering's reserved

FIGURE 55. James Deering's sitting room. This Italian Directoire room was Vizcaya's finest interior. (Photograph by Mattie Edwards Hewitt, Vizcaya Museum and Gardens Archive)

FIGURE 56. James Deering's sitting room. The yellow silk panels, white and gold woodwork, and mahogany furniture manage to be both masculine and extremely delicate.

FIGURE 57. James Deering's bedroom. According to Chalfin, Deering's bed belonged to Maria Louisa, Napoleon's second wife, and was from the Château de Malmaison. The carpet was an eighteenth-century Aubusson.

FIGURE 58. James Deering's bathroom. This exquisite room, paneled in black, white, and gray marble, includes a tented ceiling and an ingenious shaving stand piped for water.

FIGURE 59. Guestroom, Galleon. The salon of this suite was decorated in the eighteenth-century style of Pisa. (Photograph by Mattie Edwards Hewitt, Vizcaya Museum and Gardens Archive)

FIGURE 60. Guestroom, Galleon. An Italian portrait is set into a wall panel marbleized in an eighteenth-century Venetian style.

FIGURE 61. Guestroom, Cathay. The room is a study in whimsical chinoiserie. (Photograph by Mattie Edwards Hewitt, Vizcaya Museum and Gardens Archive)

FIGURE 62. Guestroom, Cathay. The Italian furniture is complemented by wall silks and decorative tassels.

FIGURE 63. Guestroom, Espagnolette. The guestroom next to Deering's suite was an exquisite eighteenth-century Venetian interpretation of French rococo décor, with carved and gilded wood furniture, panels painted in the style of Watteau, and an extravagant canopied bed.

Down East disposition, and their voluminous correspondence, while rarely warm and never intimate, was collegial.* They were clearly embarked on this fanciful quest together.

In March 1923 Deering's early traveling companion and close friend, Gari Melchers, and his wife spent ten days at Vizcaya. By then the Melchers had moved back to the United States and were living in a rather grand house in Fredericksburg, Virginia. Corinne Melchers, trained as a painter, has left a vivid description (never before published) of the visit that is worth quoting at length.

> This place is beyond all expectations lovely. The photo does not give you the slightest conception of its charm. In driving here from Miami, the very impressive high irregular, pink walls on both sides of the wide highway, broken with big vases & carved ornaments, tell you that something extraordinary is behind them. . . . The grounds are very wonderful even now with only two years work, but Versailles is going to be put in the shade someday. This photo shows the house from the

* Deering's will, drawn up in 1922, left generous bequests to no less than thirty friends (in addition to numerous relatives), including painters Walter MacEwen ($10,000) and Gari Melchers ($4,000), but did not mention Chalfin nor Vizcaya.

FIGURE 64. James Deering, c. 1917. Deering rarely allowed himself to be photographed. This portrait was taken at Vizcaya by Mattie Edwards Hewitt. (Florida Historical Society)

water—but the approach is from the other side. The house being a lovely pink with blue striped curtains blowing. Everything in the way of ornament is of the most wonderful & the house is really too full. A big square court in the middle, with a cloisterlike gallery around it on the second floor and a perfect blue sky overhead framed by the irregular tiled roof, is a congregating place [fig. 66]. To sit there in the evening & see the moon come up over the tops is a sight for the Gods.

The upstairs apts. are all on the gallery except two which are in the two towers, one of these being ours. My bed was Lady Hamilton's—one of the most beautiful I ever saw. Over the doors & windows are old frescoes. The mantle is the most exquisite piece of delicate Italian carving like a piece of gray lace reaching from floor to ceiling. The doors are painted with quaint figures dancing and are very quaintly paneled, etc. etc. I wish you could see the view from my window over the water. An enormous pavilion is being completed out in the water—of stone, in the shape of a great ship. There are statues and latticed summer houses & greenery ornamenting it. Under my side window, with a grotto extending under the house is a swimming pool [fig. 67] & yesterday a party from a neighboring villa came to swim & luncheon, after which we all were taken in their yacht for a little outing. . . . The large grounds are like paradise. The climate here naturally adds a lot of charm as one can be out of doors in the thinnest clothes all the time.[31]

"This place is beyond all expectations lovely." And so it is, which makes it all the more difficult to characterize Chalfin's achievement at Vizcaya. What to make of the mixture of

FIGURE 65. Paul Chalfin, Deering's artistic alter ego. This photograph was probably taken in the late 1920s, with most of the work on Vizcaya behind him. (Vizcaya Museum and Gardens Archive)

periods, both inside and out, for instance? In *The Decoration of Houses*, Edith Wharton and Ogden Codman, Jr., were critical of eclecticism and the ignorant application of historic styles, and insisted on conformity to the particular demands of a style.* "There is one thing more to be said in defense of conformity to style," they wrote, "and that is, the difficulty of getting rid of style. Strive as we may for originality, we are hampered at every turn by an artistic tradition of over two thousand years. Does any but the most inexperienced architect really think that he can ever rid himself of such an inheritance?"[32] Chalfin was definitely not ignorant about style, and on certain aspects of Italian decorating history he was exceptionally well informed, but his approach to historic style can hardly be described as conformist. He was influenced by his old employer, Elsie de Wolfe, who advised her readers in *The House in Good Taste*: "Don't go about the furnishing of your house with the idea that you must select the furniture of some one period and stick to that. It isn't at all necessary."[33] Not that as outré an individual as Chalfin would ever be constrained by bourgeois notions such as good or bad taste. The décor of Vizcaya, unlike that of, say, Whitehall, was not intended merely to please the eye or to demonstrate current fashion. Chalfin was up to something far more complicated.

"Chalfin was a funny fellow," Hoffman told James Maher, "but he had great artistic perception. He knew good things. He had great imagination and wonderful taste."[34] Taste is what

* Although Wharton's The Mount is, in fact, an eclectic mixture of English architecture, French décor, and an Italian garden.

Chalfin explored at Vizcaya, though not in the limited sense that Hoffman alluded to. Geoffrey Scott called the architecture of the Renaissance "pre-eminently an architecture of Taste."[35] He meant that Renaissance architects were not driven by theory but by a partiality for certain shapes—a "disinterested enthusiasm for architectural form," as he put it.[36] Scott acknowledged that taste was a slippery notion. "Taste is supposed to be a matter so various, so capricious, so inconsequent, and so obscure that it is considered hopeless to argue about it in its own terms."[37]

And what was Chalfin's taste? The answer to that question lies not in the past, however much Vizcaya seems to pay obeisance to history, but in the present, that is, Chalfin's present. He was an exceptionally sophisticated turn-of-the-century American, attuned to the latest artistic fashions. Through his reading of Edith Wharton, through his own experience at the École des Beaux-Arts, and thanks to his association with de Wolfe, he was particularly interested in France, which is something that he shared with Deering. Their France was the turn-of-the-century Parisian *haut monde* that produced figures such as the couturier Paul Poiret and the *ensembliers* Maurice Dufrène and Paul Follot. One sees the influence of proto-Modern French styles such as Art Nouveau and the Empire revival at Vizcaya. In some rooms, notably the entrance hall and Deering's personal suite, Chalfin even anticipated the luxurious geometrical abstraction of French Art Deco of the 1920s. Chalfin's taste was refined and continental, which is why he found the mainstream interiors of an American rich-man's house such as Whitehall to be shallow and gaudy. What is most striking about Vizcaya's rooms, no matter what "period" Chalfin was performing, is his sure touch.

At the same time, Chalfin's taste was greatly influenced by Isabella Gardner, despite the fact that by 1910 she represented an idiosyncratic and now old-fashioned approach to decoration. What Chalfin seems to have picked up from Gardner were two attitudes. The first was an unrelenting demand for the highest standard of execution, whether it was the quality of the cabinetry, the upholstery, or the window treatments. Nothing but the best. The second was an apparent contradiction. Certain wealthy individuals—and Gardner was one—sometimes exhibit

FIGURE 66. The court, 1923. Gari Melchers visited— and photographed—Vizcaya. His wife, Corinne, described "a perfect blue sky overhead framed by the irregular tiled roof." (Courtesy of Belmont, The Gari Melchers Estate and Memorial Gallery)

a degree of self-confidence that allows them to ignore and even flaunt convention. Chalfin, while hardly rich, practiced a similar insouciance in his work for Deering. He combined luxury with extreme simplicity, polish with roughness, and a refined aestheticism with natural effects that one would call "modern," though that word would probably have irritated Chalfin.

The interiors of Vizcaya are a tour-de-force, unmatched in other American country houses, perhaps unique in the history of décor. Chalfin did not simply provide a variety of rooms in different historical styles, nor did he merely mix and match. He once wrote to Deering that "the house would have been hopelessly hybrid if we had admitted many of the agreeable things that we have thought of."[38] What made his approach to decoration unusual was his overarching goal. Chalfin called Vizcaya "a partial evocation of the city of Tiepolo," for despite his eclecticism and—at first glance—his self-indulgence, the house was a highly disciplined meditation on La Serenissima.[39] (That is why the last decorative period represented was Biedermeier, which coincided with the demise of the Venetian republic.) Chalfin structured this meditation as a narrative: the story of a Renaissance villa in the Veneto that had been occupied for centuries and had accumulated layer upon layer of artifacts and memories. The result is a curious blend, part simulation, part historical reproduction. As Harold Acton put it, a palimpsest. Vizcaya is an imaginative reconstruction of the past that creates a historical mood, what Aline Saarinen perceptively termed "periodicity."[40] The narrative is not alluded to in any literal sense, but it gives a subliminal sense of continuity to the startlingly different series of rooms. It is tempting to characterize Chalfin as a set designer. But while he could be theatrical, he was never stagy. When he could not find old things, he used new ones, but he had them made from old patterns and insisted on traditional techniques and craftsmanship. Vizcaya is sometimes not real, but it is never fake. "It is also characteristic of this house that hardly a piece of contemporaneous furniture has found a place in any of its rooms," Chalfin wrote, "nor a single commercial lighting fixture; not a material has been purchased from a dealer's stock, not a fringe, not a tassel."[41] Not a tassel.

FIGURE 67. The swimming pool. The basement pool, half indoors and half out, was Vizcaya's most fantastic interior feature. The shells and plants in the grottolike ceiling were cast from nature in the Florida Keys by Robert Chanler. The shells in the walls were collected in the British West Indies. (Photograph by Mattie Edwards Hewitt, Vizcaya Museum and Gardens Archive)

PART II

Garden and Landscape

Laurie Olin

chapter 5

FLORIDA, THE DEERINGS, GARDENS, HORTICULTURE, AND LANDSCAPE

James Deering chose to make a vacation place for himself in what is for the United States an absolutely unique ecological setting. The landscape of Florida, which seems so different from other parts of the country, is so in part due to its geological history. Several hundred million years ago two tectonic plates, one of which holds modern Africa and the other, which holds modern North America, moved toward each other. The slow, steady grinding and merging eventually led to what amounted to a giant continent referred to today by geologists as Pangaea. Later they moved apart again, forming the Atlantic Ocean. Parts of what had been North America stuck to what is now northern Europe. One could think of Northern Ireland, the Highlands of Scotland, and a large portion of Norway as being displaced pieces of America. Florida, along with Long Island, southeastern Newfoundland, and the Boston region, are in fact dislodged bits of the African plate. Modern Florida is a truly special place, consisting of a long, flat shelf of sand and recent seabed in the form of various densities of limestone atop ancient Paleozoic rocks from Africa.[1]

The southern boundary of a warm temperate magnolia climax forest lies near Palm Beach on the Florida east coast. South of this one finds tropical species on small raised ridges called hammocks. There are marked similarities in topography and climate with Cuba, British Honduras, Guatemala, and the Yucatan, with extremely low, wet, sandy plains and dry limestone ridges leading to similarities in the native vegetation. Lower areas inland are commonly inundated and covered with rushes, sedges, and grasses, most notably the saw grass so characteristic of the Everglades. The region normally has more than 50 inches of rain from February through October. From November to February, however, a dry period occurs with only about 10 inches of rain in three months. From spring through summer it gets progressively hotter and more humid as well as rainier, with a hurricane season officially running from June 1 to November 30, often with a flurry of storms between mid-August and mid-October. From this it is understandable how a winter vacation season could have evolved and why the wealthy individuals who came here in the early days left by mid-February for the Southwest or the Mediterranean. The interiors of the hammocks south and west of Palm Beach are also frost free, which, as every citrus grower knows, unhappily is not true of most of Florida.

The tropical and subtropical areas of south Florida and Miami that lie upon limestone ridges rarely rise more than 23 feet above sea level. These upland patches are covered with heavy vegetation, the most common trees being gumbo limbo, slash pine, West Indies mahogany, lignumvitae, strangler fig, and a mixture of palms, predominantly royal palm, thatch palm, and sable palm. Along the shoreline and tidal areas two species of mangrove are ubiquitous. Of the thirteen most common trees in the area, nine are evergreen; and of the twenty-seven species of understory trees and shrubs common locally in the hammocks of the Miami area, twenty-three are evergreen.[2] In these areas one also finds numerous ferns, vines, and air plants. Among the latter are many orchids, some now quite rare.

The Deering brothers were among the first of the wealthy northern immigrants to south Florida to realize how special and fragile the natural setting, the ecology and creatures of the region were. At a time when many others saw the area around Miami to be an undifferentiated jungle or swamp ripe for development if only it could be cleared and drained, Charles and James Deering, who had grown up in the agricultural machinery business and the long-since cleared and domesticated landscape of the Midwest and Northeast, were attracted to the possibilities for horticulture and to the native flora and creatures. They saw the subtlety and unique beauty of Biscayne Bay, and as they came to understand it, both brothers became avid conservationists in concert with other wealthy and prescient neighbors such as Dr. David Fairchild and William Matheson.

Their father, William Deering, had been the first to arrive in 1870, establishing a small agricultural equipment plant. It was logical that he would be interested in Florida, which owing to its climate was to become a vast agricultural enterprise. The 1909 edition of *Baedeker's Guide to the United States* notes:

> The orange is believed to have been introduced by the Spaniards, and about 5 million boxes (ca. 175 to a box) were annually produced before the severe frosts of 1894, 1895, and 1899 killed most of the trees. The yield sank to a few hundred thousand boxes; but the groves have generally been replanted. In the S. part of the State, especially on the E. coast, large quantities of pineapples are now profitably raised. Strawberries and vegetables are also extensively produced for early shipment to northern markets. Tobacco, cotton (including the valuable sea-island cotton), rice, maize, oats and sugarcane are also grown, and extensive beds of phosphate are worked.[3]

This combined with the well-publicized knowledge that "Its mild and equable winter climate has made it a favorite resort for invalids and others who wish to escape the rigors of the North, while the beauties of its luxuriant semi-tropical vegetation and its excellent opportunities for shooting and fishing are attractions."[4]

Prior to the successful merger with McCormick in 1902 and establishing his sons in the management of International Harvester, William Deering began to winter in Coconut Grove, where he came until his death in 1913. Both sons followed, purchasing land of their own on Biscayne Bay, Charles first at Buena Vista, north of Miami, and then James at Brickell Point in Coconut Grove south of the Miami River.

Charles Deering's first venture was to acquire a tract of undeveloped land north of what is now downtown Miami in the first decade of the century.[5] Here at Buena Vista he began experimenting with various crops and ornamental plants, giving 25 acres to the U.S. Department of Agriculture for its uses while retaining about 200 acres for his own experiments. Within a few years he began laying out gardens and drives, bringing O. C. Simonds (1855–1932) down to oversee development. Simonds was a landscape architect prominent in Chicago and now associated with the origins of the Prairie Style. He had been an early partner of William Le Baron Jenney, who developed the suburban community of Riverside with Olmsted, and had been a partner of Holabird and Roche, before taking over the reins at Graceland cemetery and the design of significant portions of the Chicago parks and Forest Preserve system, as well as north shore estates for the wealthy.

In a memoir published in 1938, Dr. David Fairchild, the noted plant hunter, explorer, and tropical garden enthusiast, writes of visiting the Buena Vista estate of the older brother in 1912: "Mr. Deering seemed much interested in plants and talked about creating an arboretum of tropical trees. His place contained the finest mangroves on the coast, an old grove of beautiful coconuts, and a magnificent banyan which had spread until it covered an area one hundred feet or more in diameter."[6] Fairchild describes visiting other sites and plants with Charles, who due to his interest and enthusiasm offered to pay for the publication of Charles T. Simpson's *Ornamental Gardening in Florida*, which subsequently encouraged others in the area to experiment with tropical plants.

Simonds brought an assistant, Frank M. Button (1860–1938), to help onsite with the work at Deering's estate at Buena Vista. Button, trained in Vermont, had been employed in the construction of the Chicago World's Columbian Exposition of 1893 as an assistant engineer, and had participated as landscape architect on private estates in the Lake Forest suburb. Working with Deering, Simonds, and Simpson, Button developed considerable skill in mixing native plants with tropical imports, a technique that later served him well in his work for George Merrick in the development of Coral Gables. The site at Buena Vista, then, prefigured aspects of Vizcaya; for instance, Fairchild would recall "beautiful canals [that] wound through the mangrove forest and beneath overarching coconut palms," as well as "a collection of succulents planted by Doctor John K. Small and an arboretum of rare trees, many supplied by our office, aviaries of egrets and cranes, and even an island with monkeys on it."[7]

The house that Clinton Mackenzie designed for Charles Deering was to sit at the north of the site near the water with garden and grounds stretching away to the south much like the later plan for Vizcaya. After Simonds' initial visits, Button carried on at Buena Vista for several years, also working for Charles Deering later at his next estate at Cutler. All that remains of this first Deering garden and park are descriptions and photos, which show it to have been an ambitious blending of geometric and picturesque modes of landscape design. There was a magnificent allée of stately royal palms along an entry drive, while the view to the south shows an undulating lawn moving off into the distance with masses of tropical trees and shrubs advancing and retreating in the manner of an English landscape park. It is a translation into a spectacular flora that anticipates the work of Roberto Burle Marx and other Latin American designers a half century later. Button was to stay on in Florida to produce a body of significant work, largely parks, gardens, and the plans and landscape design for commercial developments.[8] Charles Deering's second estate at Cutler, although interesting from the perspective of preservation and horticultural experimentation, did not replicate the ambitions of his first garden at Buena Vista and was to be completely overshadowed by the artistic vision of his brother's estate in Coconut Grove. The move south was precipitated by the phenomenal development in local real estate, which he found offensive and which intruded upon both his privacy and his conservation.

In 1910 James Deering began to purchase land from Mrs. William Brickell in a large hammock south of the Miami River that would become Vizcaya. The real estate market, which had begun to accelerate following the arrival of Henry Flagler's railroad in Miami in 1896, now virtually exploded. While the rail line was continued south toward the Keys, one of the biggest land speculation bubbles in American history was in full swing. Almost overnight the Buena Vista estate was engulfed by development, much of it tawdry and obtrusive. Charles eventually decided to move away from Miami and its increasing urbanization, successfully purchasing a former hotel, the Richmond Inn, and its adjacent property known as Cutler. This pioneer settlement further south on Biscayne Bay had been bypassed by the railroad, which was proceeding to the west, thereby leaving it cut off from development interest. He moved significant portions of his plant collection from Buena Vista to the new property, again establishing farmland and experimental plots. Selling his original property at an opportune time, he made more than $6 million, a substantially more dramatic sum then than it is today. At the same time he began with his new neighbors, David Fairchild and William J. Matheson, to acquire large portions of the remaining hardwood hammocks and shoreline around the bay in an effort to preserve them from real estate development. His brother, James, and Matheson also purchased Key Biscayne Island, which forms part of the eastern side of the bay including Cape Florida, its southernmost point, much of which remains in natural condition and in public use today.

Another of Charles Deering's advisers on plants was John Kunkel Small, a noted tropical plant hunter and curator for the New York Botanical Garden. The two men carried on a considerable correspondence, and Small seems to have taken great interest in the development of the Cutler garden, becoming an adviser not only on the plants and their cultivation, but also on the trails in the hammock and the management of the hardwood groves. In 1916 another friend, Charles Torrey Simpson, a conchologist and authority on local plants and marine life, who shared Deering's interest in preservation, dedicated his book *Ornamental Gardening in Florida* "To Mr. Charles Deering who, instead of destroying the hammock, is creating it."[9]

Also in 1916 their botanist friend David Fairchild purchased for himself a narrow property fronting onto the water along the bay between James Deering's property on the north and Charles Deering's several miles to the south, where he began to develop what was to become the

Kampong, his own research and pleasure garden. While public figures and wealthy individuals like William Jennings Bryan were purchasing nearby land on the bay for homes and pleasurable retreats, others, like the Deerings and Fairchild, were interested in aspects of preservation and tropical horticulture. Paul Chalfin continued to pursue the acquisition of additional shoreland for James Deering from the Brickells, and William Matheson and his son Hugh acquired 87 acres of shorelands south of Vizcaya. One of only two surviving beach venues, and now known as Matheson Hammock, it was donated to Dade County in 1930 to become one of the key holdings in the extensive County park system of today. Their neighbor, Col. Robert H. Montgomery, likewise gave 83 acres, and subsequently another 58 acres, for what was to become the Fairchild Tropical Garden, designed by landscape architects William Lyman Phillips and Noel Chamberlain.

Other visitors to Miami and south Florida in the early decades of the twentieth century were also taken by the natural beauty and by its fragility in the face of rapid development. One was the poet Wallace Stevens, who first began traveling through the region in 1916 in his role as a director of the Hartford Fire Insurance Company and its new subsidiary, the Hartford Live Stock Insurance Company. His first letters to his wife on the subject describe it as a paradise of sorts.

> This is a jolly place—joli. It is alive. It is beautiful, too. The houses are attractive, the streets well paved, the hotels comfortable and clean. All these things count almost as much as the tremendous quantities of flowers. . . . I got here at midnight last night, the air was like pulp. But there is a constant wind that keeps stirring it up. To-day I expected to roast. It has, however, been cloudy. . . . The beach is deserted at this season. . . . The best residence section is toward the South on the shore of the bay [Coconut Grove]. The houses are not pretentious. Their grounds are full of oleanders as large as orchard trees, groups of hibiscus, resembling holly-hocks, strange trumpet vines, royal palms, cocoanut-palms full of cocoanuts, which litter the ground, orange and grape-fruit trees, mangoes in bloom, bougainvillea, castor beans, etc. etc. You soon grow accustomed to the palms. The soil is utterly different from ours. It seems all sand covered with sparse grass and the surrounding jungle. After all, the most important thing in Florida is the sun. It is hot as a coal in the day-time. It goes down rather abruptly, with little twilight. Then the trade winds quickly blow the heat away and leave the air pulpy but cool . . . here I am compelled—alas, alas—to stay in one of the most delightful places I have ever seen.[10]

Ten and twenty years later Stevens describes the changes, noting that he no longer enjoys Miami: there were "mobs of people . . . a jamboree of hoodlums," and the Florida he had valued was now threatened by Miami Beach ("the land of Oz").[11]

The instinct of the two Deering brothers to preserve land for its ecological value has made an enormous difference in the nature and quality of Biscayne Bay as it is today; on a recent visit toward evening to Charles Deering's estate at Cutler, three manatees were grazing in the boat turning basin, and a large group of egrets and other birds were arriving to settle in for the night in rookeries on an island at the end of his channel and further off to the west in the extensive hammock on the property. How much better it would have been if the southern portion of Vizcaya had not been sold off and so sadly filled in for development, which could and should have occurred somewhere else inland where it could have been more appropriate. Although this estate may have been a small fragment of what once existed in the region, still it was important, and it afforded, as many wealthy individuals have always wanted, a buffer against an unwelcome and changing world.

As became industrial tycoons in an age that combined laissez-faire mercantilism and monopolies with a sense of noblesse oblige, the Deerings were involved in civic projects of their day that entailed significant landscape development. In Portland, Maine, the city where their father had begun his business, the family underwrote Deering's Oaks Park, designed by the Olmsted firm. Likewise, the sons were supporters of the Chicago World's Columbian Exposition and of the remarkable Burnham and Bennett Plan for Chicago of 1909, where the hand and influence of the Olmsted office were pronounced. Charles Moore's biography of Daniel Burnham notes on several occasions that Burnham had lunch or dinner with Charles Deering while going to or coming from meetings with Frederick Law Olmsted, Jr., Augustus Saint-Gaudens, and other figures in the art and design world of Chicago and New York in a period of enormous productivity regarding the Fair, the Chicago Plan, and the Mall in Washington, D.C.[12] It is with this general background and interest in landscape, whether of natural preservation, agricultural experiment and productivity, or artistic design and aesthetic pleasure, along with disdain for speculative urban development, and the circumstance of virtually having been put out to pasture in late middle age, while enormously rich and ambitious, that we find James Deering in 1910 launching into his greatest personal project, the estate of Vizcaya.

chapter 6

A GARDEN TOUR TODAY

A visit in 2004 begins, as it did in the past for most people, by driving south from downtown Miami on a street known as South Miami Avenue. Entering Coconut Grove the
road jogs west between low walls and enormous trees, then turns south again, only
to come quickly to a pair of handsome pavilions and tall stone piers and gates flanking the
road. The gate to the right, or west, leads to a group of small buildings known as the Village.
The gate on the left, or east, leads into dense woodland and the house, gardens, and Biscayne
Bay. The public road stretches south into the distance framed by low walls of terra-cotta color
with an interesting design or pattern in sgrafitto (fig. 68). At intervals along this route the walls
are punctuated with baroque apsidal spaces replete with gates and rococo openings in lemon-
colored walls filled with wrought-iron grills. There are sidewalks and ornamental plantings
along the curb and base of the wall. Fragments of brilliant bougainvillea that once grew in
swags on frames and wire that stood behind and above the entire half-mile length of the estate
wall on both sides can still be found where they have not been shaded out by the carefully preserved dark tropical hardwood forest.

Entering the estate through the eastern gate one begins a relatively short journey south-
ward on a narrow drive through the cool vegetation of one of the few surviving tropical hammocks in the region. Gumbo limbo, cocoloba, strangler fig, mahogany, lignumvitae, palms
and palmettos, mangrove, and numerous other trees and vines filter the light. A couple of
white Italian marble figures punctuate the passage and turns. A sequence of odd low, square
stone lanterns with dark blue and amber glass accompany the road through this jungle.

At last one enters a broad paved octagonal clearing between gigantic carved figures; pairs
of large rustic herms, ancient male and female figures of nature and agriculture, growing from
tall limestone plinths, frame different avenues and paths, which come together here (fig. 69).
This area, referred to by Deering and his designers as the Piazza, is the beginning of a sequence
of integrated architectural, sculptural, and landscape features that lead to the house, through

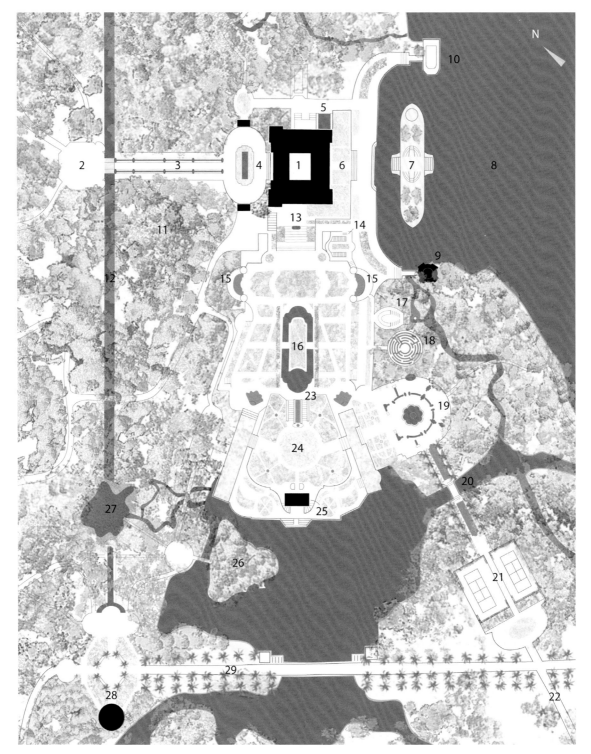

Vizcaya House and Gardens, 1921

1 House, 2 Piazza, 3 Approach Allée, 4 Arrival Court, 5 Swimming Pool, 6 East Terrace, 7 Barge,
8 Biscayne Bay, 9 Tea House, 10 Boat Landing, 11 Hammock, 12 Canal on Old Miami Trail,
13 South Terrace, 14 Secret Garden, 15 Semicircular Pools, 16 Center Island, 17 Garden Theater,
18 Maze, 19 Rose Garden and Fountain, 20 Marine Garden and Peacocks, 21 Tennis Courts,
22 Lagoon Garden Drive, 23 Cascade, 24 Mound, 25 Casino, 26 Monkey Island,
27 Cascade Pool, 28 Casba and Piazza, 29 Causeway and Bridge

FIGURE 68. Wall with sgraffito decoration along South Miami Avenue adjacent to one of the exedras that provide a view into the woodland portion of the site.

FIGURE 69. View from the entry drive through the hammock to the entry piazza with its herms and sculpture.

it, around it, and out toward the bay, gardens, and former lagoon park. Today one turns off to the right to a parking lot that was cut into the trees after the property was turned over to Dade County for public use. Walking back one considers a pair of male statues placed between the gigantic herms, one labeled Ponce de León, the other Bel Vizcaya, which further serve to establish a romantic and vaguely historical mood. Here visitors pay for their tickets and set off down the driveway toward the house.*

* In fact these appear to have been originally intended to have been portraits of the seventeenth-century sculptor/architect Gian Lorenzo Bernini and the sixteenth-century architect Andrea Palladio, which Chalfin purchased on one of his shopping sprees in Europe that he has reattributed to add to the mood of his quasi-historical myth-making endeavor with Deering.

Just inside this entry point is a feature easily missed today, a deep excavation stretching off into the forest to the left and right. Although dry at the moment, this great ditch was once filled with water that passed under a "natural" bridge of monolithic limestone. In Deering's time, water was pumped up into the north end of this moat or canal, which then ran down a cascade at its southern end into the lagoon garden. This canal was hand dug by laborers in 1914 along the higher part of a limestone ridge in what had been the right-of-way for the old jungle trail (now South Miami Avenue), which the City of Miami allowed Deering to move to the west where it currently remains.

Crossing this bridge one finds a shady lane leading downhill to a forecourt and the house's entry façade. On either side of the lane is a sequence of carved stone basins and troughs set in vegetation. These are superb adaptations of a familiar theme and feature of some of the very best Italian villa gardens of the sixteenth and seventeenth centuries. Although most people today walk down the middle, this was once a carriage drive in the form of a triple allée. The original pedestrian paths, no longer of gravel, remain to the left and right of the stone runnels. The twin water sequences separating this de facto nave and side aisles end in a pair of gate piers that sport familiar fountain basins and large grinning satyr's heads (fig. 70). At this point the visitor steps out of the tunnel of trees into a clearing to confront the house, which, hardly visible till now, is suddenly close and large. To the left and right is a pair of monumental stone arches (figs. 71, 72). The entry forecourt is empty today except for a shallow basin, a clear simple effort. It once had lilies and clumps of tall thin native hardwood trees as well as a hefty amount of shrubs and bulbs, part of the adjacent forest before the house and drive were carved out.

On entering the house it is immediately clear that there is a large courtyard ahead. To enter one must move to the left or right, as a wall fountain and plants have been used to block the visual axis from the drive, protecting the sense of privacy and enclosure of the courtyard.

FIGURE 70. One of the twin cascades on the drive that leads from the entry piazza to the arrival court.

FIGURE 71. The arrival court, looking north.

FIGURE 72. Triumphal arches
at north and south frame the
arrival court. Like its pendant to
the south, this gate—derived from
the Palazzo Bevilacqua-Lamassa
in Verona—features mythical
trophies, rampant seahorses, and
urns added by Chalfin.

Here there are general "oohs" and "aahs" from guests. The courtyard, open to the sky until the 1980s, is marvelously proportioned, with large planted areas in each of the four corners. Here much of James Deering's social life and entertaining took place when he was in residence.

Passing through the eastern loggia of the courtyard, visitors step out onto a broad terrace to a panoramic vista of Biscayne Bay. Below the balustrade, down a flight of steps, is a small harbor with a curving stone bulkhead and flanking allées of palms. A small domed pavilion and water stairs stand at the end of the southern arm. A stone wharf terminates the northern one (figs. 73, 74). Both are reached over small arched stone bridges, reminiscent of those in Venice, which at one time allowed small boats and gondolas to pass from this harbor into

FIGURE 73. The northern sea arm, looking out to Biscayne Bay and Key Biscayne, past one of the pair of Venetian bridges and the yacht landing.

FIGURE 74. The southern sea arm with its Venetian bridge and lattice-domed tea house in the foreground, with Biscayne Bay and mangrove beyond.

canals beyond, which in turn led away into the shade of the hammock. In the center of this handsome harbor is an astonishing work of art and construction, a breakwater in the form of a double-ended limestone and marble boat, or barge, bedecked with huge carved figures, garlands, obelisks, urns, railings, stairs, and basins (fig. 75). At one time it also carried full-grown trees, flowers, a latticework pavilion, and fountains. Although these furnishings were swept away in hurricanes, the sculpture and masonry have been restored. It is truly a wonderful vision, or grand folly, and there is nothing quite like it anywhere in the world.

Descending from the broad terrace on this eastern side of the house, and walking to the left, or north, one finds a swimming pool in the form of a large rectangular tank that slides under the house into an arcaded gallery space in the manner reminiscent of the water entries and stairs found under all the palaces along the Grand Canal in Venice. Today there is also a convenient café terrace and recent orchid collection in an undistinguished and poorly proportioned pergola located here next to the house. A water landing to the northernmost canal of the surrounding park and a circular glade once framed by statues, along with a path leading off to the north, have disappeared. So, too, has a rustic portion of the hammock beloved by Deering, which has been destroyed and severed.

If, retracing our steps, we turn right within the courtyard and step through the doorway from the south arcade opposite the stair to the second floor into what has been called the tea

FIGURE 75. The Barge, or island breakwater, as it appears in the villa harbor today without its summerhouse, planting, or fountains.

room, a new and dramatic vista opens. Here a view commensurate with the surprise and grandeur of the Barge appears, but now it is of an Italianate garden (fig. 76). In the foreground is a broad terrace with a grand stair at the top of which is a fountain incorporating an antique sarcophagus (fig. 77). Beyond, avenues of live oaks lead into the distance. To the left and right are raised walkways lined with antique marble figures, framed by clipped evergreen hedges, stone steps, curbs, and sills. At the bottom of the broad terrace stair are elaborate parterres of low evergreen hedges and colorful annuals in the spirit of seventeenth-century rococo planting once common in Naples and Sicily or in the Bourbon-era gardens in the north of Italy (fig. 78). In the center of the garden is a green island framed by small canals and bridges, balustrades, and obelisks, which lead the eye to a bold cascade and stair on a small hill, or mound, crowned by large evergreen oaks (fig. 79). To the left and right of the water stair are a pair of grottos, themselves framed by pairs of grinning classical rustic creatures, delightful oversize caryatids of nymphs and satyrs carved from rough local limestone.

One passes now into the garden between two walls with brilliant bougainvillea grown both as standards and vines. Hidden on the right is a service building known as the "Laundry." Opposite, on the left in a similar wall of lemon-colored stucco and stone trim, a doorway leads to a secret garden room with a rustic grotto, a wall fountain, and planters that once housed orchids and ferns (figs. 80, 81, 82). Next, as the garden opens out, on each side are a pair of

FIGURE 76. The radiating walks and vistas of the "Italian" garden and south terrace, as seen from the breakfast room on the second floor of the house.

FIGURE 77. Chalfin combined an antique sarcophagus basin and jets with lead lizards and frogs by contemporary sculptor Charles Cary Rumsey to create a focal water feature on the south terrace.

FIGURE 78. Entering the "Italian" garden with the view to the Mound, cascade, and stair as seen across the central island.

broad, shallow apsidal basins with cascades and a polychrome array of antique marble columns, topped with urns and busts (figs. 83, 84). At their southern edge, forming a proscenium of sorts for the green world one is about to enter, perched atop the curving walls are twin miniature pavilions, lattice-domed garden seats of sorts, covered with vines (fig. 85).

The choice of which way to turn next, which side of the island, left or right, hardly matters, as retracing one's steps, choosing an alternate route at another time, is part of the whole idea of such a garden. The path to the right once continued past the Mound at the end of the island, beyond and along a causeway to a lagoon garden, a piazza with a cypress-lined pool and tile-covered domed pavilion known as the Casba. Today these have been lost and the vista blocked off. The radiating walk to the left (fig. 88) gives onto another parallel path, which was once more heavily framed by the vegetation of the hammock, that in turn provides access to a series of garden rooms, no longer clearly separated from each other visually and physically as originally intended. The first is an elliptical green theater with stage, seats, and eighteenth-century figures from pastoral comedy (figs. 89–91). Next is a circular hedge maze, and finally one comes to a large open space, originally known as the rose garden, containing a parterre formed of small water channels rather than the usual clipped hedges and bedding plants (figs. 87, 88). These small stone-lined canals were once filled with lilies, lotuses, and other water

FIGURE 79. The central island and basin in the garden, showing the turf-covered bridges, obelisks, and topiary framed by live oaks that emphasize the view to the axial cascade on the Mound.

FIGURE 80. Entry to the secret garden is through a rusticated grotto in the form of a curved arcade.

FIGURE 81. The secret garden—originally intended for orchids—with its heavily rusticated stonework, wall planters, and stairways with iron railings by Samuel Yellin.

FIGURE 82. The central niche and wall fountain in the secret garden take the form of a miniature grotto, surmounted by a handsome shell and satyr, and framed by brackets in the form of female herms.

FIGURE 83. The cross axis of the main garden is formed by a pair of semicircular basins, seen here with the principal remaining floral parterres, looking west toward the hammock.

FIGURE 84. Above and behind the semicircular basins stand antique columns surmounted by busts and urns purchased from the wreckage of the Messina earthquake of 1908. Small gazebo-like garden seats covered in creeping fig terminate the ends of upper walkways beside these columns. The Spanish baroque-style railing is one of many different items in the garden by the great ironworker Samuel Yellin.

FIGURE 85. The view from one of the raised fig-covered garden gazebo seats to another, located on axis across the main garden parterre.

FIGURE 86. View into the maze garden
from the north-south woodland path showing
its connection to the eastern elevated garden
walk with its Classical figures.

FIGURE 87. The view from the top of the eastern cross-axial stair on the Mound to the rose garden,
with its antique fountain.

FIGURE 88. View east along the elevated eastern radial walkway with sphinxes purchased by Chalfin and Deering.

plants. There are some interesting antique figures and ancient furnishings around the sides, but the centerpiece is a superb tall marble fountain formerly reputed to have been designed by sixteenth-century architect Giacomo Barozzi da Vignola for the town of Bassano di Sutri north of Rome (fig. 92).* From here a topiary gate once gave access to a path leading off into the hammock to a spot on the bay that Deering gave over to his servants. This delightful beach now covered by mangrove was the location where John Singer Sargent made several superb paintings of bathing figures on a visit in 1917.

At the center of the main garden is a quiet and simple island of lawn with topiary, accessed from the sides by a pair of small turf-covered bridges (fig. 93). At its southern end stands a small hill or mount referred to by its designers as the Mound. Three generous stairways lead to the top, one on either side to the east and west, and one on the north facing the villa. The latter

* It is no longer believed that this fountain came from Bassano di Sutri (now known as Bassano Romano) but rather from Sutri, nor does it appear today to have been designed by Vignola. Chalfin referred to it as the "Rose garden fountain" and did not seem to be overly concerned with its origin, only its character.

FIGURE 89. The garden theater with its pastoral and commedia dell'arte figures, as seen from the entry redesigned by Chalfin in 1936. Note the column in the background on axis is in one of the canals created in an early phase of the construction. A recent storm was the source of the water seen standing in the parterre of the "orchestra."

FIGURE 90. Eighteenth-century English lead pastoral garden figures of a shepherd and shepherdess on the stage of the garden theater.

FIGURE 91. A small lead version of the commedia dell'arte character Pulcinella mounted on a miniature marble column in the garden theater.

FIGURE 92. The central feature of the rose garden is this fountain and basin once thought to have stood in the main square of Bassano di Sutri. The ornamental metal spout with its rampant lions was designed and added by Chalfin in 1920.

FIGURE 93. The view north from the Mound to the house along the tranquil basin and island with their ornament of obelisks, scrolls, urns, and bridges framed within an allée of clipped live oaks.

FIGURE 94. The view south across the central basin and island to the Mound, its cascade stair framed by a pair of rusticated grottos.

climbs the central axis, accompanied by large basins and a cascade (figs. 94, 97). Twin grottos flanking this central stair form cool, shady shell- and coral-encrusted garden seats with superb views back into the garden and to the south façade of the house. In the foreground to each side is a pair of shallow rustic basins in the form of seashells with delicate arching jets (figs. 95, 96).

Climbing to the top of the Mound, one finds a generous clearing paved in concrete with four groves of shady trees beneath which are fountains and tropical planting. A handsome and tall, open pavilion stands on the southern edge of the Mound facing the central axis. Known as the Casino, it is composed of stucco with rusticated limestone trim for its triple-arched openings and windows and its balustrade and figures above (fig. 99). From this loggia visitors once would have been surprised to discover a view over a vast water park of lagoons, islands, tropical planting, paths, and bridges. In the distance was an elegant bridge connecting two portions of a causeway lined with royal palms, which led to a large boathouse farther off to the left on the bay. To the right one would have seen the domed Casba with its cypress.

FIGURE 95. This central jet, located at the base of the main axial cascade from the Mound, is one of many installed within the fountains of the garden.

FIGURE 96. The right-hand (western) grotto of the pair of rusticated grottos flanking the main cascade with the figures of a couple of herms acting as caryatids carved by Edoardo Cammilli; inside each grotto, a shell-encrusted ceiling rises above twin stone seats, a wall fountain, and central basin.

FIGURE 97. The basins and plinths, with great pots, of the cascade that defines the central axial stair leading to the top of the Mound.

FIGURE 98. The view to the south façade of the house from the top of the main axial cascade with the small jet accenting a delicate sixteenth-century marble font in the foreground.

FIGURE 99. The Casino on the Mound, developed as a focal point of the vista on the main axis from the house. Principally an open loggia, the Casino also served as a tea house and shelter—complete with fireplace—once offering panoramic views of the extensive southern lagoon garden with its islands, bridges, and palm-lined causeway.

FIGURE 100. To both the east and west, cross-axial stairs lead down from the Mound to the radiating vista walks, framed by rusticated stucco and stone walls which support the groves of live oak that in turn frame the central clearing above; the stairs are accompanied by ramps to accommodate gardeners' carts and wheelbarrows.

Today all of this is gone. A dense wall of mangrove stands about fifty feet away across a narrow stretch of residual backwater from the bay (fig. 101). The entire expanse of Deering's spectacular lagoon creation—every last bay and bridge, tree, vine, and shrub, every path, stair, road, and dock—disappeared under landfill after its sale to the Catholic Archdiocese of Miami, which built a hospital, parochial school, and residences there. Descending and walking around below the Casino, a stair for a water landing, which once offered an invitation to explore the watery landscape fantasia, is a sad remnant, now facing the impenetrable tangle of mangrove rather than an entrancing view into the distance of a lush tropical lagoon. The lower part of the Casino facing this stair takes the form of a rustic portico, a grotto nearly, with appropriate grinning antique faces. It also contains a once convenient toilet and pump room and controls for the waterworks that lie above and on all sides.

A last place to visit is reached by the radial path east of the Mound and south from the fountain or rose garden. Passing another ancient vessel and descending steps, one finds a urious tank in the middle of the walk at the end of which steps lead up to a raised bridge over the remains of a canal (fig. 102). Here, at the top of the stair, are four elaborately decorated and twisted columns each surmounted by a larger than life, gracefully carved peacock astride a globe (fig. 103). At the far end of the bridge, steps descend again to another long rectangular tank in the path that once led to tennis courts and the boathouse. This ensemble, once known as the Japanese bridge (also known as the peacock bridge) and marine garden, was an entryway by land or water into the lagoon garden as well as a setting to display fish and water plants. A few feet further, where once were the tennis courts, are the unpleasant fence of the church property and a view of the dismal structures within. It is almost worth skipping this charming bridge to avoid such a disturbing conclusion to the tour. The walk back toward the house, however, and the almost inevitable choice of a route and walk different from the one taken while coming out away from the house, dispel the anticlimax of this end of the garden, for the views to the sunny south façade of the house across the terraces and basins, framed by the oaks and sculptures, are masterful compositions combining the art of both architecture and gardens.

Once there was, and still is, more to the estate. Returning to the entry from South Miami Avenue, crossing the road and passing through the opposite gate on the west, one enters a cluster of buildings. Like owners of other estates around the world since Classical antiquity, Deering required a sizable staff and services to run Vizcaya. As a man who had spent his working life with farm machinery and horticulture it was natural that he would create a small farm with livestock, orchards, large kitchen gardens, and a plant nursery. To tend this he needed staff and buildings, a carpenter shop, machine shop, greenhouse, shadehouse, barn, dairy, stable, poultry buildings with outdoor runs, paddocks and pasture, a garage and carriagehouse for the various vehicles, and housing for the hired hands, the superintendent, and their families (fig. 104). This area, which also included an undisturbed portion of pinewoods and a large waterworks, was called the Village. Unfortunately, like the lagoon garden to the east of South Miami Avenue, the majority of this landscape has also disappeared under disappointingly dull development that could have gone anywhere. Deering's extensive gardens and orchards have

FIGURE 101. The main boat landing south of the Casino, once one of many on the lagoon. The dense wall of mangrove immediately beyond screens the unfortunate development that has replaced the former water garden.

FIGURE 102. The view to the rose garden and its fountain from the top of the bridge over a canal that divided the more formal Italianate garden from the southern lagoon garden. In the other direction the bridge gave access to a path leading past the tennis courts and beyond to the boathouse. This basin, decorated with shells and another of Yellin's railings, was one of a pair designed to hold exotic fish. The whole ensemble, which also had eight baroque columns surmounted by carved peacocks, was referred to as the marine garden.

FIGURE 103. Two of the eight stone peacocks carved by Gaston Lachaise in 1920.

been displaced by a local science museum, which looks like a motel accompanied by the usual barren parking lot. Having obliterated the historic estate nursery and spectacular vegetable and flower gardens and orchard, it is now planning to decamp to occupy precious land in yet another park in downtown Miami.

The loss of integrity of Deering's creation is lamentable, but it could have been far worse. All the buildings and some of the trees that made up the Village remain, except for the water-works, a Lord and Burnham greenhouse, and its larger companion, a splendid propagation house. What does remain was saved by a few farsighted citizens and used by the Miami Dade Park and Recreation Department, which for many years used the Village as its headquarters and service yard. Although not open to visitors at the time of writing, this charming ensemble of buildings, loosely based upon vernacular buildings in Lombardy and northern Italy, is in the midst of being physically repaired and stabilized (fig. 105).

FIGURE 104. A view toward the wagon shed in the central court or farmyard of the Village with its heroically proportioned water trough and stone ornaments.

FIGURE 105. A droll version of Neptune with seaweed mustachios that transform into architectural scrolls, supporting an obelisk above the entrance to the secret garden. The figure is typical of the remarkable, witty, and deeply informed Classical imagery that suffuses the gardens of Vizcaya.

chapter 7

A WATERY WORLD

As the most recent portion of North America to have emerged from the sea, south Florida has little topography, and most of the communities that have come into being are adjacent to water, whether the Atlantic, the Gulf of Mexico, rivers, or lakes. Its reputation as a sybaritic tropical resort or playground has been associated with water-based recreation for more than a century. As a fundamental aspect of the landscape, water naturally came to influence the sort of residence and gardens that both of the Deering brothers were to design and build on Biscayne Bay, and provides the most significant and extensive element of the Vizcaya site.

To truly appreciate the "genius of the place," one must first know Biscayne Bay and see and approach Vizcaya from the water. James Deering's favorite way to arrive was by boat, and the estate was partially conceived as a Veneto villa on a lagoon. After the main house was completed, Deering and Paul Chalfin continued construction for the next six years of an extensive water garden consisting of canals, bays, and islands to be experienced by boat.

The wealthy have always liked the latest and sporty in transportation, whether it is fast horses, dashing carriages, elegant automobiles, or sharp-looking, fast boats. The Deering brothers, indeed, loved especially handsome, powerful motorboats. Charles had attended Annapolis, graduated second in his class, had been highly successful and well liked by his peers and superiors at sea and on land, and had been designated by the navy as personal escort for General Ulysses S. Grant on a trip around the world. He rose to the rank of captain. However, after twelve years in the service he was persuaded by his father to give up the navy to return and take over the reins of the family business in Chicago. As president of the corporation he was instrumental in its worldwide affairs and in solving problems of logistics in the manufacturing of their machinery. He was an expert at shipping and material supply. When he was able finally to take time off from the business, he made certain that it was spent on the water and that he could have boats. Likewise his younger brother, James, loved boats and always had several around once he began coming to Florida, where fishing was and still is an attraction to visitors and vacationers. As an early Baedeker guide to the United States remarked in the section on south Florida, "its excellent opportunities for shooting and fishing are additional attractions . . . while the fishing for tarpon (Megalops thrissoides), the largest and gamiest of the game-fish (sometimes 200 lbs in weight), has its headquarters in this state."[1]

One of the principal reasons anyone came south of the Miami River was to boat and fish, and both brothers joined the Biscayne Bay Yacht Club founded in 1887 by Ralph Middleton Munroe. In 1916 with the house barely finished and major construction work under way in the landscape and garden, James Deering commissioned two boats to be built for his use in Florida. His favorite, the *Nepenthe*, an 80-foot boat with living quarters, which he used for traveling about and visiting the Keys with guests and friends, was built in Atlantic City in 1916 and sailed down, arriving in February 1917 (fig. 106). Described by Deering and others as a houseboat, it was a long motor cruiser with a covered but open veranda-like space behind an enclosed bridge set atop a suite of cabins and rooms. Another vessel, the *Psyche*, a powerful 40-foot cruiser used for fishing, running about the bay, and day trips, was also built in 1916 in Morris Heights, New Jersey (fig. 107). In addition, there were also the *General* and the *Blue Dog*, another houseboat Deering allowed Chalfin to commission and build for himself and his staff as a floating apartment for their use when on site and staying in the area, supposedly as a cost saving over local hotels (fig. 108). While authorizing Chalfin to go ahead with the *Blue Dog*, which was built in the Miami Yacht and Machine Works, Deering comments in a letter that he thought such a solution to temporary accommodation would be too cramped for himself. There were also the *Granville Bacon* (a coastal schooner), the *La Singerie* (another houseboat), a motor-driven gondola of sorts, and the *Parthenon*, as well as several work barges or scows. Records of the Vizcaya staff list ten names of employees exclusively detailed to work on the boats. All of these boats were wrecked, along with the boathouse, the year after Deering's

FIGURE 106. The *Nepenthe*, 80 feet long and outfitted with comfortable living quarters, was James Deering's favorite boat for cruising and fishing along the south Florida coast and in the Keys. (Vizcaya Museum and Gardens Archive)

FIGURE 107. The *Psyche*, a powerful 40-foot-long cruiser built for speed, seen here on an early run in the Hudson River before its delivery to Vizcaya. (Vizcaya Museum and Gardens Archive)

FIGURE 108. The *Blue Dog*, Chalfin's Coconut Grove houseboat residence, with its awnings and carefully tended windowboxes. (Vizcaya Museum and Gardens Archive)

death, in the Great Miami Hurricane of 1926, although the *Nepenthe* was eventually salvaged, rebuilt, and taken to Long Island.

Photograph albums at Vizcaya include many pictures of the boats and what must have been pleasurable outings. The senior captain, Joseph Santini, who came from an old seafaring Key West family, recalled in an interview that James Deering liked to go out for week-long or ten-day cruises around Key West or Shark River.[2] He loved to fish, mostly for tarpon and bonefish, but because of his poor health tired easily and had constantly to rest, for which he found boating particularly conducive. Boat trips also provided pleasant relief from the stress, constant wrangling, and mess of the lengthy construction project. Deering's private physician, who accompanied him to Florida, staying at the old Royal Palm Hotel when Deering was at Vizcaya, would join him on the cruises along with friends, his two nieces, and guests. Santini described one particular "rollicking time" when his nieces, Barbara and Marion, were on board with their husbands, Richard Danielson and Chauncey McCormick. The two men were in a rowboat off the *Nepenthe* trying to harpoon sharks, apparently ineptly, as Santini recalled, and he and the women nearly died laughing.[3]

Given this activity and investment in boats, both of the Deering brothers became involved in building bulkheads, docks, landing stages, and boathouses that became major features of their landscapes. The Vizcaya boathouse also held living quarters upstairs where Santini and his wife lived, much as chauffeurs commonly lived over garages (fig. 109). Because Biscayne Bay is extremely shallow, both Deerings ended up having to dredge channels for their personal use; these are still maintained and in use today by recreational and commercial traffic. Documents depicting the main east-west channel to the outer bay, a large turning basin by the landing at the north sea arm, and another channel parallel to the shore leading to the boathouse and its maneuvering space are among the earliest engineering drawings in the archive at Vizcaya.[4] Today the channel, which once led from the boathouse to the main harbor in front of the house, has been extended around the church property and connects to the residential docks and marina areas to the south, thereby connecting them to the Deering Channel at Vizcaya and the bay. As in the great French châteaux where one approaches from a great distance along a stately allée of trees, here, too, one moves along a nearly invisible but implacable axis. This channel, 70 feet wide and nearly a mile long, approaches Vizcaya from the open water of the bay with only occasional buoys to mark it off. One must stay focused and approach the house straight on without deviating or risk running aground.

FIGURE 109. The boathouse, seen here in March 1917 with the *Nepenthe* docked alongside, was one of the first structures completed at Vizcaya. (Vizcaya Museum and Gardens Archive)

Mixed in with the hundreds of design and construction drawings in the archives at Vizcaya are numerous documents, drawings, sketches, construction plans, and details related to the boats. These include details for vegetable lockers and chart (map) cases on the *Nepenthe* and various specifications for interior furnishings, as well as construction details for dolphins and other piling arrangements, lanterns for navigation, as well as mooring facilities, boat landings, water stairs, and related details.

This interest and focus upon boats and the water, which is part of the character and purpose of settlement in Coconut Grove, led James Deering to ask his designers to create a series of canals through the mangrove north and south of his villa, and eventually to the lengthy construction of the lagoon park south of the Italianate gardens. Like the house, these became more interesting and ambitious as well as far more expensive and problematic than he had originally envisioned, but contributed considerably to making Vizcaya the unusual and extraordinary place it was to become. At the same time this involvement in the bay and boating also led the Deerings to more pragmatic issues, such as the repair of the foundations of the lighthouse at the tip of Cape Florida, which marks the southern end of Key Biscayne and the entry to Biscayne Bay opposite Vizcaya (fig. 110).

In addition to documents relating to such practical features, the Vizcaya archives preserve several sheets of more lighthearted items with a nautical theme. Some of the most whimsical are a series of masts and pennants and gonfalons by Chalfin to line the small harbor's seawall and arms, which were to be emblazoned with different motifs (figs. 111, 112). These included a seahorse, a caravel, the name Vizcaya, and Deering's motto, *J'ai dit*, "I have spoken," which he and Chalfin created as decorative motifs, the latter certainly an appropriate one for the personality of an individual who was used to commanding others and creating such an estate.[5]

FIGURE 110. The Cape Florida lighthouse on Key Biscayne, February 1917. (Photograph by Mattie Edwards Hewitt, Vizcaya Museum and Gardens Archive)

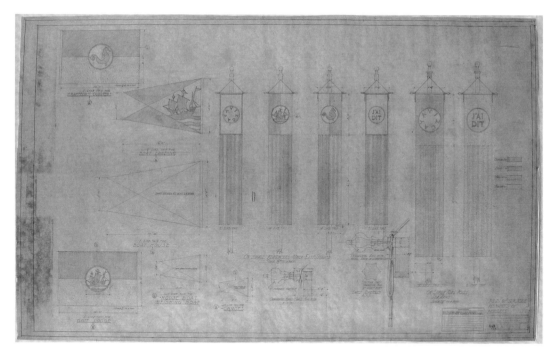

FIGURE 111. Design drawing from Chalfin's office for pennants, flags, and gonfalons for the harbor. Pencil on linen, drawing G69, November 16, 1916. (Vizcaya Museum and Gardens Archive)

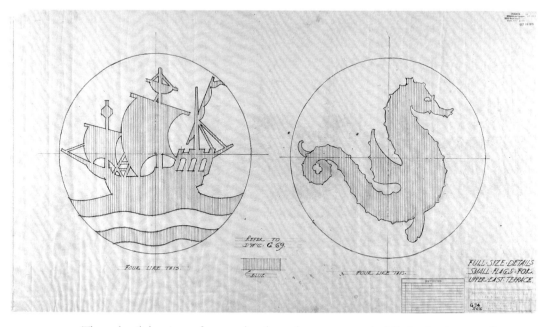

FIGURE 112. These detail drawings of a caravel and a seahorse were made full size for the manufacture of the pennants. Pencil on tracing paper, drawing G74, November 1916. (Vizcaya Museum and Gardens Archive)

chapter 8

IMAGINATION, DESIGN, AND CONSTRUCTION

A MEDITERRANEAN MOOD

Americans of means have long created country retreats with European pedigrees, as exemplified by many of the homes of those who participated as leaders in the revolution of the eighteenth century. By the last decades of the nineteenth century, numerous estates and gardens of the wealthy had reached great size, scope, and ambition. Outside Philadelphia on the Main Line and along its river valleys, outside New York, in New Jersey, Connecticut, and on Long Island, in Newport and Bar Harbor, outside Chicago, Cleveland, Detroit, and Pittsburgh, imposing structures in English, French, and Italian architectural revival styles were built by the dozens. Eclectic gardens were built, with mixtures of styles and periods, their elements derived from Spain and Italy, French baroque, and English cottage gardens. Some, such as Biltmore in Asheville designed by Hunt and Olmsted, or Lynnewood Hall by Trumbauer and Greber, were truly grand and coherent, although flagrant displays of wealth and power. Architectural firms such as Carrère and Hastings, Horace Trumbauer, and Richard Morris Hunt emerged, specializing in such creations.

As the Olmsted firm succeeded Andrew Jackson Downing, and was in turn succeeded by the firms of Platt, Duchêne, Shurcliff, Manning, Farrand, Shipman, and others in the design and planning of estate landscapes and gardens, by the first decade of the twentieth century an interest in and growing understanding of Italian garden design permeated buildings and gardens throughout the United States. Although one finds Tudor, Norman, French Renaissance, Spanish Colonial, even Bavarian styles in American estates at this time, it is increasingly to Italy and its gardens that patrons and designers looked, spurred by increasing travel and a series of books, articles, and lectures by American journalists, literary figures, artists, and designers. The two most prominent books were Charles Adam Platt's *Italian Gardens* of 1894 and Edith Wharton's *Italian Villas and Their Gardens* of 1904. Both were illustrated, Platt's with his own photographs, and Wharton's, which had originally run as a series of articles in the *Century*, with reproductions of paintings by Maxfield Parrish. Both volumes presented a selection of sixteenth-century villa gardens partly overlain by design additions and revisions from the seventeenth and eighteenth centuries, softened by time and in many cases in a state of attractive dishevelment and decrepitude. Other influential works were Edith Wharton and Ogden Codman's *Decoration of Houses* of 1902, Kenyon Cox's *The Classic Point of View* of 1911, and Geoffrey Scott's *Architecture of Humanism* of 1914.

Cox's treatise, less well known today than those of Platt and Wharton, is a compilation of a series of lectures he gave in 1911 at the Art Institute of Chicago. Ostensibly lecturing on matters relating to painting and sculpture, Cox put forward ideas and concepts related to the aesthetic goals of those about to create gardens.

> It is not only your lines and masses that must be composed, but your light and shade, your color, your very brush marks must be arranged; and the task of composition is not done until the last touch has been placed upon the canvas. . . . As design is the underlying and unifying principle of every work of art, so it is the classic principle par excellence, the principle which makes for order and stability and clarity and all that the classic spirit holds most dear. It is conservative in its nature, and tends to preserve the old molds even when new matter is put in them. . . . Great and original power of design is more rare than any other of the powers of an artist and a radically new form of design is nearly inconceivable.[1]

Cox was a close personal friend of Augustus Saint-Gaudens and a member of an art colony made up of kindred spirits gathered around Cornish, New Hampshire, which included Wharton,

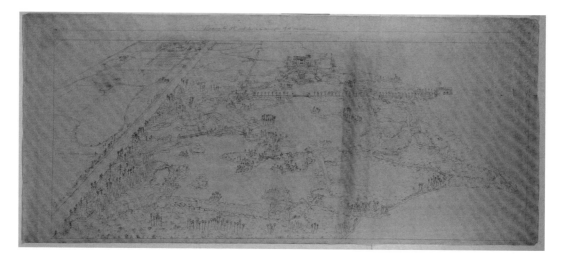

FIGURE 113. A rendered plan of Vizcaya produced by Hoffman's office after the evolution of the scheme. To date none of the earliest design or presentation drawings has been found. Pen and ink. (Vizcaya Museum and Gardens Archive)

Platt, and Parrish, all interested in country living, gardens, and Italy; he also taught for a brief period at the Art Institute, with which James Deering was for a time associated. Deering's brother, Charles, had met Saint-Gaudens, along with painters John Singer Sargent and Gari Melchers, in Paris during a youthful bohemian sojourn there, becoming lifelong friends with them all. The closeness of the two brothers, and the intertwining of their interests and lives, lead to the obvious conclusion that both were not only fully aware of the ideas emanating from this influential group of artists and tastemakers, but also among those who acted upon them.

Deering and Chalfin had been buying books on the subject and studying them throughout the course of the project. That Chalfin, not trained in either architecture or landscape architecture, made use of them is evident in a letter of 1919 when he was engaged in the execution of the ambitious south lagoon garden and also trying to complete the Italian garden. Deering asks for the return of some of these books to lend to a friend who is also thinking of building, to which Chalfin responds that "the books on gardens will be greatly needed here [his New York office]. . . . For that reason I should be very glad if you would [eventually] return the two volumes of 'Gardens in Italy,' and the smaller 'Italian Villas.'"[2] On an earlier occasion in 1914, as the design for the garden is beginning to take shape in his studio in New York, Chalfin wired W. D. Sturrock, a landscape architect in Miami hired by Deering to assist on the site: "Mr. Deering left wooden box filled with books in the Brickell house he occupied last winter [1913–1914]. Open same and express me at once all books on architecture and gardening."[3]

Sturrock responds and sends them with an inventory, which includes Sir George Sitwell's *On the Making of Gardens*, H. Inigo Triggs's *The Art of Gardening*, Platt's *Italian Gardens*, Wharton's *Italian Villas and Their Gardens*, as well as books on forestry and the Everglades and general histories of architecture.[4] The following summer Chalfin continues to correspond with Deering about purchasing books, implying that they would be helpful not only in the course of the work, but also in building a library. After asking if he already has *Calli and Canali di Venezia*, he mentions Letarouilly's three-volume folio edition of *Edifices de Rome Moderne*: "would it be too much to pay $90 . . . showing the famous palaces of Rome with plans, sections and what not. They are in fine outline. It is one of the great classics of an architectural library." He also suggests purchasing a reprint of *Renaissance Architecture in Spain*.[5]

Platt's text extolling Italian gardens is brief and pithy with a portion of the message carried in his illustrations, and reads as an agenda for Deering on embarking upon the creation of Vizcaya.

> The first steps of one interested in the formal style of landscape architecture should be directed to Italy, where at the time of the Renaissance the great gardens which have ever since served as models of this method of design have come into existence, the form they took being the natural outgrowth of the architecture and art of the period. . . .
>
> It should be said here that the word "villa" is used in the Italian sense, implying all the formal parts of the grounds arranged in direct relation to the house, the house itself being as much a part of it as the garden or the grove. The evident harmony of arrangement between the house and

surrounding landscape is what first strikes one in Italian landscape architecture—the design as a whole, including gardens, terraces, groves, and their necessary surrounding embellishments, it being clear that no one of these component parts was ever considered independently, the architect of the house being the architect of the garden and the rest of the villa. The problem being to take a piece of land and make it habitable, the architect proceeded with the idea that not only was the house to be lived in, but that one still wished to be at home while out of doors: so the garden was designed as another apartment, the terraces and groves still others, where one might walk about and find a place suitable for the hour of the day and the feeling of the moment, and still be in that sacred portion of the globe dedicated to one's self.[6]

Wharton, too, spells out exactly what was to be learned and emulated from Italian gardens: "The inherent beauty of the garden lies in the grouping of its parts—in the converging lines of its long ilex-walks, the alternation of sunny open spaces with cool woodland shade, the proportion between terrace and bowling-green, or between the height of a wall and the width of a path."[7] She also makes the following telling remark directed at her wealthy contemporaries: "Certain effects, those which depend upon architectural grandeur as well as those due to colouring and age, are no doubt unattainable; but there is, none the less, much to be learned from the old Italian gardens, and the first lesson is that, if they are to be a real inspiration, they must be copied, not in the letter, but in the spirit. That is, a marble sarcophagus and a dozen twisted columns will not make an Italian garden; but a piece of ground laid out and planted on the principles of the old garden craft will be, not an Italian garden in the literal sense, but what is far better, *a garden as well adapted to its surroundings as were the models which inspired it*" (Wharton's italics).[8]

By the time Deering, Hoffman, Chalfin, and Suarez came to work on the garden design, Charles Adam Platt had designed, built, and published numerous influential estates with gardens and houses inspired by his travel to Italy, among them the dramatic and elegantly integrated ensemble of garden rooms, terraces, and buildings of Gwinn for William G. Mather, overlooking Lake Erie outside Cleveland, and the immense Villa Turicum for Harold and Edith Rockefeller McCormick in Lake Forest north of Chicago. Both estates were well publicized in the architectural press, were built by individuals in Deering's milieu, and were undoubtedly known to some of the design team. Although Vizcaya evolves into a truly unique composition with its own character, it would be wrong to underestimate the influence of Wharton and Platt in its inspiration as well as of another less well known publication of this period, Sir George Sitwell's *On the Making of Gardens* (of which more below).

ASSEMBLING TALENT

While the house appears to be largely the product of the imagination and talents of Hoffman and Chalfin, the landscape and gardens, as is often the case, must be seen as the product of the interaction of a larger group of people. This consisted of Hoffman and Chalfin; a talented young South American landscape architect named Diego Suarez (1888–1974); Phineas Paist, an architect who acted as project architect on site for Chalfin; Fred Starbuck, Chalfin's clerk of the works; James Deering himself, who was deeply involved in every aspect of the project; and eventually a series of landscape contractors and gardeners hired by Deering. Hoffman departed for France and the war in 1917 after having been pushed aside by Chalfin. Suarez was involved for a key period of three years from the autumn of 1914 into 1917 during which time he devised the concept, basic layout and character, and many of the details of the Italian garden. Chalfin stayed on, as did Paist—who remained in Florida even after the project was over—adding details, completing construction documents for the entire ensemble, as well as developing the scheme, structures, and planting for the lagoon gardens and farm. Although correspondence between Deering and Hoffman amply demonstrates that it was Hoffman who began the design of nearly all of the Village structures as well as the boathouse, the final construction documents now in the archives at Vizcaya were all produced by the talented draftsmen and designers Chalfin employed in his office, which grew substantially to accomplish the enormous volume of work.

Hoffman had been engaged by Deering to design the house in 1912, and a general notion of a garden in a Mediterranean manner was anticipated, but no substantial design for it had been developed by the time the house began construction. In June 1914 when Chalfin and Deering were in Europe buying furnishings, they stayed for several weeks at Arthur Acton's estate, La Pietra outside Florence. Acton introduced them to Diego Suarez, a designer whom he had engaged to help in restoring its gardens. Suarez was a young landscape architect who had studied engineering in his native Colombia. Upon the death of his father, his Italian mother returned home from South America, and Diego accompanied her. In Florence he enrolled in the Accademia di Belli Arti to study architecture; however, his interest seems to have been captured by the historic gardens of the sixteenth and seventeenth centuries. Soon he was working at several that were in the process of renewal and restoration, at least three of which, the Villa Loeser, the Villa Schifanoia, and the Villa Selva e Guasto, were in the Italian Renaissance tradition. At Acton's suggestion, Suarez acted as a guide for Chalfin and Deering to visit a number of private gardens and villas to which he had access, such as the Villa Gamberaia and the Villa Caponi. Suarez later recalled: "Acton was a disciple, you might say, of the great Henry Duchêne, and he had been engaged for several years in restoring the superb renaissance gardens on his estate, some parts of them going back to the seventeenth century. They had been destroyed during the stupid craze for naturalistic English gardens. Arthur Acton was my tutor. I went to his villa four or five times a week while he was at work carefully supervising the restoration. He gave me my teaching in classical Italian garden design, and he taught me Duchêne's ideals."[9]

What may have seemed to expatriates like Acton and Suarez in 1914 to be "Classical" Italian style in the work of Duchêne looks decidedly seventeenth-century baroque or rococo, even "French" today. Certainly it is a development, if different from that of sixteenth-century Italy. Regardless of matters of style, the work of Duchêne and his son Achille was elegant. Both were involved in the restoration of numerous gardens and parks originally designed by André le Nôtre, and both produced new work of their own in his manner, with the son working as well in England and America for some of the wealthiest of Deering's contemporaries. An impressive series of Duchêne terraces and parterres may still be seen today at Blenheim and Castle Howard in Britain and at Vaux-le-Vicomte and Chantilly in France. Like Russell Page a half century later, he knew his craft, had a great eye and judgment, and moved easily from estate to estate and country to country among the very wealthy.

What Suarez may have forgotten, or was never made aware of, is that it was Cecil Pinsent, an English expatriate and architect who worked for many in the Anglo-American community around Florence repairing and restoring their houses, villas, and gardens, not one of the Duchênes, who had done the design for Acton's "restoration" in 1911. Pinsent was introduced to Berenson in 1907 and started work on his garden at I Tatti two years later, his collaborator on the project being Geoffrey Scott, who was to become Berenson's librarian and later to marry Sibyl Cutting and publish *The Architecture of Humanism* in 1914.[10] Like many of Pinsent's other projects—whether restoration at the Villa Medici in Fiesole for Cutting, new work at Le Balze in Fiesole for Charles Augustus Strong and at I Tatti for Berenson in Settignano, or at La Foce near Chianciano for Cutting's daughter, Iris Origo—Pinsent's gardens have weathered well and today seem always to have been there, to be as Italian as gardens can be, with their clear, strong organization, simple yet elegant palette, and baroque touches over traditional Renaissance-plan types. It is not surprising that Suarez was unaware of his efforts for Acton that preceded his involvement. If Suarez took a certain French rococo and baroque flavor from the Duchênes, it was only reinforced by the baroque overlays and somewhat Art Deco touches that Pinsent quietly layered onto sixteenth-century classical Renaissance models. La Pietra was so attuned to its cultural topography, and so thoroughly and seamlessly combined motifs and elements from several centuries such as one finds in genuinely historic gardens, as to feel complete, full, and authentically old.

Like Chalfin, Berenson was himself a protégé of Isabella Stewart Gardner, and from 1910 would welcome Edith Wharton as a frequent visitor at I Tatti. And it was in this intellectual and artistic community that Arthur Acton, of Italian/English parentage and married to an American from Chicago, had gathered around himself at La Pietra that Deering and Chalfin found the person who was to become their landscape architect.

The story of how Suarez came to work on the garden of Vizcaya has been told several times, largely as a result of trying to correct the record as it had become obscured by Chalfin's unfortunate behavior after the young man's departure. In an interview with James T. Maher in 1965, Suarez told of his experience and how he came to America and Vizcaya. It is worth quoting this interview at length.

> I had designed eight gardens by that time. Two of them were important—to me that is—and I took Mr. Deering and Mr. Chalfin to see them. One was at the Villa Schifanoia, which was then owned by Lewis Einstein and was later owned by Myron C. Taylor, and the other was a garden for Charles Loeser, the son of Frederick Loeser, the storeowner. . . .

When we were visiting the villas and gardens, Mr. Chalfin told me that Mr. Deering was building a great house in Florida, and he said that if I happened to come to the United States I should call on him and we could talk about the gardens. Shortly after that Lady Sibyl Cutting, who owned the Villa Medici at Fiesole, said to me, "We're going to the United States and you're not doing anything here, so why don't you join us?" Lady Sibyl was the widow of Bayard Cutting, an American, and she was planning to take her daughter, Iris (you've read her I'm sure, Iris Origo), to visit her grandmother to Bar Harbor—at Northeast Harbor, that is. It seemed sensible to join Lady Cutting's party; to go to New York, and then on to Colombia, where I wanted to look into some family property. We were hardly on the ocean when we heard that the war had started.

I was young and green when I arrived in New York, and I had very little money. I first stayed in a hotel on Broadway around Twentieth Street. Then I met a friendly Italian boy and we found a rooming house in Brooklyn where we could live for six or seven dollars a week. I addressed letters for the New York Telephone Company to earn my board.

Then one day I was having lunch at the Ritz with Mrs. Albert Gallatin, whom I had known in Florence, and on the way out I ran into Mr. Deering and Chalfin in the lobby. Chalfin asked me to come to see him at his office. I remember there was a tremendous amount of furniture, and among other things, a sort of warehouse. He first showed me the general layout of Mr. Deering's estate and then took me to the office of the architect, Mr. Burrall Hoffman. There I saw the architectural models of the splendid villa with its approaches, terraces, farm buildings, gate lodge, and boathouse. I could see at once it was a project conceived in the great Italian classical tradition—the stately house and terraces, the loggias and lofty rooms.

The models fired my imagination and when Mr. Chalfin asked me if I thought I was capable of designing Mr. Deering's gardens I knew it was an opportunity to use all the knowledge and experience I had gained in Italy. Chalfin told me that my name would appear with his on the working drawings, but we had no formal agreement and anyway, I was too young to think much about things like that. He paid me $25 a week and later I was getting $50.[11]

It was in Chalfin's office that Suarez was discovered by a correspondent of Deering's (Jaquelin Rice), who wrote, "I found him at work making a model of a beautiful garden which he said was yours."[12] For all of the work described below, his name does not appear on any of the working drawings. Chalfin virtually expunged Diego Suarez from the record once he left the project in 1917, until many years later when Suarez forced the *New York Times* to print a correction.[13]

ON COLLABORATION

It has often been said that behind every great project there is a great client. Nowhere is this more true than at Vizcaya. James Deering must be seen as one of the key collaborators and designers of the landscape. His concepts and vision of what he wished to make, his selection of Chalfin and subsequently Hoffman and Suarez, his insistence upon the location of the house and development of the overall parts of the estate, and his constant oversight and control of the project had everything to do with what was produced. Difficult as it appears to have been for some of the participants at the time to work with Deering, there is no question that he engineered and sustained an extraordinary and successful collaboration with talented artists, while never himself far offstage.

Successful projects of the scope of Vizcaya generally result from an iterative process with different individuals taking the lead on different issues at different times with ideas going back and forth in a teamwork of sorts in an effort to achieve a commonly understood and shared purpose. Without some individual or group to finance the effort, all would be impossible. Also, almost inevitably, the entire project begins with a need, a dream, an idea. In this case that was clearly James Deering's decision to build a place for himself in Coconut Grove, Florida, and to do it with designers who could give him what he wanted and not force upon him some hobbyhorse of their own. As it developed, his choice of Chalfin, who then brought him Hoffman, Suarez, and the others, appears to have been a success in nearly every way. Each individual contributed, in particular ways at various moments in the history of the project, to the creation of something none of them could possibly have done alone nor ever was to do again.

In the case of Vizcaya the number of individuals, disciplines, and personalities, many of whom were used to working alone or being in charge of their own work, led almost immediately to conflict and disagreement over who should be coordinating and directing operations. In early 1915, to end the wrangling, Deering agreed to establish a committee representing all of the parties, designers, and builders, to meet regularly to address matters of progress, control, and coordination with Chalfin and his office in charge. In many ways this is standard procedure for most architectural and landscape architectural projects today, with weekly job meetings taking place on site once construction commences. Everyone along the way constantly makes design decisions and reformulations; design never stops, and, in the case of Vizcaya, the landscape design and development went on continuously from 1912 until Deering's death in 1925.

Although the principal players in the earliest stages at Vizcaya certainly were Chalfin, Deering, Hoffman, and Suarez, many others added their judgment, skill, and on-the-spot decisions in its achievement. Starting in 1912 with virtually no staff, Chalfin had acquired sufficient architectural draftsmen by 1914 to begin producing construction documents for the garden terraces and interior details, eventually supplanting Hoffman and his office. Other key participants were H. R. Allen, who handled project management in New York, August Koch, his chief assistant designer, and Fred L. Starbuck, who Chalfin sent to Florida to live on site to act as his clerk of the works, or project manager. Significant contributions to the landscape work, which was in constant need of design decisions to be made in the field in Florida, were supplied by Phineas Paist, an architect also sent to live in Miami on Chalfin's payroll. There also was William D. Sturrock, a local landscape architect hired by Deering to assist on site, and eventually more gardening staff working directly for Deering, one of whom was named Sykes, and William McLean. Voluminous correspondence between them, especially between Chalfin and Starbuck—at times several letters per day—contains requests and receipts for drawings, sketches, details, and answers to questions and problems, as well as notification and receipts for the flood of materials and supplies shipped for the landscape, outbuildings, roads, bridges, utilities, fountains, basins, furnishings, sculpture, walls, and planting.

DESIGN OF THE GARDEN AND LANDSCAPE

The initial site Deering purchased from Mrs. Brickell consisted of three ecological communities: on the north and east a hardwood hammock atop a limestone ridge; on the west a sandy pine woodland; and to the south a frequently inundated wet prairie of grasses with mangrove along the shore. Deering elected to place his house to the north on the edge between the bay and the hammock, giving it a waterside location. At the same time he wished to relocate to the west the Old Miami Trail, a public road leading south from the city toward the Keys, and to redirect it through the pine woods, thus giving more privacy to the house and enabling him to create a longer transitional drive from an entry gate to the house. The more open pineland, being less valued than the hammock, was selected for the extensive clearings needed for agricultural fields, orchards, pastures, service buildings, and yards of the "home farm" he envisioned to support the estate. At some point the shift of the public highway out of the hammock led to the idea of utilizing its former clearing as a place to excavate a large quantity of stone to be used as fill for the house site and garden. This resulted in a vast linear trench, which could then be filled with water to form a canal in the trees.

How these ideas were first developed can only be conjectured, as there is no record describing these early decisions. The many conversations between Deering and Chalfin on their travels, and the dialogue between Hoffman and Chalfin as they began work in New York, have passed unrecorded. The documents and record concerning the gardens largely begin with a few letters in 1913, continue with drawings by 1914, followed by a profusion of records, documents, drawings, telegrams, and letters from early 1914 on.

Burrall Hoffman first visited the site in 1913, the same year he traveled in Italy, visiting the Veneto to see particular sites, buildings, and gardens that Deering and Chalfin were interested in using as sources of inspiration. On his return he and his staff began a concentrated effort to develop the plans for the entire estate. By that autumn he was instructed by Chalfin, who had brought him into the job, to focus on the house and wrap up and send the studies for the rest of the sitework as he, Chalfin, intended to take over the design of the grounds and gardens himself. Shocked and perplexed how to proceed, Hoffman wrote:

> Of course I have always understood that the development of the Gardens, as well as other parts of the Property, was a matter which would be carried out later, but at the same time some more or less definite scheme would be arrived at now, so that we would know what relation the work we are doing now would bear to its ultimate surroundings.
>
> As both you and Mr. Deering had spoken to me quite frequently about these proposed developments and I have made some studies and suggestions concerning them, I had naturally hoped, that when this part of the work had materialized I should carry it out.

> I strongly feel that it would be for the best interests of uniformity of this development, that
> all Architectural work, even in connection with the Grounds, should be done by the same person.
> I am, at your suggestion hurrying the sketch for the layout of the Grounds.[14]

What we know is that Hoffman had by then produced plans for the house with large terraces facing the bay and gardens, as well some notions of the site to the north and the entry sequence. Some sort of plans had been developed for the farm, roads, and boathouse. Photographs of plaster models made at this time show the house as it first appears in the construction documents of February 1914.[15] Up until then emphasis had been upon the house itself, and site development beyond it was limited to extensive yet simple rectangular terraces with stairs leading to the water, garden, and a service wing, all of which were to change later under the control of Chalfin. Pressure was placed upon Hoffman to begin developing the boathouse and Village layout as well. Deering, working directly with local engineers and contractors he had located, began efforts to move the Old Miami Trail to the west (now called South Miami Avenue, which connects to the north with what is now Brickell Avenue) and to start work on access roads, clearing the house site, and the creation of a causeway to give vehicular access across a tidal marshland to the boathouse site. The first completed construction drawings from Hoffman's office are all dated February 21, 1914. Within a month, clearing and grubbing had begun. The final revisions to the building elevations are dated a few months later in June.

Until someone finds any of the early studies we cannot know exactly what the first version proposed for the Vizcaya gardens and landscape was, but with a few notable exceptions they almost certainly contained several of the elements and ideas of the final scheme. One thing is clear, however, that one of the most remarkable elements of the scheme, the great breakwater in the shape of a double-ended limestone boat (later also called the Barge), was one of the earliest ideas. This feature appears on the very first drawing of Hoffman's, which is a general layout plan used to request a set of borings throughout the site in particular places to help the engineers design foundations. The Barge is clearly shown in simple outline form almost exactly as built. Other features of the site are also shown: the entry forecourt, the east and side terraces, and two irregularly shaped canals cut into the hammock to the north and south of the harbor with the sea arms in their current extent and shape. In concept, a lot had been decided already.

The arrival of Suarez in late 1914 coincided with the need to develop the garden and overall estate plans. Construction had started several months earlier, and work had begun on the site. Contractors had arrived with their crews. A quarry was opened, and a stone yard to receive and work it was established just south of the house. Engineers were pursuing ongoing survey and boring information to assist in the design of foundations and the shoreline reconstruction. A floating dredge had arrived to begin work in the bay and south of the intended garden. An approach drive was cut through what the workers referred to as "jungle." The dramatic linear excavation, which was to become the "waterway," in the former right-of-way of the Old Miami Trail, had begun on the north within the hammock. Aerial ramps and cart ways on high timber trestles resembling rustic roller coasters had been erected through the woods and in various directions to and from the house. (Deering had made it clear that he wanted the native vegetation saved and protected; the contractors were not to cut through the woods or create additional roads and areas of destruction.)

It was now time to lay out the Village, where the future staff and employees would live and the production gardens for food and flowers for the house and garden were to be located, as well as the buildings, yards, and paddocks for livestock and poultry, and to establish the main well, water storage, and pump house needed to supply irrigation for the gardens and water for the fountains and domestic use. Hoffman was busy and besieged with requests for drawings and information. Chalfin was busy hiring staff to meet the increasing workload while trying to keep Deering placated with the speed and extent of developments as he continued to search for furnishings and maneuvered to keep overall control of the project. Suarez' arrival was a godsend at this moment. Here was a young single person who could work long hours eagerly, who had talent and was deeply informed about Italian gardens and the craft of their making, who was indebted to Chalfin for helping him out with employment when he needed it, and whom Chalfin could direct.

From statements he made later, it seems that Suarez rapidly developed specific ideas and plans for various parts of the garden and island that were translated into model form in Chalfin's office and by the Menconi Brothers, art and architectural model makers who were in constant demand for several years on the project. By December 1914 Deering, Hoffman, and Chalfin had agreed to the scheme that emerged, and it was past due for Suarez to go to the site to verify particulars of the scheme and to make whatever adjustments might be necessary prior to the working drawings for this part of the project.

Years later Suarez recounted what happened next as he went to Florida.

A few days after these preliminary models and designs had been completed Mr. Chalfin told me that it would be necessary for me to go to Miami and to see for myself the characteristics of the site and property. I went down to Florida in the early part of 1915 with Mr. Chalfin. We met Mr. Hoffman on the site.

No sooner had I seen the land and the house then under construction I realized that the scheme for the garden which we had completed in New York was fundamentally wrong. For one thing, it had a series of terraces and levels gradually descending to a lake at the Southern end of the property. Standing in one of the main rooms in the Southern section of the house, and look-ing in the direction of the proposed gardens, the light was so blinding and the glare so strong, that it would have been impossible to see anything without the shade of dark glasses.

I told Mr. Chalfin that the scheme for the gardens which we had made in New York should be, in my opinion, radically altered. I immediately saw the necessity of having a high curtain of trees in the distance, rather than a succession of terraces leading down to the lake. This obser-vation gave me the idea of the "fan-like" plan which we ultimately carried out in our final design; I visualized two long vistas directing the eye as far as the lake, leaving between them a higher level of terrace crowned by thick foliage and trees which would act as a screen against the glare of the Southern sun.

. . . This idea was the basic scheme for the plan of the gardens of Vizcaya such as they stand today. I came back to New York and drew the plan accordingly to this new conception. This plan was gradually developed into models of the different elements which composed the gardens; we planned the long reflecting pool and the water cascade for which I used measured drawings of the one at the Villa Corsini in Rome; the pavilion on the lake; the baroque contours of the terraces on the lake; the ramps in the Italian manner, one of them leading down from the terrace toward the rose garden in the midst of which a fine old Italian fountain was erected; the "rocaille garden" [secret garden] to the left of the main vista; the "Theatre de Verdure" and the oriental Kasba. Finally, I personally made the design and the working drawings for the entire parterre work and scroll box designs of the garden as can be seen today at Vizcaya.

I made the initial drawings for Mr. Chalfin for the great baroque stone barge or breakwater still standing on the Eastern side of the main house and terraces. Mr Hoffman later developed these designs and completed their execution.

I worked for more than two years in Mr. Chalfin's office and I must pay tribute to his kindness and consideration; to his inspiring enthusiasm; his unerring appreciation of beauty; his constructive criticism. I finally wrote for him the first article ever published on Vizcaya which appeared in "Scribner's Architectural Magazine."

However, as a very young man and a complete newcomer to this country, I had no practical experience whatsoever as to how to direct building operations or handle the practical details which were necessary to bring to completion the ideas and schemes still in the draughting board or model stage.

Mr. Chalfin therefore called to his assistance a group of men who had never seen an Italian Garden but who had the practical experience to translate into final form ideas and creations of his or of my own. Mr. Chalfin had verbally promised me to have my name included with his on the working drawings as an *associate garden designer*.

I never pressed him on this point nor ever had a written agreement with him. Furthermore, perhaps due to my inexperience, I did not at that time realize the importance which this recognition would have meant in my later career as an architect and garden designer.

The men who Mr. Chalfin called in to organize his office gradually took over control of the situation; they undoubtedly persuaded him not to have my name attached to the final project then well under way. Their aim was, after having used my design and ideas, to gradually eliminate me. This they finally did very successfully. In a few months I was relegated to the role of an ordinary draughtsman in an office. These men even succeeded in depriving me of the authorship of my article on Vizcaya. I was destined to be the anonymous contributor to the design of the gardens of Vizcaya . . .

Mr. Chalfin *was not* an architect; he was originally a painter, and he knew nothing of the technical end of architecture.

. . . During the years I worked with him I never saw him make any but the most elementary sketches in order to express his ideas; to my knowledge he never sat at a draughting board to draw an architectural layout or scheme.[16]

By the autumn of 1914 the character and design of the house were well established. Deering and Chalfin turned their attention to the garden—to what should constitute its elements and their spatial nature. Chalfin wrote to Deering:

> What strikes me in your letter as a discrepancy between your ideas and mine is your speaking of separate and distinct gardens; the rose garden, the gardenia garden, etc. as well as the flower garden, now under drafting, is an alternation of parterres, some green and some very gay with flowers and another alternation of dry land spaces and water features. In these flower parterres, some of which are quite separate from the main disposition of the garden, that is to say our small gardens thrown out on the side, such things as gardenias, oranges and roses might be put if it were desirable but as the rose and gardenia are neither of them very prepossessing in Florida even when healthy, I am disposed to put both in the pineland and as oranges will be used purely for decorative effect they will be largely kept in pots. We should want to use for the parterres such plants as are certain to bloom in that period you are likely to stay.[17]

It is also clear from another letter a week later that he sees the structure of the garden as driving the scheme, not the selection of plants, and that he is relying upon Suarez to be his pencil and to give his ideas form.

> I note your idea for the formal garden on the slip of paper which you enclose and have asked Suarez to draw the roughest kind of sketch of his disposition of the garden to show how to some extent it already conforms with your idea. I am sending a drawing of Suarez that in a measure corresponds with your idea. It is true that there is no garden especially devoted to orchids, but the garden which can be called the house garden and a garden devoted to roses connected with the formal garden is indicated. I should suggest to you myself that orchids would be more interesting on the trees in the formal garden than in a garden by themselves, and gardenias might form some of the parterres rather than to have a garden exclusively devoted to them, although I know they are somewhat of a menace to other plants.[18]

Three days later Deering, more practical and knowledgeable about plants, and more concerned for his own pleasure and that of his guests, tells Chalfin to pay attention to his concerns and wishes.

> My idea about orchids was to have a place where they could be raised for the use of the house. I am very fond of them, and would have an ample supply if possible to have it. I, of course, expected them on the trees for the pleasure they would give to me and my guests, but not for plucking, except if it be necessary to pluck them for their own good. I do not, of course, care particularly whether gardenias for the house and my friends come from the formal garden or a garden devoted to them, but as they are a delightful flower, I want plenty of them. We will not, of course, raise them at all unless we can do so without breeding white moths, which I think I understand to [be] their chief injury to citrus fruit.[19]

Suarez was talented but young. He had been treated well in Florence. What he thought of his treatment in America we can only conjecture, but we do know that after three years he left the project. Later he was shocked and outraged when Chalfin took sole credit for the landscape design. The truth is that they both did it. Suarez does seem to have been the original genius of the scheme, but it was Chalfin who saw it through and who produced the final designs for the lagoon gardens and continued to develop and refine it over the next two decades. There are designers, especially some architects, who cannot leave anyone else's work alone, but have to take it over, fiddle with it, control it, and make it theirs.

Hoffman was a good and serious architect but no match for Chalfin, who was a remarkable artist, as deeply gifted in the matter of aesthetic judgment and theatrical effect as he was flawed in matters of fairness and giving credit to others. Two examples from this period that clearly contributed to his ascendancy was the rivalry with Hoffman over the design of the entry sequence and over the island or Barge that was in fact a breakwater in the bay. In fairness it must be said that the space at the top of the entry drive, with its octagonal clearing, gate piers that metamorphose into ancient satyrs, nymphs, and sylvans, and the pair of Italian sculptures passed off as Spanish forebears, with the threshold of pergola and natural bridge across the remarkable and surprising waterway in the woods conjured by Chalfin, is much more dramatic, far superior in imagination and effect, than a much more tepid proposal by Hoffman for a rectangular basin extending back to the west into the hammock. So, too, although a breakwater in the outline form of a double-ended boat shape referred to as the "central island" is depicted in the harbor on the plan drawings of Hoffman as early as February 1914 and must have resulted from a conversation between Deering, Chalfin, and Hoffman, it was in the hands of Suarez and Chalfin that this idea took flight, leading to the spectacular scheme we see today. Hoffman and his partner, Ingalls, did eventually document it, but by then they were simply in the position of helping to execute the artistic vision of Chalfin and his young assistant.

The work continued for more than five years after Suarez and Hoffman departed; Chalfin was still on the job, cajoling the client, producing drawings, and directing workmen. Deering continued to fret over the ambitions, scope, and expense of what Chalfin was pressing forward with in the landscape, pleading on numerous occasions that there must be some way to save more of the existing situation and to create less.

From 1914 to 1922 a truly remarkable stream of design development and construction drawings poured out of Chalfin's New York office—page after page, at times one every two or three days, based upon the dates on the construction documents and detail sheets that were produced. Bridges, foundations, railings, balustrades, fountains, walls, tile work, gates, paving, flagpoles, flags, metalwork, garden seats, planting, lighting, drains—it was an astonishing array (figs. 114, 115). As early as 1914 Chalfin maneuvered to secure for himself all the sitework and landscape, as well as the Village and South Miami Avenue. Hoffman's scope was reduced to the design and oversight of the construction of the architecture of the house and the preliminary design of the buildings in the Village. Chalfin had the rest, which kept growing. He also took over project management and oversight of the entire ensemble with his employees in New

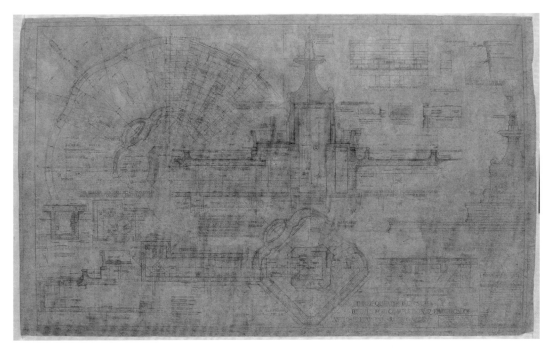

FIGURE 114. A drawing from Chalfin's office explaining how to integrate the historic stone basin with its new concrete foundation and twentieth-century plumbing. Graphite pencil on linen, drawing G192, January 8, 1920, revised February 2, 1920. (Vizcaya Museum and Gardens Archive)

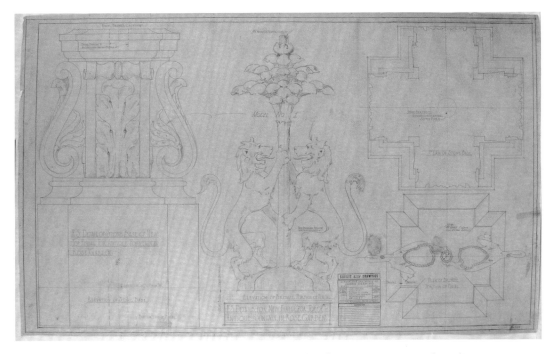

FIGURE 115. Detail drawing for the finial of the rose garden fountain consisting of two lions rampant about a nozzle. Graphite pencil on tracing paper, Chalfin's office full-size drawing G201, January 8, 1920. (Vizcaya Museum and Gardens Archive)

York and Florida. By 1916 Chalfin's office was producing the final construction documents for everything that was under way, whether interior furnishings and details, site walls, grading and planting plans, bridges, fountains, farm buildings, or site lighting. Different as they were in age and background, all of the designers were talented, all gave Deering everything they had to offer at that moment in their career, and all left exhausted. The project would never have turned out as well as it did if each one had not been there and done so.

CONSTRUCTION

Suarez was correct in that he had little experience with handling many of the details and logistics for the sort of undertaking that Vizcaya was becoming. This was a project beyond the mere restoration of an existing garden. Also it was far more than a garden. The scope and complexity of great estates is something few people contemplate. It is one thing to say that they must have cost a lot, or that they are unusual. It is another to comprehend fully what it takes to create an ensemble such as Vizcaya, one of the most exceptional in American landscape history. But twelve volumes of photo albums filled with construction photos carefully compiled and labeled between 1914 and 1922, many of which were originally sent to Chalfin and Deering to keep them apprised of progress on the site, convey what they and their associates were engaged in, day and night, year after year. While the photo albums of construction end in 1922, documents, letters, and diaries show that planting and adjustments to the site continued until James Deering's death. Another collection of photographs records the devastation of the 1926 hurricane and subsequent repair, replanting, and adjustments made. Drawings and correspondence further relate Chalfin's return in 1934, 1935, and 1936 to make additional repairs, replanting, and refinements.

A construction project that goes on continuously for more than eight years requires a constant flow of construction supplies and materials (fig. 116). In the case of Vizcaya this involved large quantities of concrete, stone, fill, topsoil, tiles, piping, trees, and other plants. For Deering, who had spent part of his career solving supply problems for manufacturing, this was part of the game. In Chicago he and his brother solved similar problems by buying the source of their steel and the suppliers of other materials. Here he purchased land to supply topsoil and coral stone deposits. He opened his own quarries, as well as mining and dredging quantities of fill from the site itself. He pioneered the use of the local stone, which has great character and is rich in fossils and coral, and is specifically known and highly regarded for what is called brain coral and fan coral. This is a very soft and rough stone, which made it particularly suitable for rustic garden ornament and landscape structures. At the same time, however, this quality meant that it was not particularly suited for fine architectural detail nor for structural elements. As the project evolved, a range of stone was employed. For some of the sculpture and fine details in the house, Istrian marble from the Mediterranean was used. Travertine from Italy was used on the house as well as the Barge. The columns of the courtyard were made from a dense limestone obtained from Cuba. The more finished garden pieces are mostly from a quarry Deering opened on Lignumvitae Key, while the roughest material came from another he opened near the site in Coconut Grove. To ship the materials he purchased and leased boats and scows and had a siding built alongside Flagler's railroad adjacent to the Village.

An example of this mixture of stone and the need to monitor its quality and use is conveyed in remarks made by Hoffman in a letter to Deering as he concluded that the carving on Center Island (the Barge) should be in native stone except for the balusters, which are to be of Cuban stone as "the native stone is now running in a superior quality and making the carving broad and simple."[20] The stone arrived at the site in blocks of varying sizes and was then sawn, turned, or cut and carved into its final size and shape by masons in a stone yard he established there. The first stone yard, where all the finish pieces for the house were fabricated and carved, was located on the site of the formal garden just south of the laundry building. As work on the house was finishing, this large outdoor workshop was moved across the road to the Village near the propagation house, allowing work to move forward on the garden.

Despite the presence of Paist, Starbuck, and at times Suarez and Koch, who were all on the site trying to direct and resolve matters of construction and design, William Sturrock was also pressed into such service, as some of his letters to Chalfin reveal: "Mr. Deering has written me about the walls in the garden. He seems to be in favor of putting in a wall of the same type of construction as the walls of Miami Avenue. I think this should be perfectly satisfactory providing it has a stone coping, as very little of the wall will be seen after the roses are planted.

FIGURE 116. The northern sea arm of the harbor, showing the concrete substructure of the connecting bridge to the yacht landing, which was already in use for construction deliveries by boat. 1915. (Photograph by Mattie Edwards Hewitt, Vizcaya Museum and Gardens Archive)

The height of the wall is only 24 inches and I expect the roses to grow at least that height."[21] Here was a matter of Deering attempting to save money somewhere. The walls along South Miami Avenue were made from rough masonry and rubble excavated from the site which were then plastered over with a heavy concrete stucco rather than being of poured-in-place concrete or coursed masonry. It was a reasonable idea, and the walls were fine; unfortunately the roses never really worked out well. Despite the heat, which they liked, the roses did not take well to the constant high humidity and salt air that characterize the site. Thus the "rose garden" never really became a rose garden, and ended up being called the fountain garden.

Deering's concern about money was not foolish paranoia. The collective costs were adding up (fig. 117). In March 1915 he became quite upset by the cost of the concrete retaining walls in the garden. The contractor had given him an estimate of $40,000. He asked both the contractor and Chalfin to find some way to reduce their height or cost, realizing that this was only the tip of the iceberg, for the stone, soil, plants, fountains, trees, and pavilions were yet to come. At the same time, the costs and arguments about the Barge were beginning to mount, while the house, utilities, and farm costs were continuing. Somehow Chalfin smoothed things over and kept him from putting on the brakes. Deering paid, and the work progressed.

In addition to the difficulty Chalfin and Deering began to have in finding, ordering, purchasing, and shipping antiques and architectural materials and supplies from Europe after the outset of hostilities in August 1914, the labor situation grew steadily worse as men were drafted and went off to war. Eventually the design team itself was affected. In late summer 1915 Suarez' brother was killed in action, and he decided to go to Italy to attend to affairs and be with his mother. After unsuccessfully trying to keep him from going, and sending condolences and

FIGURE 117. Workers lining up to receive their wages in cash from the pay shack, October 23, 1915. (Photograph by Alice Woods, courtesy of Arva Moore Parks Collection)

$1,500 to Mrs. Suarez, Chalfin accepted his desire to go but also suggested he make some detailed studies of particular gardens while in Italy.[22] On this trip Suarez did visit several gardens, in particular making sketches of the cascade at the Villa Corsini in Rome (the home at the time of the American Academy in Rome and of Chalfin's earlier sojourn there as a fellow) as an aid toward the development of the design of the cascade for the Mound at Vizcaya. In early 1916 he returned to America and to Chalfin, who clearly needed him, working for another two years on the development of the garden. Although the work never completely stopped, things progressed more slowly than Deering hoped. By 1917 landscape and garden construction was finally under way, and the house virtually complete.

Careful study of construction photographs shows an interesting side effect of the war. In 1913 and through most of 1914 they show a handful of black laborers with shovels, pickaxes, and barrows. There are also numerous white supervisors and skilled workers (masons, stone carvers, carpenters, drivers, and machine operators. A few years later, by 1917 and 1918, there are almost no white personnel in sight, and the men doing the masonry, carving, and working much of the equipment are black. In an attempt to keep things going they had been trained and pressed into service in trades and skills from which discrimination had barred them before the war. Many blacks originally imported from the Bahamas to work on the railroad brought an exuberant flavor to the work and elements of the décor, such as the inlaid shellwork in the grottos and the sgraffito designs on the walls along South Miami Avenue. The main effect from Deering's perspective, however, was that everything was taking a painfully long time to be done.

Despite considerable effort, not many early design drawings have yet been found by the authors. The few that have surfaced are revealing, since there has been considerable speculation about authorship and who did what regarding Vizcaya. One group of drawings labeled Job Set #1, which contains several undated drawings, all from Hoffman's office, was undoubtedly made (judging from the contents) sometime between mid-1914 and late 1915 at the latest.[23] Here one finds a sketch treatment of the natural bridge and the circular court and pool; a ¹⁄₁₆″ layout for the Village; a plot plan for a gas line and its relationship to the Village; drawings for the plaza and entry drive, the laundry yard, and superintendent's house, 1″ = 50′; ¹⁄₁₆″ and ¾″ drawings of channel work and details of wooden piles (fig. 118). The most interesting drawing in the set is a general layout of the property (Drawing #2, 1″ = 50′). It does not show many of the garden features, which apparently were introduced by Suarez. Notably it does not show either the maze or the theater and secret garden. There is no development of the Mound stairs nor of the grottos. It shows long pools, which eventually became the marine garden with its bridge as well as canals through the mangrove east of the garden. A small wing is shown on the southwest of the house, and the piazza in the south lagoon area is shown but the Casba is not. The gate lodges, the pump house, and South Miami Avenue are all depicted much as developed. The island in the garden, which is on axis with the Mound, is still in its first primitive rectangular form. There is also no indication of the cut-through for water on the causeway where a handsome bridge was later developed, but the pools and cascade eventually developed at the north and south ends of the waterway in the hammock do appear on one of these drawings.

Among the many things these drawings reveal is that they were made by Hoffman's office at a time when Chalfin had not yet built up his staff, and that Hoffman and his staff were producing what was needed. Here, at the end of 1914, is also the moment when Diego Suarez enters the picture and the landscape design takes a leap forward.

An excellent demonstration of the relationship between Chalfin and Suarez in these years can be deduced from a series of notations on one of the drawings of this period now in the Vizcaya Archive (fig. 119).[24] While Chalfin may not have drawn much himself, he had a remarkable eye and sense of flair, and, as Suarez admitted, functioned largely through critiques of the work developed by his staff.[25] Made sometime after Suarez' return from Italy in 1916, this undated study depicts the overall layout of the south garden. It is an ozalid print of a sort once quite common.[26] Among other things it shows the cascade Suarez drew after measuring that of the Villa Corsini. This has been carefully inserted into an earlier drawing, which depicted the entire layout of the Italian garden. This earlier drawing was a rendered plan made with pencil, pen and ink, brush and ink, and wash. A principal feature of the first draft of the drawing is the careful and precise layout of the planted scrollwork in the parterres and a

FIGURE 118. The first construction drawing produced by Chalfin's office, one of the hundreds that were to come in the development of the garden. This earliest one sets out the axes, angles, and dimensions for the geometry and control points that would enable the sketches and studies of Suarez and the other draftsmen to be built. Ink on linen, drawing G1, September 1, 1915. (Vizcaya Museum and Gardens Archive)

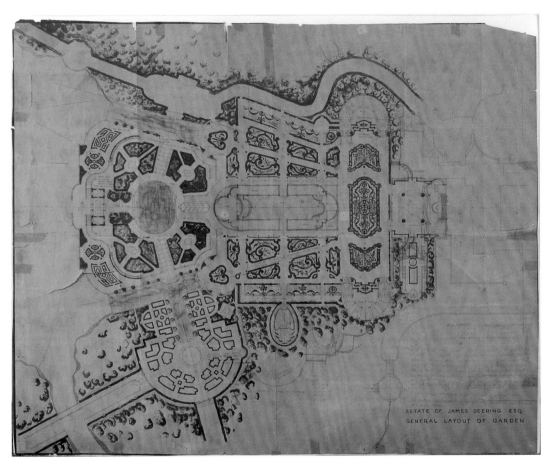

ESTATE OF JAMES DEERING ESQ.
GENERAL LAYOUT OF GARDEN

FIGURE 119. A design study of an early version of the central garden by Suarez with his annotations in red ink, and design modifications by Chalfin and another designer in pencil, made after Suarez returned from his brother's funeral in 1915. This rendering shows many features that were later changed, for example: the laundry wing is still attached to the main house; the south terrace stairs are still the first version proposed by Hoffman; the Barge is undeveloped; the stairs from the upper walks at the semicircular basin that were built and then ripped out later are shown; the theater garden occupies the site where the maze would be added later; and the pattern and shape of the parterre beds would later change considerably. Pen, brush, and ink with pencil and ink annotations. (Vizcaya Museum and Gardens Archive)

concern for the masses of vegetation. Suarez has used this print of it to develop annotations in red ink regarding detail development for the planting and character of the parts. That it is Suarez' writing is clear from the awkward English and misspelled words: "sorrounded" and the Italianate spelling of "acquatic." Two other hands are also present. One is most certainly Chalfin's in his role of mentor as well as supervisor, as he circles and corrects several of Suarez' spelling errors. More interesting and more important, however, are design changes he suggests which were subsequently made. Drawing with a soft pencil or crayon right on the print, he suggests moving the elliptical garden theater to the north to its final location, while making a circular annotation in the space left between it and the rose garden. This circle was to become the maze. Another major change proposed was that of reshaping the end of the grassy central island in the garden. Several versions are sketched for the south end. This particular edit absolutely improved the design Suarez had proposed for this central space about which the entire garden revolves. Suarez had drawn a perfectly regular rectangle. Chalfin reshapes the ends, giving it the curved shapes it has today. Here is an example of the iterative progress of a design, wherein numerous versions take place before all the parts fall into place and a final product emerges. The work is literally a product of both Suarez and Chalfin.

This rare surviving design study entitled "Estate of James Deering Esq. General Layout of Garden" is interesting for several other things it reveals about the evolution of the garden design during 1915 and after, and how the garden evolved into a more coherent and integrated composition. The hand of a third person can be detected in the lower righthand portion of the drawing, writing out preliminary specifications for planting methods and soil depths in pencil in an elegant and spidery longhand script, most likely while talking to Suarez and/or Chalfin.

This drawing also shows several features of the earlier collaboration of Chalfin and Hoffman that are apparent in the plaster models of the year before. Some, like the sea arms, boat landing, tea house, and Barge progressed into design development and were built much as envisioned here. Others changed considerably in the next two years as the scheme became fully developed and built, only to have parts subsequently ripped out and rebuilt differently. These include the two large rectangular terraces on the east and south with stairs, which are considerably weaker and less direct than those finally selected. On the north of the house, the drawing shows a baroque double-curved stair leading to a lawn that leads off into the hammock. This was actually built, but was also quickly demolished and replaced a few months later by a simpler, straight stair. So, too, a pair of curved stairs spilling out from the raised arms of the walks behind the twin semicircular basins for aquatic plants on the east and west sides of the south terrace are indicated for the location where one enters the garden from the house. These were also built only to be torn out and replaced by the pairs of garden pavilions, which frame the view and form a broad vine-covered proscenium to the vista.

The rose garden is shown much as it was built, but the drawing indicates a broad (and rather too short for its width) avenue leading off eastward into the hammock toward the bay. This wholesale clearing of native trees was rejected, undoubtedly by Deering, and was subsequently replaced by a modest path leading to the servants' bathing pavilion, dance floor, and beach in the mangrove along the shore. The rose garden, which turned out not to grow roses very well, was eventually framed on the east by a tall clipped hedge of casuarina with three arched openings and a graceful ramped stair leading to the sandy path in the woods. The maze had yet to enter the scheme, and the theater garden, derived from those at Villas Gori and Marlia near Lucca, is shown about where the maze was eventually located.

Following the easternmost radial walk leading south from the rose garden one also sees in this drawing an element that Chalfin and Deering disagreed about and that was eventually transformed into a special feature known as the marine garden. In this first sketch of it, Suarez and Chalfin show a canal entering from Biscayne Bay into the large lagoon or "lake" then under construction south of the garden. The radial path leading to the boathouse, also under construction at the time, crosses this canal on a bridge, with a high arch sufficient to allow boats to enter the lagoon. Parallel to this path is shown a pair of symmetrical extensions of the canal to the north and south. Letters between Chalfin and Deering discuss the feasibility of these twin basins for holding aquatic plants and fish. This conceit—that of garden pools adjacent to the ocean containing a collection of visually fancy or suitably edible fish for the table—was a favorite of Romans at their seaside villas during the first centuries of the empire. Deering was skeptical that it would work here and in particular did not think it would work if the basins were connected to the tidal waters of the bay, with the frequent inflow of flotsam and trash. Chalfin's response was to hang onto the concept but to change the execution. This was eventually transformed into the marine garden basins in the middle of the path and the stepped or Japanese bridge, with its gateway of twisted columns and carved peacocks by Gaston Lachaise that remain today.

Also in this drawing, the service wing, sometimes referred to as the laundry wing, is still shown as an attached appendage on the southwest corner of the main house. Chalfin has also drawn over this part with a soft pencil or crayon, proposing the baroque concave curved walls of the laundry and the secret garden, which now frame the terrace and garden stair on the east and west.

At the same time that Chalfin was editing his work to make the garden more baroque, Suarez was setting the character of the planting (fig. 120). His notes in red read in part as follows: "Enclosing hedges 10′ high and Borders and Flower beds 2′ high—outside bed built up within a higher level"; "It is desirable to know this distance"; "All beds @5′ level surrounded by low hedges and planted with small trimmed trees."[27] One further example of interaction between the various participants concerns the introduction and realization of the canals. It was Deering's idea to have canals presumably as a thematic accompaniment to the Venetian character of his villa. He instructs Chalfin, who in turn asks Suarez and Starbuck to help him figure them out. On Suarez' first visit to the site Deering asks him to attend to them, but Suarez returns to New York without doing so or reporting on the topic. Deering is outraged and writes Chalfin, "doesn't he know who he's working for?"[28] Since Suarez has gone back to New York by then, Deering turns to the engineers and Starbuck to get the canals going, and, as more correspondence demonstrates, the north canal and main waterway were rapidly advanced in the field with a minimum of design documentation.

Even so, there is a drawing dated February 12, 1915, labeled "Sketch Showing Location of Canal through Mangrove Swamp," that shows the first series of canals to be developed (fig. 121). Although there is no author indicated, it appears to have been drawn in Miami either by one of Chalfin's or Hoffman's staff, or even possibly by John Bennett, a talented young civil engineer of the Biscayne Engineering Company who was in charge of the many civil and marine works needed, including the dredging, fill sections and seawalls, pilings, and roadways. The drawing shows canals both north and south of the villa harbor and its sea arms. The northern one begins immediately north of the outlet from a spring adjacent to the boat landing and winds into the hammock and returns to the bay with two more outlets. The canal south of the harbor begins by passing under the small arched bridge to the tea house and takes a similar looping trail into the shorelands emerging just above the boathouse on the north. The canal referred to in the title of the drawing is another broad one leading more directly from the bay inland to a large lagoon, sometimes referred to as the "lake" in later times. This new canal, obviously designed to take larger boats such as the *Psyche*, crosses the earlier, smaller and more irregular one.

Based upon the drawings (see fig. 118), it is obvious that after Suarez' return from his first visit to Florida a concentrated effort was directed toward setting the geometry and defining the garden and landscape; nevertheless, it was not until September 1915 that Chalfin authorized a

FIGURE 120. Diego Suarez on site, c. 1915. (Photograph by Alice Woods, courtesy of Arva Moore Parks Collection)

drawing with the radiating axes set out and dimensioned. In October the layout for the walls of the rose garden was also issued, and finally a layout for the entire property was sent from Hoffman's office on October 8, 1915. While Hoffman and Chalfin were trying to establish fundamental layout and elements of the larger site so that they could move on to the development of details, Deering was pursuing his ideas about boating in the garden, pushing Sturrock into an exploration of gondolas, and how to build a boat that would be appropriate to the canals he was constructing. As a result, by November Chalfin was trying to obtain survey information about the canals that Sturrock had built so that he and Suarez could do a layout for the maze and theater gardens (fig. 122).

One aspect of all this that needs to be recalled today is the state of the art of construction technology at the time of Vizcaya's creation. On the one hand, today we can hardly produce such remarkable stone carving and details as was realized by the collective assemblage of carvers, masons, and designers; on the other hand, while less subtle, the mechanics and machinery of contemporary construction are both more powerful and accomplished. Looking

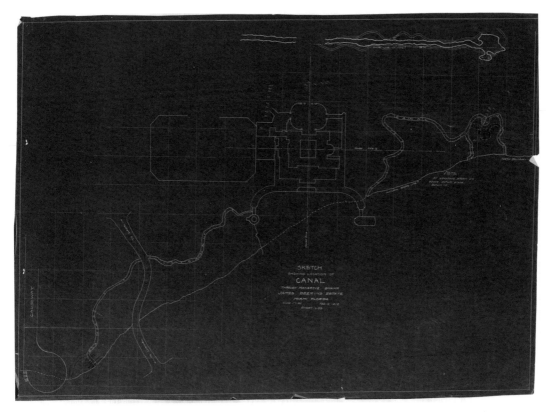

FIGURE 121. Deering's interest in creating canals in the mangrove and hammock led to this early drawing, depicting canals to both the north and south of the house. Note that the undeveloped garden is represented simply with a rectangle south of the house. Blueprint, February 12, 1915. (Vizcaya Museum and Gardens Archive)

at photographs of the construction site, one sees mule-drawn wagons and carts, donkey engines, steam-driven equipment, workers' bicycles, and a motorcycle. In a photograph made three days after Christmas 1916, twelve men can be seen unloading topsoil from a barge by hand with shovels, while a mule team and barrows with nine more men are leveling limestone base courses at the plaza adjacent to the Casba. Some mules and skids and other men are on the adjacent island with a huge mound of dredged material. The causeway and a work camp can be seen in the distance and beyond that South Miami Avenue with the wall and entry gate construction. Though Deering complained that progress was slow, part of why he received such a fine product was precisely this slow process and the careful hand methods. Modern construction equipment such as bulldozers and chain saws can destroy a site in a matter of days, if not hours. Laborers with picks and shovels, axes and wheelbarrows move and behave in a different way. Even so, advanced industrial methods of the time were employed. Photographs show dredges sucking up material from the bay and prairie south of the Mound and "fluming the tennis courts." This was a technique developed for marine and harbor work and large placer mining operations that consists of mechanically taking up sand and moving it with water under pressure through large hoses, pipes, or wooden troughs (flumes) and blowing it out the end in whatever location is desired. In mining and harbor work it is used to remove material, either spoiling it in waste heaps or filling barges and hauling it away. Here it was used simultaneously to create water bodies and to build land features in the former marsh. Likewise

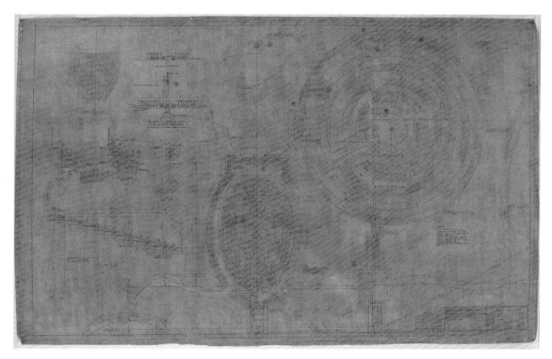

FIGURE 122. Layout drawing showing final revision of the theater and maze gardens. Pen and ink on linen, September 19, 1917. (Vizcaya Museum and Gardens Archive)

the extensive use of reinforced concrete structures throughout the project for buildings and garden alike was a relatively new development pioneered only a few years earlier in France. The waterworks, with its group of enormous buried tanks cut into the rock south of the Village in the spring of 1916, is another instance of Deering's application of industrial methods to his needs.

THE STORY OF THE BARGE

For many people their first view of the Barge is stunning. There it sits out in the bay, a gigantic stone boat encrusted with figures, balustrades, obelisks, urns, great-carved swags, and enormous masks, with huge mermaids at each end. Visitors can be heard to wonder, "how did they build it out there in the water?" The answer for the most part is that they did not. Further study of Drawing 1, and of a later drawing by the Biscayne Engineering Company, done in conjunction with the expansion of the garden south into what is referred to as the lagoon garden, reveals that the Barge was built upon the middle one of a series of three small high spots that had been surveyed along the shoreline. It turns out that the Barge sits upon a small sandbar attached to the land adjacent to the house. The curved sea arms and seawall were built behind it on what was dry land at the time, and then the strip of tidal land in between was removed, allowing water to surround it. This was not only a practical way to build both the seawall and the Barge, but was also partly driven by legal considerations, as one of Deering's early letters reveals. In December 1913, two months before the first drawings for construction were completed, he wrote from Miami to Hoffman: "If our island extends beyond the shore line it seems probable from what I hear here it will be necessary to get a permit for it from the government."[29]

By June 1914 significant sitework south of the house was proceeding, as can be seen in photographs and from correspondence about the causeway. Chalfin, privileged to be traveling in Europe with Deering, writes to Hoffman with specific thoughts on how to rework particular aspects of the landing and harbor based upon his observations. In the letter he sent a sketch (fig. 123) and a second smaller plan with annotations to help him describe the arrangement and character of the details.

> Dear Hoffman—It was splendid to get your letter with all its details. . . . I send you a sketch made on my knees in a gondola at the famous landing before St. Giorgio Maggiore in Venice— Scamozzi or more probably Longhena.
>
> At any rate it seemed to me the perfect solution of the steps going down to the basin opposite the Island. The plan gives three steps returning on themelves at a curved angle.
>
> These are under water except at lowest tide. At mean level there is a wider step, which serves as a platform for ordinary landing. But to reach the level of the piazza itself there are three risers at the return of each B C you can also land.
>
> The details are superb. The blocks are cut so as to end showing two risers in one block or the whole of A in one block. Each end toward the water is molded.

Then the three monstrous heads end the system of steps on either side with a superb crown molding above into which their manes break. This carries along about fifteen feet either side of the landing and ends on a third head, the two heads near the steps are closer together than the distance to the third head. Beyond this a plain wall begins.

It is all in Istrian marble and looks singularly like our Florida stone. I hope to send this to you in time to alter it to modify the plan we now have where the steps break out beyond the wall. In this everything made straight at H. I have a lot of things to say to you but Mr. Deering is waiting.[30]

The stair Hoffman had originally drawn would not have worked with boats moored or landing alongside the seawall as the one in Venice did. Chalfin realized it upon seeing this stair in Venice, and, therefore, this is how the water stair at Vizcaya was eventually built. The fact that Chalfin was traveling abroad with the client, had constant access to him, could point out such architectural features, and suggest changes to the architect's plan that would improve the project shows what a disadvantage Hoffman was at in comparison, and why, or at least how, Chalfin came to wield so much power and design control. As it turns out, no such similar carved heads appear on this stair at Vizcaya (perhaps because visitors would hardly see them), but they do become a major feature of Calder's handiwork on the Barge immediately in front of the landing.

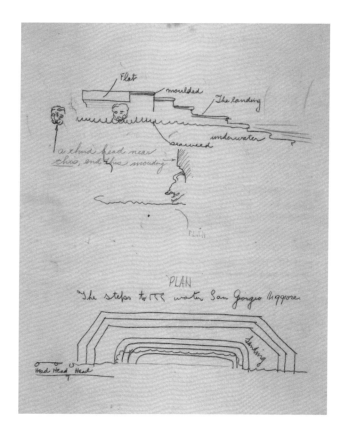

FIGURE 123. A sketch of the water-landing stair at San Giorgio Maggiore in Venice that Chalfin included in a letter to Hoffman as a suggestion for the revision of the main harbor landing on the bay, which would accommodate the tidal fluctuations and a boat alongside better than those drawn initially. June 10, 1914. (Vizcaya Museum and Gardens Archive)

It is unknown who first thought of the concept of developing a breakwater to protect the shore and house in the form of a great antique boat. There is precious little correspondence on the subject before 1913, and to date no preliminary design drawings have been found prior to the commencement of construction documents. The Barge, originally referred to by Hoffman and Chalfin as the "central island," appears on the very first construction drawing of February 1914 in simple outline form, almost exactly as it is today. After the initial flurry of activity to get the house documents to the engineers for their development of foundations and structure, Hoffman turned his energy to the design development of terraces, seawall, and this island. In June 1914 he sent Deering three alternative design schemes for it in the form of a boat.

#1, shows the Island treated as a boat, the walls being made of concrete covered with stucco, the balusters, coping, and string course, being of native stone. The plan for this is the same as shown on scheme #2, with the exception that the lower platform of steps leading into the water and forming the boat landing is not shown in this plan.

#2 shows the island built entirely of stone above the water level. The foundations of this will be of concrete resting on piles. The plan shows a long pool in the centre with a planting strip on the edge. The north and south ends are raised five steps and a little trellis and summer house is shown at one end.

#3 shows the island treated like a terrace rather than a boat, the steps also projecting out beyond the main lines of the island. Will you let me know which one of these you prefer that I may proceed with my working drawings and the specifications for this work.[31]

Thus it is clear that Hoffman began work on the Barge or island while Chalfin and Deering were traveling in Europe that summer. Deering replied a few weeks later.

I would say that while wishes are in vain, I am sorry your letter and drawings did not arrive early enough so that Mr. Chalfin and I could have discussed them together. I do not feel I can give you a final answer in regard to the Island in his absence. He has a final copy of your letter and I am sending him a copy of this one, and am willing to say to both of you that you and he may decide the shape of the Island.

I am as you both know—much inclined to make the Island in the shape of a boat, if it is not so exactly the shape of a boat as to be commonplace and undignified.

You will remember that we discussed at considerable length the idea of making a swimming pool in the middle of the Island? I liked this idea providing it could be made large enough so that no other swimming pool—aside from that in the house—would be required. Mr. Chalfin made some objection to this plan, which I do not now recall.

It would seem a pity to make a pool here unless it was a swimming pool. If the water is salt water, as I suppose it must be unless we pump water into it, it would be difficult to grow anything that would be attractive in it.

I am not much disposed to extend our water pumping arrangements to the Island—and therefore not much disposed to have the fountain that you propose.[32]

The final design for the island was still many months away, but as it evolved, it ended up with a concrete structure clad with stone. There was no swimming pool, but there were to be great grotesque masks (faces) spouting seawater, as well as two groups of basins forming cascades with seawater, and the plumbing was extended from the mainland to bring fresh water for the irrigation of planting. Among the topics taken up by Diego Suarez in the autumn and winter of 1914–15 as he began work on the garden was that of this island/boat. As Chalfin and Suarez advanced their ideas, the problem of control, which had been simmering for some time, began to come to the surface. By February 1915, within a long letter covering many topics regarding the house and grounds, Chalfin complained to Deering: "I do not know at this moment what provision Hoffman has made, but all these matters depend somewhat upon the treatment of the Island. It is not my fault if the Island is being held up but it is a triumph of Hoffman diplomacy if it is. You know how little they like it in the office and how perfectly your hesitations have played into their hands. I do not say the hesitations are not highly justified, but the delays inherent are not of my making." He goes on that he is having "somewhat of a struggle with Hoffman over the boat house," which he accuses Hoffman of wanting to "prettify and elaborate in the most eccentric and costly manner."[33] Despite this, five days later he wrote: "I learn from Hoffman on Saturday last that the drawings for the foundations of the Island are well under way, and contain a number of suggestions in the direction of economy."[34] At the same time he agrees with ideas that Carl Fisher, another early visitor to and influential builder of Miami, had suggested to Deering about the use of lights on some of the Venetian pilings as an aid for night navigation.

Although a lot else was happening, the ambitious undertaking of the island was of great interest to Deering, along with explorations of boat or gondola traffic into the canals he had initiated. In March he put Chalfin on notice regarding his understanding of the cost he was expecting (this was to become a problem later when additional costs for sculpture were added): "Dear Mr. Chalfin, I wish to make a record of what was told me in regard to the cost of the island; as far as I know, no other record exists: This I understand covers the whole structure except such things as may be placed upon it like arbors."[35] Two days later Deering sent another plea to Chalfin: "I beg also that the place be made as little costly as possible."[36]

During this period the island became entwined with his conception of the whole enterprise. The Barge and its design could contribute to the story or narrative that he and Chalfin were using to develop the program—an imaginary history of sorts that might have given rise to the parts and character of the house and estate. In June he wrote Chalfin from Chicago: "the following reflection passes through my mind: since the shape of our shore island is a ship, an appropriate name for it would certainly be one of Ponce de Leon's or Vizcaino's ships if the name were a pretty one. For the three sand islands the names 'Pinta,' 'Una' [sic] and 'Santa Maria,' the names of Columbus' three caravels, might not be inappropriate."[37] A month later he wrote again on the topic, this time suggesting that "I should be glad if Mr. Suarez, when he has the opportunity, will learn if he saw the names of the boats of Ponce de Leon in his Florida explorations. If there is one that is appropriate it will be a good name to give to the island [the Barge] between the two sea arms."[38]

Suarez, Chalfin, and Hoffman continued developing the design of the island/Barge (fig. 124). As becomes clear in subsequent correspondence from Hoffman, it was Suarez who gave it character and expression with the critiques of Chalfin, and it is Hoffman who executed the working drawings. Because the scheme called for a series of striking classical figures at various scales, a sculptor was needed. Chalfin settled upon Alexander Stirling Calder (1870–1945) from Philadelphia, the father of Alexander (Sandy) Calder, noted for inventing mobiles.[39] The elder Calder's brother Ralph was at the time working in Chalfin's office as the lead draftsman on the Vizcaya project, which partly explains the choice and his ability to locate him in California where he was working on the Panama Pacific Exposition in San Francisco. On October 5, 1915, Chalfin wrote a lengthy description of the current state of the Barge design.

6/11/15

FIGURE 124. By January 1915, the concrete substructure of the Barge had been completed, the stone cladding of the seawall and its arms as well as the balusters and trim for the northern Venetian bridge were in place, and dredging was under way to create the harbor. Note the overhead track to transport men and construction materials to the Barge. (Photograph by Mattie Edwards Hewitt, Vizcaya Museum and Gardens Archive)

The other day I sent you a scale model of the prow of the island I am constructing in the water in the front of Mr. Deering's house in Florida. The idea of the island is that it should be remotely boat-like, and that it shall sustain a park of trees and fountains at a level considerably above high tide. There are steps approaching the island, and there will be a summer house and waterways upon it, and a general design of pavement stairs, which viewed from the windows of the house will tell as a piece of form lying upon the water. However, the island is supposed to tell in a vertical sense, and the stern and bow are raised, as you will realize upon measuring the middle. The stern and bow are practically identical in the features sent you. I am only presenting you with these few facts and photographs and sketch model in order that you may exercise your imagination upon them, and not lose time in exercising it in directions other than will serve you when you come in contact with the final work.

My idea was to place great masks under a very overhanging cornice, and actually beneath piers in the balustrade. These masks, would not, I think, be, as I have represented, in the middle, planted directly upon the courses of stone in the island, which, by the way, are broken up in blocks as really constructed, and are not continuous like ship sheathing, as in the photographs. The heads, I repeat, will not be placed directly on the courses, but upon some sort of cartouche. I am hoping that the whole island will have a character of the middle Sixteenth Century, Venetian sculpture of the type of San Sovino's [sic] pupils invented, and which Longheni [sic] perpetuated. I am going to have, as you see, a mermaid, wing, tail and all, raised with dolphins at the bow, or maybe more than one, if you like; or maybe a Triton instead of a mermaid. The only idea is to have the figure make a block mass, as I have represented in the profile of the boat.

There will be a number of heads on the island, all different I hope, and above the line of cornice and balustrade. You will see some little formless lumps of clay, which I want to have transformed into somewhat confused masses. I am not yet sure what character these should have, perhaps something will suggest itself to you. I do not want, in fact, to tie down your imagination too much, and I should like to preserve throughout a certain sense of scale, as, for instance, these groups should not contain figures out of scale with the mermaid or Triton. They might, therefore, have to be baskets of sea fruits, or trophies of sea treasures, like corals and pearls and things put in a basket, who knows what. At any rate it must be a confused mass.

Your brother tells me you are coming east some time in November, and I trust you will have had your imagination much excited by this large enterprise.

The sculpture will be executed in a very porous native coralline stone, and to be conceived in the largest plane and mass, but the heads if necessary, can be of a harder stone, which you will make the acquaintance of when here, and which will take considerable detail.

There is considerable other sculptural work to be done in Florida on these premises, and I am hoping that it will cause you considerable interest to make some essays.

I am trusting to hear from you on the arrival of the model and the photographs.[40]

From this letter we learn that the Barge, largely as we know it, had been fully formed in Chalfin's imagination and that Suarez' earlier sketches had been translated into a model by the Menconi Brothers, who created many study models for the project, ranging from the entire architectural ensemble and details of particular elements, to the garden, and nearly all of the sculpture to be made. Despite the press of decisions on the house and other buildings, Deering followed developments of the island eagerly but began to grow alarmed about the rising costs of yet another aspect of the project. On January 8, 1916, he wrote: "Dear Mr. Chalfin, Replying to yours of the 4th inst. I suppose I understood somewhat vaguely that there would be sculpture on the island. I had no idea, even vague, that it would be so serious a financial matter; I am considerably staggered by it. You do not estimate the total cost. It will evidently be found by adding a considerable figure to that which you made in the letter. I would like to have a little more time to think over this and wish very much that I had a model to look at or a photograph of it."[41] One hears the voice of innumerable clients throughout history who feel their designers have no sense of what things are really going to add up to, have no ability to control the costs, nor sensitivity to their emotions let alone their pocketbooks, and offer little to the client to have or see to make them feel better about what they are being asked to support. The next day Deering shot off another telegram to Chalfin: "Can you not devise satisfactory scheme ornamental sculpture on island less costly than present proposition JD."[42]

On the defense, Chalfin responded on January 18 that he was pricing sculptors, one of whom, George Barnard, produced statuary for the Pennsylvania State Capitol for a cost of $25,000 per figure, and that he was trying to contact Daniel Chester French to get a cost proposal from him. The next day he also wrote: "Dear Mr. Deering, I am sending you two photographs of the middle of the island, about which I wrote the other day. The Prow is on a large scale, and the profile on small, but I notice in the profile that the jet of the fountain is absent, and the photographer in blanking the background has ruined the profile of the clipped trees, and of the statues at the steps. He has also cut down the profile of the sculpture on the bow and stern. You can imagine both divisions of the clipped trees to have a level top like the one on the right."[43]

Despite Deering's reluctance, Chalfin was moving forward. On the following day he wrote to his man in Florida: "Dear Mr. Paist, Menconi Brothers advise me that they have shipped on the 18th inst. Model of the mermaid figures for Mr. Calder."[44] To further insure that the route he had taken with Calder was fiscally prudent, Chalfin passes on to Deering the following on January 22: "Dan French did a sculpture for Marshall Field costing $50,000.00 so Calder is a bargain at 8,000.00."[45] Deering, not fully understanding that Chalfin was pressing forward regardless of his reservations, had simultaneously written in a peckish mood about several things, including: "If I understand it, you have a complete model of the garden and a complete model of the center island. Even while the Winstons were here, you were expecting a photograph of the island. None has ever come to me. I should be much gratified if I could have both of them."[46] Nevertheless, he gave Chalfin permission to proceed in soliciting prices from sculptors for the work as proposed by Chalfin, who subsequently responded in the same courteous language of gentlemen doing business at the time.

I am awfully gratified that you let me go ahead with the sculpture for the island. I wish I could always be prepared for your conclusions, [illegible] than I am, but, for instance, it did not occur to me that coarse sculpture would be cheaper than fine sculpture, and I am afraid that when I said coarse sculpture I only meant that it would be coarse in texture, and sculpture of a garden character, that is to say, not the most serious kind of an artistic effort. Perhaps you will be struck with some of the figures I sent you about the remuneration received by sculptors, even those not so awfully well known. We shall not get off with $8,000.00 of course, because there will be the execution of the sculpture still, and there is beside the modeling of the masks, which must be done by the regular architectural sculptor.[47]

At this moment the house was virtually complete, Deering was in the process of buying more land at the southern end of his property, and Chalfin's office was overloaded with tasks as the gardens were growing and under continuous development. Hoffman's office had less to do and was being used by Chalfin to handle engineers and mechanical services as well as a miscellaneous drafting service. Tensions rose with outbursts in the committee set up to coordinate the various firms, consultants, and contractors. When Hoffman laid claim to authorship of the design for the Barge, Chalfin appealed to Deering, who dismissed the tiff: "I read with interest what you had to say about the committee work, also what you say about the boat island. If I were you, I would ask for the original drawings of the island that you sent Hoffman's office; if you receive them, and they are properly dated by you; also if the drawings of Hoffman's office are properly dated, you will have the perfect documentary evidence. If the drawings cannot be returned to you, I think you would be entitled to demand other evidence."[48] Five days later Chalfin happily wrote back: "I have an understanding with Mr. Hoffman about the island. Using the new work on the façade more or less as a lever I presented my contention to him, and received from him direct assurance in the most overt possible terms on last Sunday that he would make no claim whatever toward authorship in the island. The documents he had to work in making the drawings have already been returned to us, and they take the form of a highly detailed small-scale model. It was from this model that the drawings were made in Hoffman's office by his draftsmen, under my supervision, and when the information in the model had been translated into the drawings, the model was returned to me."[49]

From the first sketches, drawings, and concept models of the barge to the finished work was a lengthy process. Once on board, Calder worked in clay. Menconi then made molds from the clay figures and then plaster models (casts), which were shipped to Paist on the site in Florida for the sculptors and carvers there to block them out. These roughed-out figures were then set in place in the walls and on the concrete foundations ready for Calder to come and finish them with fine detail carving. Photographs and one of Sargent's watercolors, done in March 1917, show Calder at work on platforms over the water under an awning for protection from the sun and glare (fig. 125). Deering writes to Chalfin on the occasion: "John Sargent is visiting my brother. They had luncheon with me yesterday and went over the house . . . You will be interested, as I was, to know that he highly approved the figures at the bow and stern of the island. Though the surfaces are rounded he said there was enough of a flat surface in them to make them agreeable and he said, as of course you and I say, that modesty has nothing to do with the matter. He did say that he thought the heads were too large. The comment that he did make upon the island was that he did not like the masks as he considered them out of scale because too large."[50] More contentiousness regarding the Barge was about to erupt, however. In this case it was over fees and sex.

Stirling Calder was an interesting choice for the project. Although he was classically trained in Philadelphia and Paris and the son of a distinguished Philadelphia sculptor, his work has an air of modernity combined with narrative illustration somewhat equivalent to the work done by other artists associated with popular publications and journals of Philadelphia and New York at the time, such as N. C. Wyeth and Maxfield Parrish. Unlike Daniel Chester French or Augustus Saint-Gaudens, whose work was deeply informed by Classical antiquity and late eighteenth-century French portraitists such as Houdon, sculptors whose careers were nearing their end, Stirling Calder's work had a more muscular and abstracted quality akin to the more streamlined Deco work soon to be produced in Europe. Part of his appeal to Chalfin undoubtedly was that his work, while highly figurative, was informed by his years in Paris, as was that of his younger contemporaries such Gaston Lachaise, who was to join the project in a few years, and Paul Manship, who might also have been brought into the mix if he had not still been studying and working at the American Academy in Rome when this project began.

As the work developed, the mermaids on the ends of the Barge were deemed too overtly sexual for the taste of Deering and some of his guests. Chalfin asked Calder to tone them down, which eventually he did. Having done so he asked for an additional payment because of the extra time and effort the project finally took, including the irritating request to mildly censor his own work. Deering balked. Chalfin found himself awkwardly in the middle. Calder responded with a marvelous handwritten note in his bold hand:

Dear Chalfin, I am called away from the City between the 26th and 30th, but either before or after then, shall be glad to have you see the models for the five groups.

I have read your letter carefully and understand your position of "buffer" as you put it, in the manifold complexities of your great work. I think I expressed to you when there as chance offered opportunity, my admiration for the ensemble—but on my side as one having no authority, I was not blind either to details that annoyed me in the sauce [sic] way perhaps that my poor Sea Girls as you and Mr Deering [refer to them].

As far as my small part is concerned I have no bitterness. Only the impersonal realization of being a victim—with my enthusiasm mainly to blame! There are however certain basic points upon which we do not yet understand each other.

To do your work, as I now understand from some of the definitions you give, you would like it, would have meant that I laid aside all other obligations and devoted myself entirely to it—and received $25,000.—You cannot expect to get results in any way comparable with the work you cite, with which I was familiar in France many years ago, and which all bear the mark of having been produced under leisurely and unforced economic conditions, when the reversal has ruled the case—

Do you not realize that I have given much for $8,000. And now you bargain with me to achieve certain changes on work done.

I am willing even to do this, if when I know exactly what you want, the result is possible and worth while.——

Faithfully

Stirling Calder[51]

Chalfin's response was to meet, to talk him into finishing the remaining figures, and to talk Deering into accepting.

Dear Mr. Deering:

I send you a copy of a letter which I have written to-day to Mr. Calder after an interview with him covering all the questions between us. He has the statue for the north prow of the island and the four pedestals which are still vacant all done. He is ready to cast in clay, but merely waiting my visit. I suggested some very small modifications in one, a single modification in another; both of which he readily consented to make before casting them. He asked my opinion about the right time for him to go down, and as I desire to talk to him about the draperies of the negroes I asked him to time his visit so as to meet him the next time I am down. Under the circumstances it does not seem fair to me to defer paying Calder's final installment to the moment when we may meet there, since he is quite ready to go now and install them if I were willing. I therefore felt it right to let him know in written form that I should consider his contract fulfilled, and I have further written him that our understandings yesterday were satisfactory regarding the modifications he will make in the present work. I did not want to define these modifications too definitely for fear my sense of what is needed should not exactly coincide with yours—I mean I do not want to define these modifications in writing, so as to give you a certain leeway finally to express yourself, but we in general understood that they will consist in the reduction of the size of the breasts of the two ladies on the south prow, and the toning down of certain lines and shadows which seem to insist a little pointedly on sexual anatomy. Calder himself suggests some modifications for the improvement, of some seaweeds, etc. and of course to take a hand in the adjustment of the draperies on the Herms. It was the tenor of his original communication that he thought his "quid pro quo" for an extra payment of $2,000.00, which he represented might be considered somewhat due him for modifications already made and for the great scope of the work, which he had hardly at first grasped, should be—I say this consideration should be—changes to be made by him with the object of removing objectionable cast of sentiment from the girls' figures. We were able to leave aside the somewhat acrimonious discussion we have had, and to agree just what elements could be modified so as to produce a less challenging result for the fastidious eye. I send you a copy of my letter, and will in a few days send you Calder's bill, which is requested in it, with my o.k.[52]

Deering's immediate response was to capitulate while complaining about the ever-increasing costs, which made him and his bookkeeper in Chicago anxious: "When may I expect estimate of costs on further work. . . . The sculpture on the island we agree about and I confess I have been not a little influenced by Mr. Sargent's judgment about it, not only by his admiration for the mermaids but by his desire that the mask next to the middle of the island on the right hand side facing the house should have its nose modified so that it would be less of a grotesque."[53] With this and the subsequent adjustments and installation of the herms, work on the Barge was complete, except for planting and the construction of the lath pavilion on the north end, which never quite satisfied Deering (figs. 125, 126). In this he showed good judgment as it was gilding the lily, an unnecessary addition that detracted from the strength and balance of what was already a rich and brilliant architectural and sculptural composition.

Finally, the creation and placement of the Barge fulfilled a fundamental purpose that is rarely mentioned. Like the Mound to the south, which Suarez explained was needed to block the glare of the reflection of the bright sun from the lagoon, the Barge fulfills similar tasks. In addition to functioning as a breakwater, thereby creating a calm stretch of flat water for the landing stage in front of the house, the Barge is perfectly placed to block the glare and reflection of light off the bay in the morning, whether one is in the east loggia, on the terrace, or above on Deering's private balcony; conversely it lies handsomely in the full sun and blue water in the afternoon when these social spaces are comfortably in the shade.

PLANTING VIZCAYA

Deering's selection of the property was originally founded in part on his interest in its natural tropical state (see fig. 12). Throughout the lengthy construction period he insisted upon the preservation of as much native vegetation as was possible. Photographs sent to him in mid-summer 1915 show how the contractors and designers had preserved 30-foot-tall oaks adjacent to the entry gates and the southwest corner of the house, tucking the new structures under particularly attractive overhanging branches (see fig. 18).

FIGURE 125. Scaffolding, staging, and Stirling Calder's assistants working on the final carving of figures in situ for the southern end of the Barge. November 1916. (Photograph by Mattie Edwards Hewitt, Vizcaya Museum and Gardens Archive)

Although Deering's ample property provided him enough material to shift about to create topography for his garden and lagoon landscape with dredges and other steam-driven equipment and a workforce of laborers and mules, there was not a great amount of topsoil. What existed had been subject to ocean flooding, was sandy or silty, and was high in salt content. As a person who had been involved in the agricultural industry, he knew some of what to do himself. To help improve the soil he not only procured quantities of manure, but also produced a volume of charcoal to mix into the soil by burning the wood he cut on the land he was clearing for the farm and agricultural fields of the Village.

Deering also consulted with several leading horticulturalists in Florida and elsewhere for both native plant expertise and the latest research in agronomy for the region. In 1915 Deering added to the cast of professionals involved in the project. Correspondence between Sturrock and Chalfin indicates that he was connected with horticulturalists and nurserymen in the

FIGURE 126. Inside the summerhouse, looking toward the southern end of the Barge and the tea house beyond. Note the new planting in the garden onshore to the right, c. 1922. (Photograph by Mattie Edwards Hewitt, Florida Historical Society)

region and assisted in plant purchasing and collecting, as well as in trying to figure out how to translate some of the Mediterranean and European plants used in gardens that had inspired Vizcaya's designers into equivalent ones in terms of color, form, and texture, which would thrive in the climate of Florida. A sample letter from him to Chalfin reads: "Replying to your letter from Savannah with specimen enclosed. The vine is one of the varieties of cypress vine, an annual, which does not bloom here in wintertime. The other low growing tree, Cephale-taxus pedunculata, is closely related to the Taxus or Yew family. I have grown it in North Florida at Griffing's place quite successfully and believe it could be grown here. I am ordering out the plants from Berkman, of Atlanta, Georgia, for a test."[54]

In July 1915 royal palms from Cuba began to arrive for planting on the causeway leading to the boathouse (fig. 128). A sequence of photographs shows how they were placed, staked, and then cleverly tied together to insure their stability, long-term growth, and health. This spectacular avenue with four rows of these stately trees was one of the most dramatic elements of the entire landscape design. At the time, these particular trees, especially large ones, were hard to obtain, and these were purchased only with the help of H. A. VanHermann, chief of the Cuban Department of Agriculture, who agreed to allow them to leave the country. After lengthy delays for permits, digging, trimming the fronds, shaving the root balls, and shipping, 265 royal palms arrived on the site. Sturrock proudly pointed out later that they did not lose a single tree in this operation.[55]

In late spring 1916, several photographs labeled "showing coconut planting on point at entrance to meandering channel," a photograph of the oaks being planted in the garden, along with those of workmen in the new stone yard in the Village engaged in the production of

FIGURE 127. A view from the villa to the concrete retaining walls of the Mound under construction with its twin grottos and cascade substructure in place. The causeway palms and open water of the recently dredged lagoon can be seen beyond, as well as a massive excavation on the left and the stone yard work shed in the right foreground. January 1916. (Photograph by Mattie Edwards Hewitt, Vizcaya Museum and Gardens Archive)

plinths for garden statuary, point to the flurry of activity throughout the site. Other photographs in the albums of the archive labeled May 1916 show barges arriving with the first group of large oaks to be planted on top of the Mound (fig. 129). These had been collected in the Miami area to the north from sites undergoing development and brought down the bay. The decision to plant the biggest trees obtainable that could be moved to this location in the garden is easy to explain. In doing so Chalfin and Suarez shrewdly placed these trees atop the Mound adjacent to the Casino then under construction; using these trees below the Mound would have made them look small, while the Mound would have seemed disappointingly short with a raw-looking pavilion atop it. Placing these largest trees in an elevated position on top made the Mound appear taller and the pavilion nestled between them look at home. Later, when they planted the rows of oaks in the foreground beside the island canals, it worked visually to use younger, smaller trees, as the contrast was acceptable, even desirable. Today both have grown considerably and look very much as originally envisioned nearly ninety years ago.

FIGURE 128. The recently planted allée of royal palms, located between the stone retaining walls of the partially filled causeway which led to the boathouse in the southern portion of the garden. In this 1915 photograph, dredging has begun for the lagoon on the left (north), and a portion of the original saw grass marsh can still be seen on the right (south); fill from the various excavations is being placed on the site of the future Mound at the far left of the photograph. 1915. (Photograph by Mattie Edwards Hewitt, Vizcaya Museum and Gardens Archive)

Although the landscape and gardens were under constant construction from the commencement of activity on site in 1914 until Deering's death in 1925, 1918 was a particularly busy year in terms of planting. There was also a changing of the guard on site. After a period of contention between Deering, Chalfin, and Sturrock, the latter left, whether of his own accord or not. Regarding the transfer of a quantity of nursery stock to Vizcaya, Deering's secretary notified Louderback, who managed his finances in Chicago, that "Mr. Sturrock is now not connected with the James Deering Property in any capacity, hence the greenhouse is now under Mr. McLean's supervision and the prices will from this [date] on be fixed, or passed upon, by him."[56] Despite making a real contribution, in the long run McLean was not to have an easy time of it either, having many run-ins with Chalfin and his associates, striving to do things as best he understood them horticulturally while attempting to please Deering. One example is Deering's displeasure with the mess that had developed along the entry drive. Photographs show that for several years a considerable amount of shrubs and trees existed in the two strips containing the basins and runnels separating the pedestrian lanes from the carriage drive in the middle (fig. 130). These were original native trees that they were trying to save and work around. Lower plants crowding the basins had been added by Sturrock before he was dismissed. A punch list written by someone (Starbuck or Paist in all likelihood) who accompanied Deering, Chalfin, and McLean, Sturrock's replacement, on an inspection tour through the property noted Deering's dislike for the planting in the entry drive and forecourt and his request to "show" the fountains and basins, and to generally clean up this area and to get rid of "Sturrock's misconceived hedges." Despite this, two years later, in June 1920, one finds Deering again directing Chalfin to cut down aralia hedges hiding the basins. A flurry of communications occurred, with Deering angry that McLean had not yet done it and had been trying to restore and improve them with young plants.[57]

FIGURE 129. One of the mature live oaks purchased from development sites in north Miami arriving at the site by barge. Note burlap protection of the enormous bare root mass of this heavily pruned tree. May 1916. (Vizcaya Museum and Gardens Archive)

Once the confusion and mess of the entry drive leading down to the house had been cleared up, Deering turned his critical eye to the oval forecourt at the front of the house where he had also attempted to retain some of the native vegetation (figs. 130, 132). Again it did not look right to him, and for a good reason. Trees growing in a forest condition grow as fast as possible to get to the light. They are often close together, which means that when they finally become part of the forest canopy they occupy a small portion of it. If later someone removes a number of trees in the forest leaving a group or a few individuals standing alone, the residual trees often are tall, scraggly, tufty-topped specimens, which have none of the pleasing visual characteristics the same species would display if planted in the open where they can fill out horizontally as well as vertically. Often such spindly specimens end up dying in slow motion. This is exactly what happened at Vizcaya in the early efforts to save native trees near the house. They looked spindly and gawky and were candidates for being scalded in the sun and easily blown over. Despite the efforts of Chalfin, Suarez, Sturrock, and McLean to retain as much as possible in this entry area, the relict trees looked rather poor compared to nursery-grown material or the remaining bulk of the forest. Although Chalfin replaced the struggling grass plot at the entry with carissa to tidy it up, by 1919 Deering was exasperated: "Dear Mr. Chalfin, You know how I feel about the vegetation in the forecourt. It was good the first two winters and bad last winter."[58]

FIGURE 130. The view from the house looking up the entry drive, showing completed runnels, basins, and native vegetation that had been retained, as well as new beds of planting. March 1917. (Photograph by Mattie Edwards Hewitt, Vizcaya Museum and Gardens Archive)

He had already written: "You asked if I wanted the landscape department to replace the trees, shrubs, etc. in the forecourt by more mature trees and shrubs. It is no use to repeat the statement that I think we ought to have done this in the first place. I would say that to the extent that these two places, about the most important if not the most important on the place, ought to have anything done to them that will make them more dignified and more attractive."[59] This interest in first impression and an overall neat appearance is understandable in a person who had spent his earlier life in sales. He told Chalfin: "All that I want of the flower beds is that they should first look healthy and happy and second pretty. I do not care how this result is obtained."[60]

One of the problems with designing gardens in Florida is that many desirable flowering plants do not bloom between late autumn and spring, which was and still is the main tourist season for those seeking relief from northern winters. Even in the tropics, most plants bloom in spring and summer. Thus we find Chalfin writing: "Dear Mr. Deering, I am so glad to learn from your letter of May 14th that the Judas trees bloom. They were an experiment. They showed a few leaves last year, which was their first year, but no flowers. I have never seen any in Miami, but as the tree flourishes in climates so much colder, I had grave fears about its sustaining the heat down there."[61] It is fair to say that a considerable amount of landscape and garden design is an experiment, and in this Chalfin was both brave and adventurous,

FIGURE 131. The completed carriage (entry) drive in the hammock with stone lanterns designed by Chalfin. March 1917. (Photograph by Mattie Edwards Hewitt, Vizcaya Museum and Gardens Archive)

having a fair amount of success and some clear failures. Fundamental to their work was testing and experimenting to see just what would and would not work in south Florida near the water, and what to substitute for traditional Mediterranean and northern garden plants. In July 1918 McLean reported to Chalfin: "The Australian pines now planted on the sea-arms are showing a very strong growth and should now be pruned in order to obtain the necessary framework for future needs. Mr. Broomfield says he planted these trees, but really no one here knows what the growth effect will be, whether these trees are to be grown with a full top and get the vistas cut out between them, or whether each tree is to be sharply pruned in cylinder form, the proper framework to be started now. I would judge that the cylinder form was the type intended, and, likewise those bordering the walk as far as the swimming pool, being planted close together, suggest the hedge treatment."[62]

McLean guessed wrong, and Chalfin's answer came back: "As for the Australian pines on the sea-arms—I beg to say that the idea was that these Pines should be trimmed in straight square columns to a height of about nine feet [fig. 133]. After reaching that height they should be allowed to come together only in rows, but across the front row to the back row, thus forming a kind of arbor of which the sides looking toward the water and balustrades are open in arches. At a still greater height the top of the tunnel will be horizontal and on the sides trimmed vertical. The arches formed by this form of the trees will not be gothic, that is to say not pointed arches, but round arches." As an afterthought, Chalfin, who had been outmaneuvering his loyal but managerial client, appends a postscript: "In looking over the plans of the property the other day Mr. Deering asked me to write you to contradict the directions he gave you while he was there to plant trees or shrubs within the oval on the further end of the Tennis Courts. I showed Mr. Deering my designs for these spaces and he recognized at once that it would be a mistake to follow his suggestion for planting these. He asked me particularly not to forget to write you these circumstances."[63]

FIGURE 132. The arrival court with lily fountain and one of the twin garden gateways showing the native vegetation that had been retained and was to become a source of contention between Deering, McLean, and Chalfin, July 1916. (Photograph by Mattie Edwards Hewitt, Vizcaya Museum and Gardens Archive)

The Australian pine, or casuarina, that he mentions, a feathery gray-green tree (but aggressively invasive and now banned in Florida), made remarkable topiary, providing a superb substitute for the live oak and laurel hedges used throughout Italy.[64] Tough and resilient, they have survived heat, humidity, and hurricanes, bouncing back afterward. While the arbors created on the sea arms in 1918 were totally destroyed in 1926 and not replanted, several other hedges of this initial planting are still to be seen doing well.

McLean replied: "Dear Mr. Chalfin, Your instructive letter arrived yesterday and the blueprint for the hedge on the sea arms arrived this morning. . . . Mr. Deering's planting suggestion—south of the tennis courts—was one of many reminders he left in writing when he departed in the spring. I had no intention of planting a lot of trees there because I knew what your plans called for in detail. You may rest assured that no radical changes will be made without your knowledge, provided I know the effect you are striving for." McLean then goes on to discuss further experiments with arborvitae, yews, and boxwood, saying that the arborvitae had come through well, so he had purchased four hundred of them.[65]

The casuarina was such a success that Deering suggested to Chalfin that they use it also for the "verdure theater" and the maze (fig. 134). On the other hand, he despairs of ever being successful with roses: "we will have to give up the name of rose-garden, for as you and I agreed the other day that probably there will be few roses in it, and we will only make the place ridiculous calling it by that name. You might call it the house-garden or something else. . . . I do not want scraggy roses in the garden." He goes on to worry also about the water plants and whether the quality of the water will support them properly as well.[66]

FIGURE 133. The northern sea arm leading to the yacht landing with the "pine [casuarina] arches" in their intended form, and with the original mast and yardarm on the landing. 1924–25. (Photograph by F. E. Geisler, Vizcaya Museum and Gardens Archive)

Deering, as a manufacturer of agricultural equipment, had come to know a fair amount about horticulture and growing plants. He also knew that Chalfin was not a plant expert and endeavored throughout the length of the project to supplement his work with the advice and help of others. At times his worries were prescient. The year before he gave up on roses he had written: "Think you should have thorough investigation made as to distance from the Sea at which roses can be successfully grown."[67]

Deering was so fussed by the thought that he sent a repeat of the telegram he had sent the day before as a night letter, adding: "and my telegram of today which reads 'East side of Garden is two hundred thirty-nine feet from ocean.'"[68]

Records in the Vizcaya archive give tallies of many of the various materials and supplies purchased for the garden as different portions were finally ready to be planted. A typical note from January 1920 reads:

64 pines
10 moonvines
100 periwinkles
20 Ficus Nitida
50 Aralia
25 Surinam cherries
4 Jasmine[69]

FIGURE 134. The maze garden as completed by June 1920, with casuarinas spaced for future growth and maximum effect as topiary. (Photograph by Mattie Edwards Hewitt, Vizcaya Museum and Gardens Archive)

That April, F. L. McGinnis, one of the landscape contractors, told Chalfin: "I have closed for five acres of Allapath land for the hauling of enough soil for at least our needs for some time to come, so that we now have secured plenty good soil."[70] At the same time he noted that he was installing three poincianas between the main gate and the house along the drive, and Bermuda grass on the rectangular terraces around the house (see fig. 29).

As with all large landscape projects, an enormous number of plants were needed and installed at a steady rate. The design team and contractors were searching near and far to find enough high-quality material. Ample evidence for this process of acquiring everything that was of decent quality and using it somewhere can be seen in the correspondence between McGinnis and Chalfin throughout 1920: "Can bring six slender Royal Palms somewhat shorter than on causeway about forty dollar each delivered Does property justify purchase?" A month later McGinnis found another thirty royal palms averaging 20 feet high, "9′ brown trunk to the butt of lowest frond," which he snapped up for the job.[71]

At that point in 1920, Deering calculated that he had already spent $334,805 on the gardens alone—a startling amount.[72] In some ways the landscape at Vizcaya may almost be seen as an "engineer's garden" in that it was so completely built upon a costly structure of concrete walls, fill, dredging, embankments, revetments, manufactured soils, piping, wiring, bridges, walls, stairs, tanks, and basins (fig. 136). Few people, when contemplating the great gardens of the Italian Renaissance, French baroque, or even the English landscape movement, notice that they are quintessential examples of the architectural and engineering aspects of landscape architecture. In addition, the planting for Vizcaya and other grand landscapes and gardens was also expensive because, although the individual plants and bags of seeds do not cost very much, the vast amount needed is staggering. Large, ambitious gardens require great quantities of materials: soil, fertilizer, stone, gravel, water, and plants of all sorts. Also, plants that may

FIGURE 135. The Casino on the Mound, nearing completion in late spring of 1918, was framed by large oaks seen on the right that were transplanted from other properties in the area. (Photograph by Mattie Edwards Hewitt, Vizcaya Museum and Gardens Archive)

be inexpensive in small sizes cost more the older and larger they are, and some less common plants, especially flowering evergreens, have always cost more. This is especially true for trees, which take years to grow into sizes desired by clients who are wealthy or impatient, or both; they tie up land and require maintenance without bringing in any revenue for the nurserymen growing them for many years. Thus the final sale price is high as is the cost of the expert crews needed to carefully dig, handle, ship, and plant larger trees and shrubs. The planting of mature stock is an art and an activity that at this scale, owing to the difficulty and expense, is and always has been indulged in by very few people.

While the work was progressing slower than anticipated, Deering's interest in native vegetation led to a desire to do more than merely preserve and own it—he wanted to show and explain it to others. Part of the original idea for the winding paths in the hammocks was to be able to explore, see, and learn about the various trees and plants, in essence to have a native arboretum (fig. 137). In September 1919, with construction of the area south of the causeway still very much in full swing, he noted in a letter to Chalfin that they were now in their fourth season at Vizcaya and that it was probably "time to mark our trees" and make a tree map. For this he recommended using labels of a type his brother had used earlier on his first estate at Buena Vista.[73]

Planting of the lagoon area continued for more than five years, partly because of the vast number of plants needed for the extensive territory. In a diary kept by one of the later resident gardeners, I. N. Court, there is this entry: "Mon 16 Jan 22, sent scow + 3 negros to Cape Fla. to dig last load of coconuts and all or part of dates. Think I will get from 50 to 75 dates of all sizes." At the end of the week this crew returned, and he noted: "Sat 21 Jan 22, scow of palms came in morning from Cape Florida. 106 coconuts + 100 dates, about 40 dates more suckers only also some neglecta."[74] Deering was harvesting these trees from his own property at the south end of Key Biscayne, where he had earlier contemplated building a resort community.

FIGURE 136. The central basin, island, and Mound of the garden, completed prior to the construction of the Casino, showing recently planted and heavily pruned trees already in place. November 1917. (Photograph by Mattie Edwards Hewitt, Vizcaya Museum and Gardens Archive)

FIGURE 137. One of several rustic bridges built over the northernmost canals to allow for winding paths through the hammock. March 1917. (Photograph by Mattie Edwards Hewitt, Vizcaya Museum and Gardens Archive)

FIGURE 138. One of James Deering's favorite areas on the property, with its rustic furniture, located at the far northeast of the hammock, at the end of the coral ridge overlooking Biscayne Bay. March 1917. (Photograph by Mattie Edwards Hewitt, Vizcaya Museum and Gardens Archive)

In all, the records indicate that at least 480 coconut trees were brought from Cape Florida alone to Vizcaya and planted in the south lagoon area.

Although the instructions for the dimensions of the stonework are quite precise and detailed on the working drawings in April 1916, those for the planting are more general (fig. 139). This was due to the fact that Suarez was still involved, the design was still evolving, and a considerable amount was being worked out in the field by Sturrock and the nurserymen. On the layout and materials drawing for the maze and theater gardens, there is the following note:

NOTE: Planting and paths by owner
Entire area planted with trees, shrubs and vines except where Maze & Theatre are shown
Fronts of Stage Wall, Theatre Seats & Steps covered with close clinging, trimmed vine
Connecting paths trimmed thru' planting
Key   Grass
          Sand
          Hedge
          Flowers
          Coral rock paths[75]

Despite all the effort and cost involved in creating the garden and tracking down and purchasing quantities of plants, David Fairchild, visiting the site in 1922, was a bit disdainful of the result (fig. 140). Writing in his journal, this botanist, oblivious to the art of garden making, remarked:

FIGURE 139. The central portion of the main garden with the layout of the parterres and the installation of the planting. Note that the semicircular basins and their elevated gazebo seat pavilions are finished, while the columns are awaiting urns to be installed. (Photograph by Mattie Edwards Hewitt, Vizcaya Museum and Gardens Archive)

FIGURE 140. Completion of the parterres on the central axis, showing the lines of clipped oaks framing the central basin and island, the hedges and bedding plants, lawns, and furnishings all in place. February 1922. (Photograph by Mattie Edwards Hewitt, Vizcaya Museum and Gardens Archive)

In the afternoon I went through the James Deering place, which I had not seen for years. It is a remarkable structure, and so far as its architecture and the furnishing of it are concerned, I doubt if anything so completely luxurious has ever been built in Europe. I certainly never saw any royal palace which compared with it. But I looked in vain for a rare plant of any kind. In respect to planting, it is poor, though the plants like Pithecolobium dulce and the native ferns and the royal palms and citrus trees are well selected as regards their suitability to the architectural plan. . . .

It seems a pity that so little attention is given to the establishment of really new and rare plants around the house. Of course, it takes much time to do this and perhaps there are more than I saw on my brief visit. It would be very desirable for us to utilize this place for all kinds of rare plants, because if people see it there, they will want them in their own yards, and a demand for them will be created. I shall show Mr. Mcginnis our Psychotria and Ficus sycamorus and bamboos, etc.[76]

FURNISHINGS

Paul Chalfin was as much an impresario and talent scout as he was a designer and decorator. In the course of overseeing the design he pulled together an eclectic group of artists and craftsmen, whom he cajoled into working on different parts of the landscape and its structures over many years. Skilled craftsmen and sculptors were needed to produce the various shapes, moldings, and architectural details as well as garden elements such as plinths, balusters, rails, benches, urns, finials, and a certain amount of rough masks and herms. John Cruikshank was the stonework contractor who rounded up the first group of masons and carvers in New England and brought them to Florida. His stonecutter-foreman was B. S. Carter. Among the most skilled carvers mentioned in the records were two brothers named Lyons. For much of the figurative work imagined by Chalfin and his staff, several Italian sculptors were also recruited: Ettore Pellegatta and Edoardo Cammilli, the two most prominent, Victor Guardi, and someone named Bucci.[77] Pellegatta (1881–1940) is probably best known for work done for Carrère and Hastings, especially for carving the lions from Edward Clark Potter's maquettes on Fifth Avenue at the New York Public Library. Trained at the Milan Academy of Fine Arts, Pellegatta had come to New York to join his brother. Chalfin persuaded him to come to Miami in 1915 where he worked at Vizcaya until 1920, both carving himself and directing the work of others on a seemingly endless number of ornaments, animals, heads, masks, finials, and architectural details from sketches prepared by Chalfin's office. He stayed on in the area to work for Carl Fisher and others, returning to Vizcaya to help with repairs and touch up the stonework over the next several decades. Edoardo Cammilli had been a professor in Florence before the war. After a brief stint in the Italian army, he came to America and, like Suarez, ended up in New York stranded and broke. In 1917 Chalfin engaged him to produce the figures that now frame the twin grottos at the base of the cascade from the Mound. These four giant, rustic, hermlike caryatid figures are truly splendid and contribute enormously to the antique pastoral character of the grottos and garden. The two on the east are a young giant and giantess, those on the west an aged couple. Despite Cammilli's departure for Italy, these sylvan figures were eventually produced in the rough coral stone by the crew at Vizcaya from plaster casts made by the Menconi Brothers from Cammilli's superb clay originals.

Two other remarkable talents engaged by Chalfin also contributed to the ensemble of garden furnishings. These were the soon-to-be prominent sculptor Gaston Lachaise and Samuel Yellin, one of the greatest and most productive metalworkers in the history of the decorative arts. Gaston Lachaise (1882–1935) was born in Paris and trained at the École des Beaux-Arts, apprenticing for a time in the workshop of René Lalique, the Art Nouveau jeweler, before coming to America with his American wife. After arriving in New York he worked for a time in the studio of Paul Manship, who, although younger than Lachaise, needed help with the volume of work that had come to him upon returning from a fellowship at the American Academy in Rome. The first decades of the twentieth century were fertile ones in the decorative arts in Europe, with both the Vienna Secessionist and Art Nouveau movements producing a wealth of furnishings, architecture, clothing, fabric, utensils, jewelry, and graphic design. In

FIGURE 141. One of the team of sculptors finishing a base in situ for one of the entry piazza sculptures. Note the bougainvillea-covered pergola over the pedestrian entryway into the drive, to the left. April 1920. (Photograph by Mattie Edwards Hewitt, Vizcaya Museum and Gardens Archive)

their work, Manship and Lachaise were very much aware of and inspired by the streamlined, somewhat rococo, and at times oriental inspiration and elegance of these movements. Likewise, Chalfin's exposure to these developments from his years of residence in Paris, study, and travels, combined with his attraction to the ideas and milieu of decoration, furniture, and the design of precious objects, can be detected in several aspects of Vizcaya. This is particularly so in his selection of Lachaise and the nature of what he wished him to do.

Lachaise was principally employed in contributing to the new oriental mood, which, by the middle of 1920, Deering and Chalfin had agreed would be the general character of the lagoon garden that was then well under way. Rather than Italy or Europe, it was to evoke aspects of the tropics and to some degree the South Seas and Asia. Thus, of the two major paths radiating from the house in Suarez' fan-shaped plan, the one to the right, or west, led to the piazza with its cypresses and Casba, while the other, departing from the Italian garden, passed over the "Japanese" bridge (so called because of its high arch and steps) to the boathouse with its Moroccan roof terrace. Chalfin had decided to erect at this spot a set of twisted, spiraling Spanish columns encrusted with vines (acquired during one of his trips) to act as gateposts into this new world, and he wanted Lachaise to make a set of peacocks to sit atop them. These were preferred to the Classical references—antique marble columns surmounted with urns and busts near the house, purchased after the great Messina earthquake a few years earlier—as peacocks had become a favorite device of symbolist poets, painters, and graphic artists in the late nineteenth century and were associated with heady dreams and the art of Byzantium, India, and Asia (even though they were also birds found on Italian country estates). Lachaise had been working with this motif for some time, having produced a single bronze peacock atop a slender stone pedestal for Philip L. Goodwin's estate at Syosset on Long Island in 1918, and a group of three begun in 1918, a gilded example of which can be found at the Metropolitan Museum of Art.[78] The twisted, baroque columns were, to be sure, reminiscent

FIGURE 142. One of the gateposts of the arrival court with its Villa Borghese–inspired basins and masks, seen nearly complete: the basin to the left is finished but that on the right is still only roughed out, as it was shipped from the stone yard. July 1916. (Photograph by Mattie Edwards Hewitt, Vizcaya Museum and Gardens Archive)

of those produced by Borromini in his collaboration with Bernini on the baldachino at St. Peter's in Rome; yet since these in their turn referred to columns used in the Temple of Solomon in Jerusalem, the motif could still be firmly associated with splendor, paradise, and the East.

Chalfin's staff developed preliminary sketches for this ensemble of bridge, basins, and columns. His assistant, Palmer Ogden, presented and discussed them with Lachaise. The original concept called for eight columns and birds, two pairs at each end of the bridge. Only the group of four at the north end of the bridge were in place by 2004, although all eight were completed. The southern four were removed in the 1970s and are in storage at Vizcaya. Each elegant and vaguely oriental bird, atop a sphere or globe, turned to face another is unique, having been finished on site by Lachaise. Like the well-known female figures he was to produce later, there is a striking contrast and tension between the elongated necks, the plump bodies and orbs, and the stretched pendulous weight of their abundant tails. The difference in sensibility and mood between this work and that of the Italian garden is striking, possibly jarring, but clearly consistent with the intent to shift from one landscape and set of forms, images, and ideas to another.

Unlike Calder, Lachaise, or Cammilli, whose work can be found in one particular part or place in the garden, that of Samuel Yellin (1885–1940) exists in many places throughout the garden and house. Yellin, a recent immigrant born in Poland, had worked in Belgium and England before coming to America in 1906 at the age of twenty-one, where he set up shop in Philadelphia, which was at the time one of the richest cities in the world and in the midst of a commercial and residential building boom. Yellin was a virtuoso metalworker capable of remarkable feats with hot iron, a hammer, tongs, and an anvil. He also was a superb artist, had studied and knew both decorative and utilitarian ironwork from Classical and medieval through the Renaissance, baroque, and rococo eras. While still in his twenties, he began teaching at the Pennsylvania Museum and School of Industrial Art (now the University of the Arts) and had developed an important forge on Market Street in Philadelphia. Leading architectural firms such as Trumbauer, Mellor & Miegs, Frank Miles Day, Zantzinger, Borie and Medary, and Will Price in Philadelphia, Carrère and Hastings, McKim, Mead & White, and Delano and Aldrich in New York sought him out. His workforce expanded beyond a hundred employees, eventually reaching more than three hundred, supplying hinges, gates, railings, locks and latches, clamps, grills, stanchions, andirons, and sconces for buildings from Maine to Florida and from New York to Chicago (fig. 143). Generally regarded as America's greatest artist-blacksmith, he described his approach as follows.

> First, draw a sketch to a small scale, so as to obtain the general composition, proportion, silhouette and harmony with the design of surrounding materials or conditions. This sketch should then be developed into full size to obtain details or ornament, various sections and sizes of material, and a general idea of the method of making. At this time careful consideration must be given to the practical use of the piece of work, so that it may serve its purpose in the best manner possible. Workers in iron should always attempt to make everything direct from a drawing, rather

than from models. When working from a model, the object becomes more or less a reproduction, whereas the drawings allow a greater opportunity to express the craftsman's individuality.

Studies or experiments in the actual material are now made, for here many things are revealed which could not possibly be shown on paper. The character of a twisted member or the flexibility of the material might be used for example to show how difficult it would be to conceive many such things in the drawings. For this reason the true craftsman should often make a fragment or portion of the ornament in the actual material first, and make the drawings later.[79]

Although Chalfin had purchased some superb pieces of metalwork in Europe, they were only a portion of what was needed at Vizcaya. In some cases a gate needed a new frame, to be repaired or set within a larger opening. Yellin adjusted and solved these problems while producing a panoply of new fittings to accommodate Chalfin's details, ranging from the metal rings that hold the braided silk ropes that serve for handrails on the stairs to the pommels that function as drapery tiebacks, rails for tapestry and draperies, and various cleats and fittings for the boats and flagpoles. This sort of background hardware is barely noticeable to the casual visitor, but is remarkably ubiquitous and consistent. Yellin's more obvious and artistically satisfying work, however, was the production and (in several instances) design of the numerous railings and balustrades employed throughout the garden (fig. 144). Major works are the

FIGURE 143. One of many full-size detail drawings made by Chalfin's office, this was sent to Yellin's works in Philadelphia for the fabrication of the railings in the orchid (secret) garden. Charcoal carbon pencil on tracing paper, November 6, 1916. (Vizcaya Museum and Gardens Archive)

railings for the secret garden and parapets above the twin basins and pavilions on the north of the garden where the hemicycles of columns are located, balcony railings in the pavilion on the Mound and marine garden basins and bridge, and at the swimming pool. His work in the lagoon area for the boathouse, Casba, and bridges has been mostly destroyed, although handsome grills in the view windows along South Miami Avenue still remain.

Some of the railings are made from square bar stock, twisted and worked in a traditional manner, straight up and down with a minimal amount of detail, some are made from flat strips worked into ample sinuous scrolls that bulge out like the late baroque railings of Spain and curve off into the distance above the water gardens. In contrast, the parapet railings at the Casino on the Mound are more in keeping with its French interior and present a series of panels in the form of baroque or rococo medallions, a repeated geometric form reminiscent of a tapestry pattern, executed in rounded and rectangular bar stock. The most unusual is the railing of the balustrade at the marine garden basins where Lachaise's peacocks are located. Here Chalfin had Yellin create a series of railings made of flat iron sheets worked into the common profile of a traditional turned stone baluster. While it is exactly what a drawing of a stone balustrade would be, it has none of the substance of one, but in this strange iron presentation is more like a shadow of one. The top surface of several of the iron railings was made of wood, however, partly to keep them from becoming too hot to the touch in the blazing Miami sun, and partly as an echo of the characteristic furnishing of luxury ships and boats.

FIGURE 144. The secret garden construction, completed, with the installation of Samuel Yellin's railings, July 1917. (Vizcaya Museum and Gardens Archive)

The combination of stone piers and frames with wrought iron infill and wooden handrails with each part well done, yet in an unexpected combination, is pure Chalfin and shows the sensibility of a decorator rather than an architect. Few designers would think of it, let alone do it. In the case of the secret garden, Suarez objected that the metal pergola and railings were out of place and should have been of stone and wood, but lost the argument.[80] Today one finds only the handrail on the stair of the secret garden, which admittedly seems out of place, despite being so lovely. Originally each of the stanchions for this railing continued vertically to support an arbor that covered both stairs; one can still see where it was fastened to the walls as it ascended to the parapet walk and pavilion above. This was an unsuccessful attempt by Chalfin to produce enough shade to grow orchids in planters set into the walls. While wrought iron railings exist in Italian gardens, they have usually been added in the nineteenth century to an older design. In gardens such as the Medici villa at Castello they are awkward and unattractive, an unwelcome intrusion. In the gardens of Spain, however, elegant metal railings, grills, and gates have been an integral presence for centuries. One has only to think of the variety of lovely railings in the gardens of Aranjuez or of the simple and elegant railings one hardly notices in the gardens of the alcazars of Cordoba and Seville to realize the source of Chalfin's inspiration. With the work of Samuel Yellin he was able to return to the Spanish theme with which he had begun the garden, thereby inflecting and overlaying the seemingly Italian layout of Suarez.

Other elements contributing to this hybrid quality were the ranks of antique Classical figures arrayed along the walks and a swing seat reminiscent of French rococo, within the rose garden and facing its fountain (fig. 145). This fanciful tall wooden swing of Chalfin's design, worthy of a Watteau painting, later disappeared in one of a series of hurricanes. The Great Miami Hurricane of 1926 also accounts for the lack of mention of the sculpture in the glade northwest of the house recorded by Sargent, for this area had also been hard hit. The large shady trees here were blown apart and statuary that could be salvaged was combined later with others that survived in the southern garden.

The following is a repertoire of the sculpture as described by Chalfin in 1934. Two rows of statues on raised plinths faced each other from the raised walks that frame the central fan-shaped space of Suarez. On the east, Autumn, Neptune, Silenus, Summer, and Apollo were located. On the west were Neptune, Zeus, Pomona, and Vulcan. At the end of both walks there was a pair of marble shepherds and shepherdesses facing each other. While most of these were seventeenth- and eighteenth-century Italian marble figures of various distinction and repair, there were also an English lead copy of an antique Narcissus and a group of smaller-scale African mermen carved from coral. In the theater one found an eighteenth-century French lead pair, also a shepherd and shepherdess. Additionally there were a genuine antique Roman sarcophagus and altar in the Bassano fountain space. Beyond, silhouetted against the railings and deep space of the lagoon at the end of the two walks, on one side were the figures of Leda and the Swan and on the other Ganymede and the Eagle.

Despite this wealth of figurative Classical sculpture there was no particular story or narrative imposed by Chalfin or Deering. An iconographical program such as those found in some sixteenth-century Renaissance and eighteenth-century English gardens was not part of the concept. Instead these furnishings helped to produce a garden of evocation, not narrative. Like his interior furnishing, Chalfin mixed periods and styles and the work of one nation or artist with another to evoke a mood and feeling, namely, that of the accumulation of time, a nonspecific but fictive past for the site, with memories of other places seen and cherished.

INFLUENCES AND PRECEDENTS

In addition to the owner, none of the three principal designers had ever done an estate like this before from scratch. Few designers get such a chance. Like many students and beginners they attempted to do everything they knew in this one project. Suarez, the youngest, who knew Italian gardens the best, was encouraged to be ambitious. Chalfin, after his years abroad, was stuffed with ideas and memories. In the scheme as it was finally built there are allusions, elements, and whole passages derived from villas and gardens, palazzi and Classical sites from Florence, Lucca, Frascati, Rome, Turin, the Piedmont, the Veneto, and Lake Como. It is a

FIGURE 145. Construction document for a garden swing erected on the edge of the rose garden. The swing shows Chalfin at his most theatrical while in a rococo mood. Blueprint, drawing G82, December 21, 1916. (Vizcaya Museum and Gardens Archive)

truism that art learns from art. Nearly all artists are a bit cagy about the sources upon which they have drawn and at times are reluctant to discuss those they feel most dependent upon. Paul Chalfin openly talked of many of the sources of inspiration and precedents for portions of the scheme that he and the others produced in a manuscript guide to a walking tour of the grounds that he wrote in 1934; even so, not everything is mentioned, remembered, or confessed.

He begins with the front entry gates on South Miami Avenue. These he says correctly were modeled after gates facing the Brenta Canal, which were added in the eighteenth century to the imposing Villa Pisani at Strà. (Edith Wharton has many good things to say about this villa, which carried weight with Deering and Chalfin, and she also included a drawing of one of these gates in her book on Italian villas and gardens.) The octagonal piazza at the top of the drive features a seventeenth-century Venetian fountain believed to be in the style of Longhena. The basins and runnels of the entry drive at Vizcaya were clearly inspired by the well-known descending water features at the Villa Lante and at the Casino of the Palazzo Farnese designed by Vignola, Giacomo del Duca, Tomasso da Siena, and others at these popular sixteenth-century sites north of Rome. Unlike these prototypes, which utilize the motifs of linked chains and dolphins, the repeating bowls and basins at Vizcaya seem more obviously to derive from a set of basins and troughs at the Villa d'Este on Lake Como, as well as the use of seashells exploited in the more baroque work of Bernini and other of his contemporaries. Chalfin, in an elliptical statement characteristic of his associational imagination and use of whatever came to hand to suit his purpose and mood, made a point of declaring the garden design at Vizcaya to be baroque (which portions of it are to a degree): "Vizcaya is a conspicuous instance of Baroque architecture. The contorted pearls of certain clamshells were called by the Italians *barocche*. Their curious curves prompted the nervous movement of the style, which thence came to be called Baroque. The Baroque might be said, thus, to have a marine origin."[81]

The gate piers of the entry court, with jets spouting from satyrs' masks into attached bowls, derive from those of the Villa Borghese on the Pincio in Rome, albeit the proportions and feeling are quite different here. Chalfin declares them to be Venetian depictions of the Four Seasons, which is hardly the case. To the left and right of the forecourt, flanking Hoffman's entry façade, are a pair of triumphal arches that at first seem familiar, but prove to be inventions. In Hoffman's first model they were small pavilions with pyramidal tile roofs and arches, more like William Kent's pavilions at the Horse Guards or Holkham Hall. What eventually was designed and constructed is pure Chalfin. They are unique with their whimsical carvings of seahorses, Spanish armor, and fictive heraldry. Chalfin said they were modeled upon the gateways of the Palazzo Bevilacqua in Verona, which may be true enough, and yet a recollection of the elegant single Arch of Titus in the Roman Forum also remains. These, however, are merely garden gates with a different meaning and purpose. Rather than a civic monument on an important urban avenue celebrating the glory of an imperial regime and the military conquest of Jerusalem, with a depiction of trophies from the sack of the city and the Temple, we have the apparatus of the imaginary history of a house, the development of a romantic narrative about Vizcaya. And even though the garden environment they lead to is more of a stage set for personal pleasure, the urge to impress and to express authority remains.

The swimming pool, which appears to slide under the building from the garden, with its shell-encrusted, fresco-decorated, arcadelike cabana beneath the first floor of the house, conflates aspects of the water entries of nearly every palazzo in Venice, entered by boat through a lower-level portico and landing, with the imagery of seaside grottos common in baroque theater and in gardens from Naples to France and Vienna. The terraces facing the bay and south garden, which originally were covered with elegant lawns stretched taut between stone trim and balustrades, were clearly inspired by the precious (and rare) lawns of prominent Italian villas. These lawns, difficult to maintain in the heat of the Mediterranean, were proud features of villas such as those of Gamberaia in Florence and Albani in Rome, and had become more common in and around Florence and Lucca in the wake of the influence of English landscape parks in the nineteenth century. They were, as it transpired, no less difficult to maintain in south Florida next to the sea.

The curved arms of the bulkhead with its landing stage and arched bridges are clearly reminiscent of the *fondamenta* located throughout the city of Venice, an echo made specific by the wooden pilings painted with spiral stripes in the colors of that city, yellow and blue (fig. 146). This ensemble has been modified, domesticated, and transformed into a garden feature, however, with the addition of planting (originally clipped hedges but now two rows of palms) framing paths along the sea arms and a small baroque pavilion with a latticework dome and water stairs known as the tea house. A broad stone stair leading down into the water of the bay at the center of the composition is modeled after those at San Giorgio Maggiore and Santa Maria della Salute in Venice. Also, as already noted, it is impossible not to think of Charles Platt's well-publicized earlier and similar curved walls and water landing at Gwinn in Cleveland.

FIGURE 146. Gondola and completed southern sea arm and tea house, c. 1922–24. (Photograph by Mattie Edwards Hewitt, Florida Historical Society)

Harold Acton's villa, La Pietra, as we have seen, provided the setting for the principal actors to meet and was the setting for some of Suarez' first practical experiences in garden craft. Although it does not in any particular way look like Vizcaya or resemble its arrangement, nor appear as the source for much if any of the imagery or design motifs developed at Vizcaya, there are several aspects that should be acknowledged as contributing or relating to the gardens of Vizcaya. First, as a quintessential scheme of Cecil Pinsent, La Pietra was eclectic, combining several elements and motifs, images and compositions from different periods of Italian villa design. Second, it was conceived as a set of separate but interrelated outdoor rooms, each with a different character, quality, and purpose (i.e., as landscape "architecture"). The whole was pulled together with a preponderance of clipped evergreen hedges and walls. Finally, there was a small garden theater derived from those at Gori and Marlia in which Acton and his friends and guests could perform amateur theatricals, skits, pantomimes, and musical evenings. In none of Pinsent's gardens did he particularly indulge in floral *broderies*, or embellishments, rather keeping to simpler geometry and monochromatic architectural planting. His clients, however, such as Acton, Berenson, and Origo, did subsequently overlay them with handsome displays of flowers. So while there are echoes of the mood and strategies of La Pietra, the gardens of Vizcaya move far beyond La Pietra in every way.

The Barge stands out for every visitor as one of the triumphs of Vizcaya. While this may be one of the most original features of the garden, it has precedents in ancient Rome with the shaping of an island in the Tiber River into a marble-clad ship, portions of which can still be seen, as well as Bernini's stone boat, *La Barcaccia*, at the foot of the Spanish Steps, or the charming *Navicella*, a Roman votive boat discovered in the sixteenth century that inspired the stone boats which appear to float in the basins of the main terrace at the Villa Lante. There was also the architectural ensemble resembling imperial ships discovered in Lago di Nemi south of Rome, used as a party venue by Nero and Caligula.

Twenty years after the Vizcaya Barge was designed and built, Chalfin wrote: "[This] motionless vessel, this Island Bark recalls in miniature the great Barromean [*sic*] garden on Lago maggiore—half finished—and bearing the palace of the family amidship. The prow of the Barromean [*sic*] gardens remains unachieved in the lake, half visible—the poop constitutes the famous terraces. It was the privilege of the Cardinalate in the 16th century, exclusively, to employ the boat in the forms of villa decoration—an allusion to the membership of the Cardinals in the manning of the Bark of Peter—the Roman Church. The present island likewise recalls the marble barge of the late Empress Dowager of China in the Summer Palace near Pekin."[82] It hardly matters how much of this was consciously in the minds of Chalfin and Suarez while working on the design as their inspiration and sources were totally absorbed and transformed into the completely fresh and delightful, bold and whimsical stone vessel we see today.

The secret garden, a small, narrow outdoor room, was intended by Deering to house a collection of orchids. It is unquestionably derived from a similar enclosed garden room at Gamberaia near Florence. Like the earlier one, it was entered through a narrow passageway, but in this case one that is also a rusticated grotto with fountains, sprays, dripping walls, and ferns. Grottos in this manner abound in seventeenth- and eighteenth-century villas, any one of which could have provided the model. Likewise, the parterre garden, with its curvilinear hedges, is in the manner of many created throughout Italy in the seventeenth century, which would have been well known to the team. Chalfin remarked later that "the gardens, in logic of plan and careful detail, recall the great Italian landscaping of the seventeenth century."[83] Particular candidates the authors all knew include the Villas Petraia, Lante, Falconieri, and Albani, although several in the Veneto, such as Villa Pisani, also possessed such parterres. This type of floral *broderie*, taken up so thoroughly by the French in their baroque and rococo gardens, was revived by designers such as Duchêne at the end of the nineteenth century. Suarez knew these parterres in their original settings as well as in restorations and gardens recently created for the expatriate community of Florence. Examples can be found throughout Italy from Villa Celsa near Siena to those of the vast Palace at Caserta near Naples, and the recently restored Villa Doria Pamphili and Villa Borghese in Rome.

The twin semicircular basins, with their antique polychrome marble columns topped with stone vases and portrait busts and enframing vine-covered masonry arms, walkways, and tiny overlook pavilions, are certainly echoes of the baroque era and the late eighteenth century. The raised pavilion on the Mound, while supposedly inspired by a structure at the Sforza villa outside Milan, also has echoes of the casino at Caprarola and, more literally, a casino also with a surprise view done for Deering's contemporary Chicagoans, the Armours, in Lake Forest in 1904. The list goes on: the twin grottos flanking the water stair (also Caprarola); the raised linear walks on the sides with their statuary and evergreen planting (Villa Albani); the central cascade of the Mound (Torlonia at Frascati, Garzoni at Collodi, and others); the evergreen theater with its stage and woods, statues of a shepherdess and young swain (Villas Gori near Sienna and Marlia near Lucca, as well as La Pietra); the maze in a clearing (Villa Lante, the Orti Farnesiani on the Palatine, Villas Valsanzibio and Pisani in the Veneto); the view windows in an exterior wall into the garden from the road (again Valsanzibio, and Aldobrandini in Frascati, also mentioned by Wharton).

The little island with its canals, bridges, obelisks, and topiary shrubs framed by live oaks in the center of the south garden, which forms a forecourt to the large cascade and the Mound, is one of the more delightful and original features of the Vizcaya garden. Yet it, too, has a pedigree. Several famous gardens in Italy possessed water features with islands and small bridges. The most obvious is that of the Isola in the Boboli garden of the Pitti Palace in Florence. Then there is the fanciful arrangement of bridges, basins, railings, and obelisks with its central island and fountain at the Villa Lante. Also there is the charming island for rabbits in the middle of a basin at Valsanzibio in the Veneto, and Gamberaia, once again, with its central walk and putti surrounded by basins and hedges, or the brilliant island with its fountains at the Generalife in Spain. This sort of conceit runs through the best of the great fifteenth- and sixteenth-century gardens. Suarez knew them all well and was able to draw upon them with a confidence that few people could have done. Chalfin and Deering, therefore, were incredibly lucky to have found him.

Influences upon the garden read like a scrapbook or course in Italian garden design, but the effect is not that of a pastiche or collage. Magically it all hangs together to a remarkable degree as a coherent and seamless composition. Suarez had taken up this material so well and so made it his daily sustenance, his life, that he was able to draw upon it with total confidence and ease. Everything was altered, transformed, or adjusted to its new context and adjacent elements. What one sees at Vizcaya is the result of someone working *in* a Classical language, not looking backward and copying, but looking forward and creating new things with a vocabulary and set of typological motifs. This is the sort of invention we see in the work of Vignola and Michelangelo, of Alberti and Bramante. It is more than working with a kit of parts, but requires consummate artistry and feeling. This is something that cannot be taught, but only discovered and learned by extremely talented individuals. Regardless of any thought we may have today about the appropriateness of such an endeavor, as with the main house, this is not copying Classical architecture, but rather *performing* it.

While the precedents for many of the particular elements of Vizcaya are quite clear as recounted above, the overall inspiration and artistic program is not so obvious, and yet here, too, there is almost certainly a primary source for Chalfin and Deering's work. This is to be found in a slender book published in 1909 by Sir George Sitwell, *On the Making of Gardens*. The only reference to it anywhere in the records at Vizcaya or by those who worked there appears to be in an annotated list of Deering's books shipped by Sturrock to Chalfin. However, the garden as it stands is a literal embodiment of this essay, paragraph by paragraph, subject by subject, one motif and detail after another. It is common for amateurs to seek guidance and formulas, to copy things they like and to search for rules and precedents when building or gardening. It is stunning to see how literally those who created Vizcaya followed Sitwell's extended essay from the overall aesthetic mood through his advice upon how to site or locate a house, to the relationship with particular specified desirable views, major elements, their location and to recommended strategies, themes, methods, and details in the garden.

Sitwell's essay is redolent with a fin-de-siècle mood, one of nostalgia and reverie. It argues for the superiority of Italian gardens of the sixteenth and seventeenth centuries over all others, whether French baroque or the English landscape style, and briefly acknowledges Wharton's earlier text. He supports the arguments advanced by Reginald Blomfeld in an attack upon William Robinson and is especially scathing in his criticism of gardens and parks that attempt to be naturalistic. Sitwell argues that gardens, like architecture, and villas in particular, are not natural products, but highly artificial cultural works and that the best of them are repositories of flights of imagination, art, and wit whose purpose is to stir the soul and memory. As John Dixon Hunt has pointed out, Sitwell implies without actually saying that gardens are as much a *Gesamtkunstwerk* as the operas of Richard Wagner, employing diverse modes of physical craft and fine arts, which speak to all of the senses and the mind.[84] Sitwell argues for representation, narrative, allusion, and sensuality. At the same time he frequently acknowledges the need to understand and work closely with the underlying natural and physical attributes of the chosen site, specifically repeating Alexander Pope's dictum to "consult the genius of the place."

After invoking a litany of well-known historic Italian gardens and an enumeration of their beauties, Sitwell discusses the nature of their appeal, employing theories of perception and reception from contemporary psychology and biology.[85] In the course of the essay he shifts from description and appreciation of gardens of the past to prescription and precepts, and finally to suggestions for garden designs, even to a few rules. It is a fascinating performance, very much in the manner of Horace Walpole's famous essay on landscape gardening. It is every bit as rhetorical and polemical. Walpole's essay, however, argued for the emerging English landscape garden style as the only proper, even "natural," way to develop a park or landscape, and in so doing helped to justify and make fashionable a seemingly new and fresh style to a class of landowners who were on the rise and soon to control the future development of a nation and the expanding economy of an international empire. In contrast, Sitwell's tract was published at the moment when the style he advocated was on its way to extinction, despite attempts by himself and others to reinvigorate it, partly because the most sympathetic audience for his message was about to be swept away by the broad economic and social changes resulting from World War I.

Sitwell's thesis that a garden provides a particular sort of setting or background for "life" must have appealed to Deering and Chalfin. Specifically regarding the location and position of the house, Sitwell suggests:

> For the spirit of man like his body abhors restraint and confinement, will not be pent up in a narrow compass, nor be content without a spacious horizon in which the eye may wander and fancy and memory move . . . for thinkers or rulers of men should look down upon a distant country where one may drink deep draughts of space and freedom, upon a bay studded with islands, or at least upon some great river which, like the stream of Time, bears onwards its freight of lives and treasure, of human hopes and fears. . . .[86]
>
> This, then, leads to what I believe to be the great secret of success in garden making, the profound platitude that we should abandon the struggle to make nature beautiful around the house and should rather move the house to where nature is beautiful. It is only part of the garden that lies within the boundary walls. . . .[87]
>
> The lover of liberty will find delight in the vast horizons of the ocean and the desert.[88]

Sitwell lists specific suggestions for elements to be incorporated into a garden, one after another of which we find worked into Vizcaya: "The Italian love of looking down from a height upon a great parterre of flowers finds its expression in the Roman gardens of the Vatican, Villa Medici, and Villa Pamphili. Another favorite motive in Italian gardens is coolness in summer heat, and few of the larger houses are without a grotto adorned with fountain and marble floor and encrusted with sea shells or fantastic pebble work."[89] He goes on to give a catalogue of items, including balustrades and statues, box hedges, sculpture on pedestals, plots of turf, pools with mermen, and a superb peroration on the role and value of water features in a garden.

Not only are all of these general effects worked into Vizcaya, but also particular details are followed: "There are many little tricks of technique by which scale may be given. . . .

A curious illusion of spaciousness is produced in some of Knyff's engravings of English gardens by a number of yew obelisks placed at equal intervals from each other."[90] Although they have been let go into shapes vaguely resembling balloons or baseball bats, the two ranks of shrubs on the island leading to the cascade and the Mound were originally and for several decades trimmed into the shape of obelisks, literally (and successfully) following Sitwell's recommendation. Yet another passage seems to have yielded a specific inspiration for Vizcaya: "Who has yet sought the summer coolness of a water labyrinth with rose bordered canals, where a great pool serves for a lawn in front of the house and boats may pass among fruit trees and flowers . . . who has worked out the possibilities of a sea shore demesne . . . ?"[91] Not only are there clear correlations with particular features such as the rose garden with its somewhat Persian pattern of labyrinthine small channels, but also suggestions for the roof garden terrace at the boathouse and the exotic, even tropical, development of the lagoon garden: "On Lake Maggiore, he may pass at Isola Madre into the Tropics, and look upon strange flowers and shrubs hardly to be seen elsewhere in Europe."[92]

Finally, there is Sitwell's recommendation which, when carried out by Chalfin and the others, produced one of the greatest of all garden follies and Vizcaya's unique signature piece: "A good effect may be produced by false scale, if the owner accepts it as a convention and is determined to be amused by the contradiction when giant figures come upon the scene."[93]

> To make a great garden, one must have a great idea or a great opportunity; a cypress causeway leading to a giant's castle. Or a fountain cave . . . or a mighty palace quadrangle lined with hanging gardens of arcaded terraces, or a great galleon in a lake whose decks are dripping with jasmine and myrtle, or . . . who has realized the full glory of vine, or clematis, or honeysuckle, wisteria, or bougainvillea?
>
> . . . where baby loves are climbing the obelisks and the flower-vases, playing and splashing each other upon the water-edge, swimming out to a marble Nef whose mast and sail and homing bows are festooned with clambering cupids.[94]

The cupids were apparently too much for Chalfin and Deering, but the galleon, sea nymphs, and giant grotesque mask as executed by Calder certainly fulfilled this vision, and then some. Most of us today are not familiar with Sitwell's word *nef*, but in the Middle Ages it meant a silver or gold table furnishing in the form of a ship, either for holding various utensils or for ornament. Deering and Chalfin certainly knew, and a great marble nef indeed has been set before the house. While words and gardens are different things, and one can never prove that any particular thing absolutely influenced or caused something else to come into being, it is generally the case that we all obtain ideas from various sources and that we then act upon them within a set of unique circumstances. In consideration of the people, the time, and the place, though it is obvious that many features at Vizcaya are drawn from different villas and gardens around Italy, this particular text of Sir George Sitwell's appears to have provided the guiding authors of Vizcaya with a road map for their endeavor, many portions of which were followed closely, whereas others provided inspiration and a climate of thought.

chapter 9

FARM VILLAGE AND
LOST LAGOON

There were two other major elements of Vizcaya, now nearly forgotten. These were the farm, or Village, and a vast water garden. The former has a long and ancient pedigree, dating from the time when the contrast between town and country was developed as a literary trope by Roman poets and agronomists—Horace with his tale of the town mouse and country mouse, the satires of Juvenal and Petronius, the letters of Cato, and Pliny the Younger. This was in part a response to the already established pattern of wealthy figures maintaining country properties as well as urban residences and businesses. These rural holdings, often inherited land from earlier generations and more humble family origins, whether large or small agricultural estates or farms, had been subject to considerable improvement and architectural enhancements by the time of Augustus in the first century C.E., and had come to be called villas. These country residences, although in some instances verging on palatial, or merely gracious and attractive in others, were in effect just an owner's house on what was essentially a farm. Most were self-sufficient in terms of food, labor, and materials, exporting for sale agricultural produce, livestock, cereal, oil, wood, and small manufactured items such as baskets, brooms, and leather goods. More often than not, these estates evolved to become large commercial enterprises with multiple dwellings, tenants, workshops, and centers of activity spread over an expanse of agricultural territory. The principal dwelling for the owner commonly retained one of these farms for its own support, supplies, food, and drink. While there have been many variations and exceptions down through the centuries, the estate with its big house, or country seat, château, or villa and its home farm has been a persistent phenomenon. Whether one thinks of the Villa Barbaro, Stowe, Vaux-le-Vicomte, Mount Vernon, or Monticello, the land development type is the same.

This Classical model is followed, too, at Vizcaya, despite its unique location on Biscayne Bay and the hybrid design style of both house and garden: to the grand owner's house, garden, and parkland is appended a functional agricultural estate. It is not surprising that a man whose family fortune was made through the manufacture and sale of agricultural machinery should choose to create a place for himself in this tradition. The development of a farm, with orchards, kitchen and cutting gardens, greenhouse, livestock pasture, poultry buildings, dairy, stable, machine and paint shops, and workers' quarters, to accompany his own house is fitting. These facilities were part of Deering's initial concept for his Florida retreat and were incorporated into the earliest site development plans prepared by Hoffman and Chalfin. So, too, the idea of public display was also in Deering's mind quite early, as his remarks to Chalfin in December 1914 indicate: "I had never thought of having an arboretum or anything like it, but I should like all varieties of trees that we can expect to grow with reasonable care, especially such as would be interesting or curious. In this connection, I think there are many things that we might have, like papyrus, rice, sugar cane, etc. I refer to such things as would be a curiosity to people who have never seen them."[1]

As early as February 1915 Chalfin was at work on this area (fig. 147). In a four-page letter to Deering on a wide variety of topics, he discusses the Village and south lagoon areas at length. It is clear that he had already begun to make plans for the farm, the public approach, and its views.

> In regard to Sturrock's conversation about the pine land I can say that my plan contemplates certain tufts of round foliage or large foliage trees interspersed among the pine trees, and a plantation, in time of other pines, including the Italian stone pine. We should have already some of these planted but we do not seem to get its species definitely. I think it is Cembra, but the Pinus Cembra obtained by Sturrock does not look to either of us like the youthful pine, which I am

FIGURE 147. A panorama of the clearing for the Village and farm, with trenches for irrigation, drain lines, and recently planted orchard visible beneath the remaining pines. Note the temporary shade house for propagation of the initial plants, 1915. (Photograph by Mattie Edwards Hewitt, Vizcaya Museum and Gardens Archive)

familiar with in Italy. I mean I am familiar with it in extreme youth. We are also certain about the species of the cypress which is grown in Tuscany. Both matters are easy to determine but have slipped us. I will look them up.

I do not wish Sturrock to make a tentative plan for the planting in these pine lands nor the treatment of the sides of the roads because I have an idea of the sentiment that such planting express, which he is, I think, not yet experienced enough to sympathize. I should feel that elaborate ideas from as young a man, or perhaps too formal or too stately, for instance his suggestion of fig or laurel trees in a line does not seem to me happy. I shall have some correspondence with him and make the primary suggestions myself.

What you quote from Mr. Gifford would seem to make four feet for garden walls excessive. I thought we had decided long ago to make an arbitrary stand, regardless of the diversity of opinions. What you and Sturrock found in regard to the absence of vista north of the north pool does not trouble me. I do not wish to have a line of sky down old Brickell Avenue at all noticeable through the trees. I do not wish either to have a structure at the north end of the north pool, I mean a building, neither did I desire a window in the wall on axe[s] with the present Brickell Avenue to show a vista. What I wanted was an architectural feature contained in a window. Some little statue might be placed in the trees, but perhaps an apparently walled up window would give the same effect of something at the end of the present Brickell Avenue.[2]

Chalfin makes clear that he does not intend to let a younger landscape architect, such as Sturrock, begin to do his own thing or to allow him to talk Deering into anything he, Chalfin, does not want. This letter goes on to take up issues such as the character of the canals and Chalfin's hope that they will be able to purchase more land to the south, and not just east of the relocated South Miami Avenue. His ability to alternately bully and cajole his client, to make overtures about saving money and using prudence in Deering's interest, while laying the groundwork for a further increase in scope and expenditure, namely, the lagoon garden, is extraordinary: "I shall be delighted if you buy 200 more feet of Mrs. Brickell's land but I do regret that these 200 feet is not added to the pine land, as you know, but we must not ruin you. What you say about any further work on the plaza, or what I properly call the kasba, is evidently just, of course, if you are to buy more land, but I can imagine no better backing for what is proposed there than the land you would buy. I do not think you need fear any modifications in the piazza, rather you might contemplate amplifying in a Southern direction, but such an amplification would not supercede [sic] the line at present established by the causeway."[3]

While Hoffman was working to keep up with the demands of the house construction and Chalfin's machinations, Deering was pressuring him to produce documents to begin the layout and construction of the Village west of South Miami Avenue. A brief note from Deering to Hoffman in July 1915 repeats a "request for something showing the general layout in the Pinelands."[4] In November that year Hoffman advised that the contract for the greenhouse had been "closed . . . in accordance with the drawing submitted to you and approved by Mr. Sturrock with modifications."[5] And one month later Hoffman sends Chalfin "a complete set of the final working drawings for the Farm Blgs. Which embody the latest corrections requested by Mr. Deering."[6]

Construction photographs verify that work on the clearing and preparation for the nursery and farm buildings west of South Miami Avenue were well under way by midsummer 1915. The gravel sub-base for the roads in the vegetable garden and the handsome shade house, which was much larger than the greenhouse located behind it was to be, were begun by July 1915. Construction in the Village continued unabated through 1916. By 1917 a significant proportion of the work here was directed toward what was to become the public face of Vizcaya, the new road (South Miami Avenue) with its walls, gates, walkways, windows, and planting, with the first of the vista gates and the easternmost wall being completed by August of that year. In the autumn and winter of 1915, when the Italian garden was slowly being raised with fill and the busy stone yard still occupied the future site of the laundry and one of the two hemicycles of columns and aquatic planting, across the road to the west at the Village the propagation house and garage were nearing completion and the gatehouses were finished.

For several years prior to Deering's death, this area and the lagoon garden were open regularly several days a week to the public, who were allowed to drive through on a prescribed route and were encouraged to purchase produce and poultry in what was arguably the most elaborate and ambitious roadside farmstand in history. Whether the idea to open the farm to visitors for tours was an original premise of Deering and Chalfin is not known, but the arrangement of the buildings and plots, being substantially different from that of the house and gardens across the road to the east, suggests their planning for such an activity very early in the project. Here a large quadrilateral layout of drives is organized around two cardinal axes that are terminated by the propagation house and the superintendent's residence. Seen axially from a view window on South Miami Avenue, the propagation house, as drawn by Chalfin's office and as built, was a reprise of a building well known to Deering—the Agricultural Building designed by McKim, Mead & White for the World's Columbian Exposition in Chicago—and featured a central pediment and dome with long fenestrated flanking wings. The superintendent's house, with its delicate tripartite loggia, became the centerpiece on the north. Native pines, which had been saved, and young orchards were used as veils to screen the less grand working buildings—greenhouse, sheds, animal quarters, workshops, and apartments—arrayed behind and to the sides of these two symbolic centerpiece structures.

As in everything Chalfin touched, aesthetics set the conditions by which things were to be judged. Persuasive in case after case, he argued and found support for his opinions and desires in practical considerations. Rejecting Deering's suggestion that the gravel roads be oiled to keep down the dust, he argued correctly that it would be bad for the trees, would give a bad odor (also correct), and that he personally disliked dark roads.[7] Deering let the idea drop.

The pressure to bring things to completion affected this part of the project, too. In October 1917 Deering wrote to Chalfin inquiring where progress on the Village stood and when it could be finished.[8] A year later, with the large vegetable gardens completed and in production, other problems presented themselves. Deering wrote of his distress that nematodes in the soil of the hedges bordering the vegetable garden had invaded the vegetables and he had been told to remove the hedges to save the produce he wants. As he put it, "I do not know what it is wise to do."[9] At the same time he concluded that the orchids will not work in the secret garden. Chalfin agreed and claimed that it was intended that the orchids were to be rotated from the shade and greenhouses to the secret garden and back, blaming McLean for the problems.[10] Deering, exasperated, let McLean go at the end of 1918 and hired yet another gardener, a man named Pierce, to take the vegetation in hand. In an interesting aside, Chalfin gave Deering his explanation of the differences between a designer, a horticulturalist, a landscape architect, and a nurseryman. Needless to say, he considers himself to be a designer and, therefore, not necessarily nor compelled to be deeply knowledgeable about the physical needs of plants, whereas McLean, whom he felt should have been more of a horticulturalist, was in his opinion a bit too much of a landscape architect like Sturrock, that is, too close to him in ambition and knowledge and neither subservient nor technically supportive enough.

The animal buildings of the Village form a compound around a courtyard (farmyard) with a large watering trough at its center. The machine shop and garage form a separate group near the entry gate with the chauffeur's lodge and employee apartment. Further to the south, adjacent to the western property line and the former rail spur and site of the second stone yard, were the propagation (shade) and greenhouses. The latter structures formed a terminus to the main east-west axis of the extensive production gardens and the view from the principal vista gate on the west side of South Miami Avenue. The structures of the Village were clearly intended to be more modest and less costly than that of the main house and its appurtenances, and as such were modeled loosely upon vernacular farm buildings of northern Italy. At a remove from all of them, near the western property line, was the paint shop, isolated because of the flammable nature of its contents and Deering's fear of fire.

The Village's staff facilities, originally planned in 1914, proved to be inadequate as the estate became operational. Chalfin added an additional residence west of the superintendent's house along the northern property line. With an exterior stair and small second-floor entry gallery, rambling plan, and roof, it is the most eccentric structure of the Village and yet closest in its resemblance to the *fattoria* of northern Italy that had inspired the ensemble. Unlike the buildings begun by Hoffman earlier, which regardless of size and purpose were classically composed and ordered, this is pure Chalfin, its composition derived almost entirely from a theatrical picturesque notion.

As with many other aspects of Vizcaya begun by Hoffman, Chalfin massaged and reworked his simple farm buildings. In so doing he managed to produce structures highly foreshadowing similar vernacular-based workers' houses and outbuildings that Cecil Pinsent produced a decade later for the Origos at La Foce in Tuscany.[11] There is also a decided touch of whimsy in their expression, reminiscent of the fictional architecture that Gustaf Tenggren was to invent for Walt Disney's animated films *Pinocchio* and *Snow White* more than a decade later. Examples of this are the poultry house with its horizontal elliptical windows highly evocative of eggs, the exterior stair and its partial arch on the large employee apartment, the heavy wooden brackets and beams on the covered walks of several of the structures, and the soft shape of the central watering trough in the courtyard. The traditional rubble masonry, seemingly ad hoc attached shed roofs, and cross-shaped openings and vents in the thick masonry walls, commonly found in the farm structures of Tuscany and Umbria, are here arranged in sophisticated decorative patterns and are combined with a careful blend of traditional architectural devices, such as stringcourses, dressed quoins, battered ground-story foundation walls, and buttresses, similar to those in the palaces and fortresses of Peruzzi and the Sangallos. In this, as in several other aspects of Vizcaya, Chalfin showed an avant-garde interest in vernacular architecture. A decade after this work, between 1925 and 1935, architectural books and journals in America and Britain were replete with travel studies, sketches, and measured drawings of such structures in Spain, Portugal, Italy, the Tyrol, and Mexico, which fed into the design and construction of innumerable residential and institutional buildings from coast to coast. In Santa Barbara, Los Angeles, Santa Fe, Miami, and Palm Beach, this trend helped shape an architecture and urban image that they partly retain to this day.

Given Deering's background it is not surprising that he attempted to run the agriculture of his home farm or Village on a businesslike basis. An industrial irrigation system with tall rotary spray heads (virtually the same as those still in use today throughout the industry) was installed and in operation by 1917. Earlier his brother, Charles, had helped to introduce bananas, papayas, and mangos in his experimental efforts at Buena Vista and Cutler. The diversity of crops at Vizcaya, while interesting, was neither specialized nor extensive enough to develop a going concern or profit from the effort. Nevertheless, James Deering did well enough for himself and the table at the house. In the accounts, diaries, letters, and reports, one finds a wide range of vegetables and fruit produced in the garden: "I sent you Saturday," Chalfin wrote, "to the office, two boxes of fancy citrus and one of grapefruit. I am going to send some more in two days. They take about a week to arrive. The fancy boxes are smaller than the grapefruit, and my idea was the contents could be put together in the office and distributed among the men."[12] Amid gardeners' orders ranging from white onion sets and shallots to strawberries, one finds basic items such as: "Dear Sirs, will you kindly rush our last order of Irish Seed Potatoes, and oblige, Yours very Truly, James Deering Property, Superintendent."[13] Or, as on March 5, 1922, the superintendent noted that he was shipping ice, milk, and vegetables to the *Nepenthe* for one of its trips.[14] Notes, ledgers, and receipts indicate that the farm activity was treated very much as a business. Even so, one reads: "While all the departments, with the exception of the Greenhouse, show a loss, still you will notice that in most cases the running expenses were less this year than last and the returns greater."[15]

LAGOON GARDEN

The lagoon garden, the most unusual portion of the landscape of Vizcaya, is now lost and gone. This extraordinary composition of winding lagoons, canals, water, islands, peninsulas, tropical planting, paths, and bridges was built south of the fan-shaped Italianate terraces and the Casino between 1917 and 1923. Chalfin wrote to Deering at the end of January 1916 that he had obtained the deeds to additional property south of the boathouse causeway and that he was asking Bennett for a survey "so that I may begin to think before I see you."[16] Two months later, in a letter to Deering that discusses a resort development project for Cape Florida that Deering was considering as well, Chalfin stated that there should be a lake with islands in the new south property along with the canals envisioned by Deering.[17] The next week he explored the topic further, proposing that the Cape Florida project employ a South Pacific island theme for its structures. This may have been as much partly suggested by the large stands of coconut and date palms then growing on that island as his personal and theatrical whimsy or sense of the exotic. As it developed, Deering abandoned the notion of a commercial venture at Cape Florida after expending considerable effort to produce a survey, lay out a subdivision, stabilize the beach with a series of jetties (or groins as they are sometimes called), and the shoring up of the lighthouse. The South Pacific theme, however, was imported into the south lagoon garden at Vizcaya.

There were few precedents at the time for such a garden in the West. True, the city of Venice had been established on a group of sandbanks within a lagoon with twisting channels, villages, remote dwellings, wild vegetation, birds, beaches, and fishermen. But the Venetian lagoon is not a pleasure garden. Many of the villas that Hoffman, Chalfin, and Deering visited in the early years of the planning and design of Vizcaya are located on or near the Brenta Canal which leads from the Venetian lagoon to Padua. Although several have gardens that lead down to the canal and have water landings, none could be said to have a water orientation, let alone a watery garden. There is a precedent in the great Chinese gardens of the seventeenth to nineteenth centuries and one or two in Japan, but they are never mentioned, nor do they seem to have been considered, even though both of the Deering brothers had traveled to Asia earlier in their career.

On the other hand, James and Charles Deering were part of a circle that had been involved in a series of projects in Chicago that in some ways were precedents that may have provided a climate of thought in which plans for a lagoon garden could easily develop. As noted above, the Deerings were on familiar terms with several leading architects and artists of the period, including Burnham, Olmsted, Saint-Gaudens, and others, who produced the Chicago World's Columbian Exposition of 1893. The Deerings were frequently mentioned as being present at various luncheons, clubs, parties, and meetings of prominent committees where matters of urban design and art were discussed.[18]

One of the central features of this enormously successful and heavily visited exposition was a lagoon and island with lush planting and a Japanese temple with gondolas and silent electric pleasure boats, planned and executed by Frederick Law Olmsted and his staff. This large water feature was a residual and scaled-down fragment of an earlier plan of Olmsted's, developed for the same site south of what was then the bulk of Chicago's urban development. The Deerings, of course, with their main factory and offices not far away, were major exhibitors of machinery at the exposition and were very familiar with it.

An earlier water park proposal for Chicago was far more ambitious than the ponds and waterways Olmsted and Vaux had already created in the great parks of New York. The Deerings would have known about this proposal, which was made several decades before the development of Vizcaya. In this project, for what are now Jackson and Washington parks with their connecting Midway Plaisance, Olmsted originally proposed a series of elaborate lagoons, islands, channels, and walkways with bridges.[19] The entire ensemble was to be planted with exotic plants, as well as local and native plants associated with wet environments. Olmsted had traveled across the Isthmus of Panama and seen spectacular lush tropical waterways, which inspired him to suggest that a similar environment would make an appropriate park for the low, flat, poorly drained land adjacent to the lake. The idea of such an aquatic park had no antecedents in either Olmsted and Vaux's work or in anyone else's. Olmsted wrote:

> You certainly cannot set the madrepore or the mangrove at work on the banks of Lake Michigan, you cannot naturalize bamboo or papyrus, aspiring palm or wavering parasites, but you can *set* firm barriers to the violence of the wind and waves, and make shores as intricate, as arborescent and as densely overhung with foliage as any. You can have placid and limpid water within these shores that will mirror and double all above it as truly as any, and thus, if you cannot reproduce the tropical forest in all its mysterious depths of shade and visionary reflections of light, you can secure a combination of the fresh and healthy nature of the North with the restful, dreamy nature of the South.[20]

Olmsted proposed cutting a channel from the low swampy land out to Lake Michigan and then dredging a series of interconnected lagoons and channels. The dredged material would be piled upon the remaining land to create islands and peninsulas upon which one could then successfully plant trees and other foliage, which would in turn be well drained. Once established he hoped to create "the finest aviary in the world. He planned numerous rushy islands without boat landings to provide isolated coverts and breeding places for birds. . . . There were to be animals in the park as well."[21]

This brilliant plan was submitted in 1870, but abandoned the following year as a result of the Great Fire, which leveled the town and redirected the energies and economic resources of Chicago for the next decade. Years later, after Olmsted's innovative landscape proposals for the flat marshland of south Chicago, one of the exposition's principal planners, Daniel H. Burnham, proposed a visionary plan for the redevelopment of the entire city and region. One of the most prominent features of his vast civic plan was a park and lagoon running the entire length of the city from a proposed civic center and a marina at the mouth of the Chicago River and Grant Park south for several miles along Lake Michigan to the former site of the exposition in Jackson Park. The Deerings, members of the Commercial Club, an influential businessmen's organization that acted as a sponsor and host for Burnham and Edward H. Bennett's proposal, were subscribers in helping to underwrite the cost of developing and publishing this plan in 1909.[22]

Finally, two other precedents for this aspect of Deering's lagoon garden are those of J. Ogden Armour's Melody Farm outside Chicago and the remarkable lake-filled landscape of James B. (Buck) Duke's estate at Somerville, New Jersey. Armour, one of James Deering's peers, began construction in 1904 of his landscape in a Classical style designed by O. C. Simonds, the landscape architect for Charles Deering's first estate at Buena Vista and with whom Chalfin had lengthy negotiations for the Deering plot and mausoleum in Graceland Cemetery. One of the Armour estate's main features was a 350-foot-long water garden ending in an arcaded casino, beyond which was a surprise view to a 20-acre artificial lake with islands. This entire garden and its meadows were lushly planted by Simonds with a remarkable combination of native and exotic grasses, trees, water plants, and bamboos.[23] Duke, who had made his fortune in tobacco rather than meat like Armour or farm machinery like Deering, hired James L. Greenleaf, who had begun designing landscapes several years earlier in 1894. Originally trained as a civil engineer with considerable experience in hydraulic design, Greenleaf had worked on projects for the Mississippi River and Niagara River and Falls, and he had taught civil engineering and hydraulics at Columbia University for the previous fifteen years. Beginning with several hundred acres that were essentially flat in the floodplain of the Raritan River, Duke and Greenleaf excavated enormous amounts of material and rearranged it into hills and valleys, creating an extensive series of lakes, ponds, cascades, and streams. In the process they developed an extensive network of aqueducts, pumps, piping, and reservoirs that took large quantities of water from the river, ran it through the lakes, and then back into the river. Over this landscape Duke and Greenleaf developed an extensive set of roads and trails with bridges and cascades with a planting scheme nothing short of re-creating native forests. Greenleaf thus became an inspired plantsman and developed a flair for working with masses of evergreens and conifers, which became a trademark of his later work.[24] From information available to date, one can only speculate whether Chalfin or Deering ever visited these two places, but surely one or both would have known of them.

Suarez may have been a consummate advocate and connoisseur of Italian gardens, Hoffman remarkably adept at neo-Renaissance architecture, and Chalfin a designer with extraordinary flair for composition, materials, decoration, and production with quality and control. But it may well have been Deering who conceived the lagoon garden, which was then taken up by the others and which took Chalfin, his staff, Harold Ley, and his subcontractors more than six years to build. Of the entire cast of characters, only Deering had long years of exposure to both built and unrealized schemes for just such a landscape. The strategy of dredging and reinforcing the curvilinear edges of the islands and peninsulas made with the dredged material employed at Vizcaya was exactly as Olmsted specified in his report to the Chicago Parks commissioners. Unlike Olmsted in Chicago, however, here the designers and contractors actually could use tropical and semitropical plants to achieve Deering's vision. Also following Olmsted's lead, James Deering, an inveterate lover of birds and other animals, planned that his lagoon park would have plenty of birds and a sanctuary, as well as an island with monkeys. It was a tropical fantasy of ambition, extraordinary effort, time, and considerable expense.

The subtle intricacies and carefully shaped landforms found in the work of Olmsted and his colleagues were the result of many long years studying nature and building parks and gardens. For all of his felicity in design, Chalfin's strengths were different. The men he hired were architects, gifted but trained to design interiors, architectural structures, and their details—masonry, cabinetwork, metalwork, and the like. The most fluent of them were trained in the manner of the École des Beaux-Arts and when challenged with drawing up a plan for a vast water garden did so in the manner of contemporary City Beautiful parks, boulevards, and parkways.

Several versions of the plan layout for this area from Chalfin's office can be found in the Vizcaya archives. The layout of one in particular is striking in its geometry and imagery, for it had evolved into a Beaux-Arts fantasy of axes, circles, radiating spaces, and promenades trans-posed to waterways encompassed by a peripheral undulating canal connected to the bay.[25] One of the only comparable plans in western garden history is that of the park of the château of Rambouillet not far from Paris designed by Pierre Descottes, a nephew of André le Nôtre at the end of the seventeenth century, which has a baroque arrangement of radiating canals and connecting basins resembling the normally dry avenues, rides, and allées of parks of the period. Looking at the final construction plan of Vizcaya from August 1920, one sees almost immediately that the designers were struggling with the need for invention in terms of land-scape form and that they had fallen back upon stock devices of contemporary urban design. The repetitive use of circles and plazas is one of the themes and weaknesses of the design. To be fair, people do not experience landscapes in plan except when flying. On the ground, if the height of the different parts were varied, and if one were to add vegetation, it could easily have seemed extremely diverse and mazelike. In time it could have become an absolutely extra-ordinary landscape garden.

Construction of this landscape of islands, bays, and lagoons was a large undertaking, and the work dragged on. Deering chafed throughout 1919 and beseeched Chalfin and the con-tractors to pick up the pace and cut back on the scope of work. As the year opened he wrote that they must try to finish in the next two years, commenting that labor and material costs would never again be as cheap as they were at that moment. Again desiring that some of this southern lake area be left in its natural state, he asked them to reduce costs, but to do nothing "shabby or indecent."[26] Seven months later he made a specific request that the hammock west of South Miami Avenue be preserved in its natural state, repeating that he wished some of the property south of the causeway to "show the saw-grass and its primitive state," and suggesting that it remain just "a river with a few bays . . . and primitive log bridges."[27] A few days later, still troubled, he sent Chalfin a telegram with a follow-up letter requesting a reduction in the work south of the causeway, demanding it be kept simple and that it not "drag along year after year," at the same time acknowledging that it was "unfortunate for me that I still have large sums to spend on the garden, but this is part of the original undertaking."[28] Nevertheless, he still wanted it to be special. Two days later Deering wrote Chalfin, "I have always been in favor of the Japanese path in the Mangroves south of the Tea House."[29]

By November Chalfin, very much on the defensive, responded in a wounded tone with a letter objecting to Deering's most recent request to make it "radically different" in terms of scope and content.[30] Deering fired back that it will cost at least $50,000 more to complete the dredging called for in Chalfin's scheme, which he feels is simply too much. To this Chalfin replied that he had developed a revised scheme with very little water to meet Deering's demand, but that he did not like it.[31] Not surprisingly, as in the past, Deering gave in; Chalfin made adjustments; work continued. Even so, a year later Chalfin wrote to explain yet another revised plan for this area in response to Deering's persistent desire to keep some acreage "natural." Chalfin noted that he and Deering would be together in Miami later in the month and that they would then go over the site in detail to discuss the paths, roads, marsh, islands, and vegetation in this area.[32] This letter is particularly interesting for some of the other details it contains. Chalfin discussed issues to do with the quarry, the amount and quality of the fresh water from the wells, and the problem of trash in the water from Biscayne Bay, which even in 1920 had already become a problem, and his notion of building a weir to keep it out of the lagoon and lake area.

Although Chalfin has written that Deering "desired to express the Tropics and the Orient here, as in the formal gardens he recalled Italy and Europe,"[33] it is more likely that it was he, Chalfin, who suggested the flavor of the lagoon gardens. Perusing the grading and layout plan from his office for the islands, canals, lagoons, and paths as revised in October 1920, one finds the following annotations regarding the major planting south of the Italian garden:

coconut palms	callas	Beach
Buttonwood	oleander	grassy plain
Royal Palms	pertium	grass or cover
"choice palms"	var of pursley	and
Washingtonia palms	group of oaks	arums and callas
Eucalyptus	"Rubbers all along shore" [of one canal]	
Sable palms	Trimmed Australian Pine [in a grid near Casba]	
Conifers, Cypress	Ficus Nitida	"Heavy leafed Hammock"
Pines	Ficus Benjamina	Cocolobo
Olives [in a grove]		Eucalyptus Avenue
Date Palms [a clump]	Bamboo	Cypress Avenue
Ficus elata	Sand	"Improve scrub" [near road][34]

What is referred to as buttonwood or button-mangrove (*Conocarpus erectus*) is not a true mangrove, but forms a transition community between the main mangrove communities and inland vegetation. The mangrove present along the shore here are largely the red and black mangrove (*Rhizophora mangle* and *Avicennia nitida*). Deering's desire to maintain at least some of the native qualities led not only to the preservation of large stands on some of the slightly elevated hummocks, but also to the creation of a large circular plantation with a clearing in the middle of what are labeled buttonwoods (one of the native mangrove species). This is structurally and ornamentally an interesting use of native plants as part of the garden.

As a result of the many changes, the difficulties and clumsiness of construction and subtraction by means of dredging, and the insistence on preserving particular fragments of vegetation and their topography, the Beaux-Arts symmetries and strict geometry of the early plans were eroded and finally nearly abandoned. The result was a looser and more irregular set of landforms, which appeared relatively "natural" to viewers of the time. Like the hairstyles of actresses that give away the period in which a film—even a historical costume drama—was made, so, too, there are stylistic touches, the fashion of a period, in landscape design that give away the date of a landscape's creation. The lagoon as it was built was a period piece of "naturalism," quite different from what a designer of the Renaissance or a restoration ecologist or filmmaker of today would create. One era's idea of "nature" and "natural beauty" is rarely the same as another's.

Landscape construction in the form of grading, major planting, and the finishing of the paths and bridges in this area continued through 1920, 1921, and into 1922, when it finally appears largely to have come to an end. In photographs of the time it still looked a bit raw and awkward, the way landscapes always do before they grow out and groundcovers spread and fill in, before trees recover from the shock of transplantation and begin to grow again, and new construction mellows with age and wear. Even after what was substantial completion, adjustments and additional planting continued until Deering's death in 1925.

chapter 10

DISASTER AND ENCORE

It is a commonplace to say that landscapes and gardens take a longer time to come to fruition than architecture, both conceptually and physically. Frederick Law Olmsted once explained about his methods in construction and planting regarding one of his parks that he was planting with the effect in mind of a forty-year time horizon to achieve desired effects. Thus it is not surprising that nearly a decade after the house was completed, work continued in the garden and large portions still looked awkward, even a bit naked and raw, although the work continued until 1925. Nevertheless, as things were settling down to grow out, fill in, and mature, the disastrous Great Miami Hurricane of 1926 nearly demolished it all (fig. 148). The city of Miami and much of the region were devastated. Although the concrete and stone structures that had been so carefully engineered withstood the fury of the storm, hundreds of trees were stripped, uprooted, and felled. The columns, urns, and busts at the semicircular basins were toppled and smashed, an oceangoing scow was driven by the surging waves across the Barge, shearing off statues, balustrades, trees, and the summer house, finally coming to rest in the garden atop the parterres at the foot of the south terrace. All of Deering's boats were smashed or sunk. Statues were toppled; the topiary arches on the sea arms and nearly every one of the giant terra-cotta pots were shattered, and all of the ornamental planting vanished. Roads and paths were impassable because of the debris that filled them. It was truly a disaster. Then his brother Charles Deering died in 1927. The property languished for a time, but was eventually taken in hand by the two nieces, Charles's daughters, whom James had doted on. One of their husbands, Chauncey McCormick, acting for the heirs, took charge, bringing back Pellegatta, McGinnis, and others from the original team to make repairs, and in the late winter of 1933–34 he asked Chalfin to visit and help with further repairs and renovations.[1]

Two interesting documents that resulted from this visit survive and provide details of what actually had been planted, replanted, and preserved. They reveal how invested Chalfin was in the garden, which in some ways was his magnum opus and last work combined. They appear also to reflect thought on the part of the two nieces' families, McCormicks and Danielsons, regarding the future of the property and their intention to open the estate for public visitation in the near future. One is the text of a guide for a tour of the house and grounds written in March 1934 during and after Chalfin's stay that February.[2] The other is a blueprint completed in June that he marked up, coloring various portions and adding annotations in pencil as instructions for repair and modification to the rose (fountain) garden.[3]

The guide begins with a walk from the entry gate to the house. After a tour of the house, it describes the principal features of the main garden, briefly visits a portion of the lagoon area, and returns. Along the way it covers sculpture and architectural features, mentioning some of the sources for the motifs and elements. Chalfin comments that there were many "curious tropical orchids and creepers flourishing in the trees" as one traverses the hammock. Along the entry drive he mentions colorful crotons, the overhanging trees, and in particular a strangler fig (*Ficus aurea*), rubber trees (*Ficus elastica*), gumbo-limbo (*Elaphrium simaruba*), pigeon plum (*Cocolobis laurifolio*), the red and white stopper (*Eugenia procera* and *Eugenia axillaries*),

FIGURE 148. Devastation from the Great Miami Hurricane of 1926, in the garden north of the house. The scrollwork in the foreground is part of the wreck of one of Deering's electric gondolas. (Vizcaya Museum and Gardens Archive)

and the sand box (*Hura crepitans*). At a clearing he describes Bermuda grass and a red-flowered border (*Russellia elata*) with yellow-flowering shrubby trees (*Cassia elata*) and Jerusalem thorn (*Parkinsonia aculeta*). Next came the brilliant royal poinciana (*Delonix regia*) and the mastic (*Sidoeroxylon faetidissimum*) and the large-leaved vine pothos (*pothos aurea*).

The octagonal piazza at the top of the entry drive with its statues was enlivened with a brilliant bougainvillea on lattice fences and an arbor. While crossing the bridge cut from the coral ridge attention is called to masses of ferns and screwpine (*Pandanus*) planted along the banks of the waterway. More *Ficus religiosa, F. elastica,* and *F. aurea* frame the avenue descending to the forecourt of the house. He also refers to "orchid-like" plants in the trees. Chalfin says the northern arch was framed with oaks, which he called *Pithecolobium dulce* (although the trees shown in contemporary photographs look like a variety of the evergreen oak common to south Florida, *Quercus virginiana*; it may, however, actually have been *pithecolobium,* which is a rapid-growing evergreen from Mexico with contorted branches planted in Florida at the time). Opposite, at the southern arch, were traveler palms (*Ravenala madagascarensis*), tropical almond (*Terminalia catappa*), Chinese fern palms (*Livistona chinensis*), and banana trees (*Musa* sp.).

On the steps leading up to the house were potted plants, including orange trees, sago palms (*Micro eyeas*), and clipped topiary of Australian pine (*Casuarina equisetifolia*), the latter in two Ming dynasty porcelain goldfish bowls. Chalfin does not comment on the planting of the courtyard, but looking at the working drawings, one discovers that the planting beds were originally edged with a low clipped hedge of ivy between the curbs and paving stones. The stones themselves had a miniscule green plant (unspecified), similar in scale to Corsican mint, growing in the joints, which softened the surface and room considerably. The four quadrilateral beds had an abundant mix of palms, ferns, flowers, and shrubs, which seems to have changed with plants rotated from the greenhouse and shade house fairly regularly.

Turning to the Italian garden, his guide remarks, "Of interest is the substitution of tropical plants for Box, etc." and the discovery of a subtropical pine that could be shaped and clipped, in place of trees usually used in topiary gardening. This refers to the Australian pine or casuarina, which can, of course, be clipped within an inch of its life, allowing one to produce extremely refined, tall, almost wafer-thin planes of green as well as large crisp volumes with it. A few of these original hedges are still in place near the house. As a substitute for boxwood, a simple shrub form of jasmine was used for the parterres. Chalfin calls it *Jasminum simplicifolium,* which was probably either *J. odoratissimum* or *fruticans.* Another hedge substitute was one of the aralias (which he called *Aralia guilfoylei*). Chalfin does not mention the creeping fig that covers the small twin gazebos with such felicity, planted more recently after the county took over. The twin basins below them are said to hold aquatic plants; he names papyrus (*Cyperus papyrus*) and exotic waterlilies supposedly from Zanzibar (*Nymphaea* sp.). The most prominent vegetation here is that of the clipped lines of live oaks (*Quercus laurifolia*). Chalfin does not specify in his guide what was used in the parterres and patterned beds beyond the hedging. Scrutiny of period photographs suggests begonias.

South of the Italian garden he does not bother to explain the vegetation, only that it contained "tropical groves." From a planting plan dated October 10, 1920, we know what was originally intended and one can see in photographs from the 1920s and 1930s that much of it was actually planted.[4] Adjacent to the marine garden, with its peacocks and bridge, and to each side were planted a group of what Chalfin referred to as "stately specimens" of Mexican fan palms (*Washingtonia robusta*). Returning to the Italian gardens in his guide text, Chalfin mentions the "secret" or "grotto" garden as "reserved for exotic plants (ferns, air-plants, etc.) The arbors are covered with the delicate foliage of *Vignonia speciosa* [*sic*]." He probably meant cape honeysuckle (*Tecomaria capensis*), which is in the *bignonia family*, or one of the trumpet vines native to the gulf. Today none of these vines or air plants remain, nor do the handsome wrought iron arbors by Samuel Yellin.

Correspondence now in the Robert Tyler Davis Papers of the Smithsonian Institution Archives records how Chalfin, true to form, not only takes on the chores he is asked to help with, but soon develops a relationship with McCormick, whom he knew years before, and launches a new campaign in the gardens for improvements, additions, and the installation of items that had not made it into the earlier work. The scope ranged from rounding up and repairing the broken and smashed terra-cotta pots and garden furniture to revisions in the planting and design of the rose garden, the creation of a new "white sand beach" in the lagoon with another stand of royal palms as a focal point for the view from the Casino, and a suggestion of a windmill. Working now in the depression without the aid of an office or staff, Chalfin proposed a revised scheme for the rose garden in March 1934. In June he sent a new plan to McCormick with the usual obsequious apologies for how long it took him to do so. Part of the problem, however, is that his eyesight is failing which he acknowledges in the accompanying letter to the large (quarter-inch scale) blueprint marked up with colored pencil indicating various plants and materials. The handwritten legend reads as follows:

1) The Hedge of Casuarina now exists
2) The phrase "Execute as Drawn" refers to parts now existing but not executed in conformity with original and existing drawings.
3) The white sand tracts are of 2 sorts. Four are marked as Paths. The other Eight, flanking the waterways are proposed so as to afford convenient approach to the jets of water, for clearance of obstructions and adjustments, and for clearing the surface basins.
4) the low Hedges or Edgings are of two sorts: High around beds for Amaryllis—to be of Trimmed Jasminum Semplicifolium: and *low* ground beds for Begonias—to be of Artillery plant.
5) The Circular outside Hedge is proposed to be of Cunninghamia sinensis clipped to 12′ high in place of the current scraggy Aralia. But at the Mermen fountain this Cunninghamia is to give way to Murcia—only as high as the Faces on the heads of the figures.
6) Metal strips in the ground to separate tracts. These strips are commonly used on drive-edges. They are sim[ilar] to the desired grade and present a narrow edge only to view.
7) Oxalis is used as a vivid green ground cover.
8) the spaces marked x are for grouped pots of Tubrose and Carnations. Those marked y are for tubs of Blue Agapanthus.

9) Beds 1-2-3-4- 1. Amaryllis - Hyb. Deep Crimson
        2., 3.   "   "   White & Rose
        4.   "   "   Scarlet
        5., 7., 10., 11. low Begonias 6. High Rose Begonias
        8., 9., 12. High White Begonias

The key on the drawing reads:

Red	*Red Sand*
Purple	*Flower Beds*
Yellow Green	*Waterways*
Gr. On Blue	*Hedge on circumference of Garden*
Yellow on Blue	*Artillery edging*
Black on Green	*Jasmine edging*
Yellow green	*Casuarina Hedge*
Grey	*White Sand*
Pale Blue	*Crushed Slate*

A   A is always a stone paving slab level to
Grade
To separate different color tracts, to accent
objects and passages.

X   Objects on Pedestals
Large pots on Pedestals
Blue of Paper—Tamped Coral[5]

Accompanying this drawing and list of June 1934 Chalfin also sent along to McCormick an eight-page memo entitled "Outline For Program of Work—Summer of 1934, *In the Garden— Vizcaya.*" The topics included: benches and chairs needed; disposition of antique objects now in the Casino and parterre (largely concerning repairs); annuals for the parterres; vines, shrubs, and trees; flowering plants to propagate; repairs to various structures—walls and paving— including portions of the seawall; regrading and replanting in various places; repairing the "busted" terra-cotta pots; replacing fill and soil that had been swept away (the entire maze garden had been lost to the hurricane); metal railings, basins, colored sand areas, and the removal of ragged and volunteer plants. It is a remarkable amount of work and was distributed throughout nearly the entire extent of the gardens. McCormick agreed to proceed with many of the tasks and decided to postpone others. From October 1934 Chalfin stayed on for twenty weeks into February 1935 engaged in the recovery.[6] Six closely spaced typed pages give details of the work and the problems encountered: "out of the twenty weeks—about eighteen will be assignable to reconditioning—reconstruction and the erecting of salvaged property: about two to aesthetic betterments—to be called beautification for clarity—and that, original purchasing

DISASTER AND ENCORE   215

agent of these antiquities, I compute the value of the restored objects I have enumerated, with individual notes on their value, as amounting to $13,000.00 purchasing value."[7]

Ironically, before this work was complete, two more storms hit Miami, in September and November 1935. Again statues were toppled, the Barge damaged, trees and planting smashed, ripped up, and portions of the lagoon garden swept away. Not fully restored from the hurricane of nine years before, the rose garden and the adjacent maze disappeared in the storm, leaving only the central fountain and a few benches standing three to four feet above the former beach sand and storm debris. The area of the Casba was particularly hard hit, and the woods on the hammock were a jumbled mess. Chalfin returned to Miami and took charge, directing repairs to the roof and gutters of the main house and tea house as well as the grounds at Vizcaya from late January through late March 1936. Extensive correspondence from January to May records the enormity of the tasks. These ranged from rounding up broken furniture and pots to working for weeks on end with crews to remove trash and debris dumped throughout the forest, gardens, and lagoons and righting vast numbers of trees—forest hardwoods, mangrove, palms, and oaks that he had planted throughout the estate—securing them with quantities of cable, rope, and rubber hoses. Portions had to be completely rebuilt with new walls, fill, soil, and paving. On the advice of Fairchild, he traveled to nurseries on the west coast of Florida that had escaped these hurricanes to purchase trees, shrubs, and quantities of groundcover, perennials, and annuals.[8] Among his many entreaties to McCormick to come down and assist him, with money and decision making, are his complaints about earlier repairs made by the staff and estate workers after the 1926 hurricane, which he pointed out were slipshod and came apart in the recent storm. While preparing his client for hefty costs anticipated for the repair of the house's roof and the new walls, he accounted for the costs of the first six weeks of his time, the materials, and the efforts of others, a total cost of $1,270, today seeming an unbelievable bargain. There is an echo of the wrangling of the previous decade between himself and McGinnis over how to do things, and of his leading the owner to further development and greater expenditures than initially intended.

> I have been away from Vizcaya a week, and I realize already how cured and calm one gets with a short absence from the imbecile and decadent naughtiness, the intrigue and idleness that reigns there. I must not let the calm overcome me. I was well aware of the cost to me of my normal life, and the perils I must encounter from my incapacity—when and if *there*—in certain fields—machines, electrical equipment—negro labor—my clerical insufficiency, and the social awkwardness of the proposed relations between me and all of you—but still—I must keep on and keep my *mad up*. I have not made immoderate judgements there, but in fact indulgent ones, and I see the obstacles that McG. Has encountered—sometimes with his eyes. But since I think, with a short tenure he will surely reduce the place to complete disarray, and to a perfected political machine with accompanying pools of filth, I do—now—promptly renew my proposal . . . [offers to meet with McCormick]. . . . Will I have raised a storm by my expenditures? I bought more soil than asked for, and more nursery stock than $400.00 would cover. And when new equipment, sound ropes, axes, and shovels, peat moss and manganese were needed I allowed these to be attributed to my activity.

In this way the gardeners got some hoes, the wood men some axes, and the diggers some shovels with unbroken handles. Trees were saved by my manganese, and the first grindstone was brought to Vizcaya,

I am not, therefore, really contrite for my sins, nor for the inconvenient manner of their commission.[9]

In January 1937 Chalfin wrote to McCormick:

My planting of last spring has thrived tremendously. The woods are full and flourishing. They show no trace of the hurricane, and—with the new soil I added are thicker than they used to be. But the overgrowth will soon be excessive. No one seems to know anything about forestry there—or lift a hand to it. But for the moment I am happy with the results. The place is far from ruinous. John West has finished all the grave depredations of the hurricanes. The Island [Barge; fig. 149], the Peacock bridge, the Sea-arms, balustrades and the Casino are all present in perfect order. Even the rose garden has a flourishing look. There is now paving work to be done I judge.[10]

FIGURE 149. The Barge in a 1934 photograph commissioned by Chauncey McCormick. By 1934 the Barge had been restored from the damage of the 1926 hurricane, with its planting full and fountains working again. Palms had replaced the topiary arches on the sea arms. They were about to be hit hard again by another severe storm. (Photograph by Frank Bell, Vizcaya Museum and Gardens Archive)

He went on to report on the intrigue among the staff and to discuss his inquiries regarding a new head gardener, listing several and suggesting that the best would be a man named Broomfield who wished to leave his current employment; however, Broomfield "would not come to Vizcaya with either McGinnis or Roberts on it—knowing them both too well. He is a very competent garden head—used to be our best man under Sturrock."[11] Soon thereafter another great war overtook America, and its social life once again was altered, even for the very wealthy. Chalfin was not to have another campaign on this seemingly unending project, his only lasting work, which was finally coming to an end.

chapter 11

SARGENT'S INTERLUDE

The records and letters of the men who made Vizcaya give facts and insight into their actions and motives, and the many photographs of construction tell us much about the process and its progress, but there are a limited number of photographs of life in the completed estate. There is, however, another source that both provides commentary and captures the spirit or flavor of Vizcaya as a place, alive and brilliant. This is a group of watercolors made by the American artist John Singer Sargent (1856–1925) even before Vizcaya was complete. They are interesting for what he selected and for what made an impression upon a person of his experience and eye. How he came to visit is also interesting and sheds light upon the Deerings' social life as well.

Like many other aging and wealthy industrialists from the Northeast, John D. Rockefeller found Florida attractive in the colder months and, partly inspired by his former colleague and confidant Henry Flagler, began to spend time there. In February 1917 John Singer Sargent traveled to Ormond Beach, just north of Daytona, to paint a portrait of Rockefeller. For Sargent, raised in Europe by American parents and devoted to the Mediterranean, especially to Spain and Italy, not only was Florida warm and a pleasant relief from winter in Boston and New York where he had been working, but it also possessed a languid and picturesque, even exotic, charm. Between sittings on the Rockefeller portrait, Sargent whiled away some of the time making studies of the local palmettos and alligators, which are among the most virtuoso watercolors he ever produced. Sargent wrote to his friend Thomas Fox: "My Rockefeller paughtrait [*sic*] is almost done—but requires several more days, after which I will pay Charles Deering a visit of a week or so at Miami. I have been sketching a good deal here, but palmettos and alligators don't make interesting pictures. Surf bathing is the best of this place."[1] Whether he was being ironic and making a joke or truly believed what he wrote, there is no question that these first watercolors he made in Florida are among the most astonishing performances in the medium of watercolor painting that he ever achieved. He also worked at them, producing at least seven separate studies of the palmettos and easily as many of alligators.

More than forty years earlier, James Deering's older brother, Charles, had met and become friendly with Sargent, even studying painting in Paris with his encouragement. After Charles Deering had been coaxed into coming home and taking the reins of the family business, he became one of Sargent's social contacts in Chicago and an important patron. Upon finishing his work at Ormond Beach, Sargent happily traveled down to stay with his old friend at his rental house at Brickell Point. While there he discovered the project that Charles's brother, James, had been engaged upon at Vizcaya for the past four years and was smitten by it. Over a period of a few weeks at Vizcaya, Sargent executed an important group of watercolors which are distributed today among the Worcester Art Museum in Massachusetts, the Metropolitan Museum of Art in New York, the Art Institute of Chicago, and the Melbourne Museum of Art in Australia. During his stay he also produced other watercolors of various subjects on the Miami River and in the Keys, a watercolor of a man reading in a hammock during the heat of

FIGURE 150. John Singer Sargent, *The Patio, Vizcaya*, 1917. Watercolor. (Anonymous loan. Photograph by Robert Lifson. Reproduction, the Art Institute of Chicago)

the afternoon, and a full-length portrait in oils of Charles Deering in white linen sitting in a wicker chair, both of the latter done in the shade of some trees at Brickell Point near the mouth of the Miami River.

Sargent was to some extent putting off a trip to Europe where World War I was destroying the world in which he, Edith Wharton, Henry James, and their circle had happily spent so much time when younger. At Vizcaya he found a freshly created evocation of aspects of the Mediterranean he had loved and painted successfully in the past, remarking that "it is hard to leave this place. There is so much to paint, not here, but at my host's brother's villa. It combines Venice and Frascati and Aranjuez and all that one is likely to never see again. Hence this linger-longing."[2] In another letter to Thomas Fox, a Boston architect and friend, he wrote that "the great big villa that James Deering has built down here (*Chalfin Architect*) is a mine of sketching. It is like a giant Venetian Villa on the Brenta with columns & loggias & porticos and ships down to the water, and dark gardens with statues just like Frascati. I can't tear myself away."[3]

While the northern portion, entry, and terraces had largely been completed as he portrayed them, the Barge and landscape to the south of the house were still very much under construction. One of his watercolors depicts Calder at work on the figures for the prow of the great stone barge under a jury-rigged awning and scaffold. At least four studies depict nude African American men relaxing in the shallows of Biscayne Bay under a group of mangrove (fig. 151). The location is clearly the area later known as the servants' beach, to which Deering had a path with stairs constructed from the rose garden. The men are almost certainly some of the Bahamians who had first arrived to work as laborers on Flagler's railroad, had stayed on afterward, and become part of the large workforce then engaged on constructing the south terraces, lagoons, islands, and gardens. In one of these figure studies, the curving stone break-water and arched bridge leading to the yacht landing can clearly be seen in the background. Deering was noted for his concern about the well-being of his workers, as many anecdotes recorded by his former employees and visitors demonstrate. Although the season of Sargent's visit was early spring, the backbreaking work in the sun necessary for the dredging, digging, filling, and construction of formwork for concrete foundations and walls, as well as the hauling and lifting of the stone employed in all the architectural features, certainly could put these men in need of rest and cooling down, which was provided by the nearby water under the shade of the mangrove. Sargent was fond of drawing the figure throughout his career, and finding this collection of muscular, naked, and unself-conscious workers on their break combined with water and dappled light, another of his recurring subjects, was an opportunity to create a remarkable group of extremely fluid and ravishing studies. In addition to being superb works of art, these sketches remind us that it was a man's world here, even during the war with so many away. With the exception of two women photographers on site from time to time, there were few women around until after the house was complete, and then only as domestics or guests.

James Deering was gratified by the attention Sargent paid to his accomplishment, writing to Chalfin the letter quoted above discussing the sculpture, and ended it saying: "So far as I know Mr. Sargent's stay is indefinite and you are very likely to see him here. He stated that ever since he has been in America he has been hungering for some architectural painting and asked permission to come here and do a lot of work. This of course I granted though to have anybody not a member of the household constantly about is not a great pleasure."[4] Despite such remarks, Deering clearly delighted in the presence of such a distinguished visitor and coaxed him into joining his extended boating and fishing trips south toward the Keys. Sargent wrote to a friend from the *Nepenthe* near the end of April: "it has seemed absurd to be lazily cruising about for ten days in these tropical waters with very little chance of sketching—and a strong moral pressure put upon one to fish"; and in an earlier letter: "By the way, I am extremely proud of having landed one weighing 140 pounds & 6' 10 inches long."[5]

Sargent was disturbed by Chalfin's insertion of canvas blinds between the pairs of clustered columns in the loggia between the court and the bayside terrace, but like everyone else since, could not think of a better solution short of eliminating them, which would cause other problems (fig. 153). To this Chalfin responded: "I am very much in agreement with Mr. Sargent about the curtains between the four columns. You will probably recognize that we are merely satisfying your requirements there, which were for a set of rain curtains and sun curtains

FIGURE 151. John Singer Sargent, *The Bathers*, 1917; Bahamian workers relaxing under the mangrove at the servants' beach with the recently completed harbor and yacht landing in the distance. Watercolor. (Worcester Art Museum, Museum Purchase, Sustaining Membership Fund)

also, and wind curtains as well. I think, with him, that the curtains can be withdrawn from the middle a great deal more, but will have to plan the matter on the spot."[6]

Two paintings of the east terrace overlooking the bay are equally interesting for they show a particular aspect of what has been lost. In one can be seen the freshly laid lawn across the entire front of the house, rather than the broad expanse of stone that today produces so much glare in the brilliant light of the region (fig. 154). Stone trim and balustrade sparkle between the blue of the water and the green of the terrace. In the other, one sees trees that were originally planted at the north and south, framing statues as well as the view (fig. 155). Several of these, too, like the lawn, have disappeared with changes in ownership, management, and sensibility.

Aside from being delightful works of art, Sargent's views give us a peek into the world of Vizcaya, its life and character at a particular moment. Although the Mound and south parterre gardens were very much still a construction site at the time, the entry drive, canals, and woodland paths with their statuary to the north of the house were complete. There are views of the arcade of the courtyard with its lamps, tile, and blue canvas drapery. The barge, even in its incomplete state, captivated Sargent, who painted it with the Venetian "barber pole" pilings conjured up by Chalfin. Although he painted them faithfully, Sargent, who had spent many years off and on in Venice sketching and working commercially, had an aesthetic problem

FIGURE 152. John Singer Sargent, *The Basin, Vizcaya*, 1917. Watercolor. (Anonymous loan. Photograph by Robert Lifson. Reproduction, the Art Institute of Chicago)

with the color palette employed on the pilings and obviously discussed it with Deering, who in turn passed his remarks on to Chalfin: "Three connoisseurs in art disagree with you as to the painting of the channel markers. Mr. Sargent expressed it in this way: The blue looks dirty when one sees the blue water, the blue sky and the blue of the house. Alongside of the blue the yellow also looks dirty. He, Charles and I have the same feeling about the matter."[7]

It is interesting to think of this trio, the immaculately dressed midwestern brothers—Charles, robust and fit; James, thin and ailing—and Sargent, bearded, roughly dressed, rotund, hard drinking, cigar smoking, a Europeanized Edwardian, sitting about debating the hues and values of colors on pilings compared with those of the sky, clouds, and reflections in the water. Nell Dorr, a photographer and writer whose husband worked for the general contractor, and whose brother-in-law, Louis Koons, worked as Chalfin's secretary and assistant while living on the *Blue Dog* for a time, recounted in an interview several years later: "I remember one day when I was in the woods with the children—they were still quite little—and they found a wonderful tramp. He had old clothes and a beard. The children played with him and climbed

FIGURE 153. John Singer Sargent, *The Loggia, Vizcaya*, 1917. Watercolor. (Anonymous loan. Reproduction, the Art Institute of Chicago)

into his lap and had such a wonderful time. When we went back to the house I got hold of Paul [Chalfin], whom we called 'Brother,' and I said, 'Brother, don't you tell Mr. Deering, but there is a wonderful tramp in the woods and the children adore him' then I described the man and told Brother what had happened. He started to laugh and he told me, 'that tramp is John Singer Sargent.'"[8]

Sargent engendered many anecdotes in his brief stay. Fond of swimming, he was in the pool on one occasion when a female guest happened by. It was Lillian Gish, who on seeing his walruslike frame sporting about asked her attendant from the staff who he was. On being informed that it was John Singer Sargent, the actress asked, "Who's he?" Later the painter asked who the attractive visitor had been. When he was told it was Lillian Gish, Sargent said, "Who's she?"

In contrast to his dazzling depictions of sea and coral stone structures, one oft-reproduced and evocative watercolor depicts the shady native hammock north of the house, which Deering had been at such pains to preserve (fig. 156). It shows a group of four white marble figures and bases framing a small, round clearing paved with the crushed cochina stone of the site. The trunks of a group of young live oak and gumbo-limbo trees twist upward in the dappled light.

FIGURE 154. John Singer Sargent, *Terrace, Vizcaya*, 1917; the northeast corner of the upper bayside terrace with its new turf and crisp stone balustrade. Watercolor. (Metropolitan Museum of Art, Gift of Mrs. Francis Ormond, 1950, 50.130.81n)

A path leads off through a gate beyond into the deep shade of the woods to the north. This was a place where Deering liked to walk, the path eventually leading to the shady spot out of sight from this view, where he installed several rustic chairs by the mouth of the creek at a point where the ridge of oolitic limestone forms a small bluff above the water. Today one can find the space depicted in Sargent's watercolor immediately beyond the northernmost of the pair of arches that frame the entry court. The low curbs, a couple of plinths, and a strangely naked and useless gate are still there. The figures, however, have been relocated, the trees and woodland path are gone. The site beside the creek to which Deering retreated to smoke and read has been separated, the canal fenced, the trees felled, and a house constructed. Sargent recorded it at a particular moment when it was fresh and as its authors intended. Now, only the ghost of this space remains.

FIGURE 155. John Singer Sargent, *The Terrace, Vizcaya*, 1917. Watercolor. (Anonymous loan. Photograph by Robert Lifson. Reproduction, the Art Institute of Chicago)

FIGURE 156. John Singer Sargent, *Shady Paths*, 1917. This view shows a small glade (now lost) immediately north of the arrival court, with sculpture now located elsewhere. A gate, located between the two farthest figures, that gave access to a path leading into the hammock still stands. Watercolor. (Worcester Art Museum, Sustaining Membership Fund 1910.37)

Aftermath

Ambitious projects often remain unfinished. Things cost more than the owner and the designers expect, construction nearly always takes longer than planned. At a certain moment, the weary owner runs out of energy, or interest, or money—or all three. Sometimes, after recovering from the initial building campaign, he returns for a second bout. But, frequently, he gives up, leaving the last phase of a project, which usually involves the landscape, uncompleted. And if the owner moves in prematurely, it is nearly impossible to finish properly.

Vizcaya was different. Work on the landscape continued for seven years after the house itself was finished and occupied. Deering was in residence for only a few months in the winter, so construction was not affected. Notwithstanding his nervous directives to Chalfin and the contractors, the pace did not slow. Nor did Deering tighten the purse strings. Despite his occasional complaints, and his accountants' concerns, he spent what it took to get what he wanted. Vizcaya did not bankrupt him, nor did it seem to affect his style of life in any way.

The fortuitous creative collaboration between Chalfin, Hoffman, and Suarez, did not—perhaps it could not—last. In 1915 Chalfin demoted Suarez to draftsman, and within two years the young Colombian had left; the subsequent work on the gardens was supervised entirely by Chalfin. In February 1917, soon after the house was complete, Chalfin convinced Deering to instruct Hoffman that he should not undertake any additional work and should only complete the ongoing electrical and plumbing installations in the house. This effectively terminated the architect's contract, leaving Chalfin in charge. Later there was a rancorous exchange of letters concerning the final settlement of Hoffman's fee, which Chalfin held to be excessive.

Three articles on Vizcaya appeared in 1917, in *Vogue*, *Harper's Bazaar*, and *Architectural Review*. *Vogue* listed Hoffman and Chalfin as "co-architects"; the other magazines called them "associated" or "associate" architects.[1] Hoffman had earlier generously agreed that Chalfin could call himself "associate architect" of Vizcaya, to enable him to apply for a New York state architect's license (which he received). When the articles came out, Hoffman was in France, serving as an officer in the Corps of Engineers. He was offended by Chalfin's self-promotion, and by his not giving credit to either Hoffman's colleague Ingalls or Suarez. "I told him what I thought of what he had done," Hoffman recalled later. "I never spoke to him again."[2]

Chalfin continued to call himself the associate architect of Vizcaya, and sometimes went further. In a 1917 letter to a prospective client, he wrote of Vizcaya: "I have built this house complete, drawn the gardens, and furnished the interior down to the minutest detail."[3] In the series of articles that he wrote about Vizcaya for the *Miami Herald* in 1934–35, he did not mention Hoffman and Suarez at all, and referred to himself in the byline as "Architect of Vizcaya." In 1954 he told Aline Louchheim (later Saarinen) of the *New York Times*, who was writing about the newly reopened Vizcaya, that "Hoffman did the plumbing, I did the house."[4] This was mean-spirited—and untrue. Hoffman threatened to sue, and obliged the newspaper to print a retraction.

Chalfin's poor behavior may be explained, in part, by the course of events. By 1917 he had devoted seven years to Vizcaya, and he imagined that this commission would be his ticket to a triumphant new career. That year he gained fame in New York City for a temporary transformation of MacDougal Alley, off Washington Square, into a picturesque French street, part of a charity benefit to aid the war effort.[5] He bought a country property in Greenwich, Connecticut (Deering lent him the money), where he is said to have entertained many "celebrities." In 1919, while still working on the Vizcaya gardens, he landed another high-profile commission: the decoration of Fifth Avenue from Washington Square to 110th Street for New York City's homecoming veterans parade. Chalfin did it all in great style, with Revolutionary War regalia on City Hall, garlands in Washington Square, and an Arch of Liberty adorned with illuminated balloons in Madison Square. He even designed the standards carried by the troops.[6]

The decorations for the parade, which was attended by more than two million people, were a great success, but other projects foundered. A $5 million resort in Cuba fell by the wayside.[7] Hollywood beckoned in the shape of Cecil B. De Mille, who expressed interest in Chalfin doing work for his studio, but that also came to naught. Earlier Chalfin had taken on a young Philadelphia architect, Phineas E. Paist, as his assistant (Paist would later design Charles Deering's interesting but stiff stone house at Cutler). In 1926 he and Paist built the Colonnade Complex in George Merrick's development of Coral Gables and, also for Merrick, designed a Mediterranean-style campus for the future University of Miami.[8] Architects such as Addison Mizner were building large houses in Palm Beach and Boca Raton, but not Chalfin. The problem was that almost everyone in Florida had heard rumors of the fabulous cost of Vizcaya, which was the worst sort of advertising. Chalfin looked farther afield. In the late 1920s, he established an office in Chicago and designed a series of domestic interiors for the Marshall Field family, and is said to have built a theater and a club.[9] Returning to New York, he decorated several Manhattan apartments, and designed theater sets. In 1929, he built an exquisite shop on Fifth Avenue for the Parisian perfumer Lentheric which Robert A. M. Stern has called "among the most elegant of French Modern Classical designs of the period."[10]

The stock market crash and the depression effectively put a stop to Chalfin's practice, since his luxurious, handcrafted brand of design was no longer in demand. Most of the great family fortunes survived, but the self-confidence that had produced the American Renaissance was gone. Vizcaya already seemed like a throwback to another time. As explained above, in the mid-1930s he spent some time at Vizcaya, putting the gardens back in order, but he was effectively in retirement. To make matters worse, this gifted visual virtuoso started losing his eyesight. Yet two small honors came to Chalfin before he died: in 1956 he was made an honorary member of the American Institute of Decorators, and the Florida South chapter of the American Institute of Architects gave him an award for Vizcaya. But by then, at eighty-two, he was too frail to attend the ceremonies. A contemporary photograph shows a well-dressed, stylish old gent with attractive, wizened features (fig. 157). The feeble eyes still sparkle. Not exactly a kind face, it radiates a sharp and quizzical intelligence.

While Chalfin's career suffered ups and downs, Hoffman's practice expanded and prospered. A comprehensive study of his commissions between 1908 and 1929 lists thirty-nine projects.[11] However, following the stock market crash, work dried up, and Hoffman also closed his office. He was not financially affected by the depression. Two years earlier, he had married a wealthy southerner, Virginia "Dolly" Kimball. Theirs was a leisurely, peripatetic life: winters in Florida, summers in France, where they owned a Parisian apartment as well as a country house, and the fall season in New York City.[12] Although Hoffman never again opened an architectural office, he did not stop designing, collaborating part-time with a New York City architect, Livingston Elder, with whom he built three apartment houses in Manhattan (he and his wife moved into the penthouse of one). Hoffman also continued to build residences, in New York, Florida, and Paris, often assisted by Dolly as interior decorator. Philip Johnson, who met Hoffman, described him as someone who "built large houses for his wealthy clients."[13] In the 1950s, one of these clients was the financier Clarence Dillon, for whom Hoffman designed a house in Montego Bay, Jamaica (later owned by Ralph Lauren).[14] Hoffman's last public project was a Federal-style ballroom addition to Gracie Mansion, the New York City mayor's official residence, on which he consulted to Mott Schmidt. In 1974, when he was nearly ninety, Hoffman designed a Neoclassical villa for C. Douglas Dillon in Hobe Sound, Florida.[15] It was an honorable if somewhat leisurely career, yet in his eclectic body of work nothing ever rose to the exquisite level of Vizcaya. The villa on Biscayne Bay was a once-in-a-lifetime experience.

Diego Suarez had a similarly unruffled life. After leaving Chalfin's employ in 1917, he worked for McKim, Mead & White and then set himself up as an architect in New York City. In 1921 his office (shared with Alfred Sides) was located at 10 East 50th Street. He designed a series of residences and gardens, mostly on Long Island. One of his works was a small house at Douglaston, Queens, on Little Neck Bay, built for Ada Louise Kendrick in 1924. The house was entered through a diminutive domed rotunda. Photographs of it in 1994 show a small casino buried in trees and lush planting.[16]

Suarez, who was described as a "charming gracious man," moved easily in society. His great-grandfather was General Francisco de Miranda, a Venezuelan adventurer and revolutionary and the forerunner of Bolívar.[17] His father was a Colombian diplomat and historian.[18] In 1937 Suarez married Evelyn Marshall, the sister-in-law of Brooke Astor and former wife of Marshall Field, the publisher and grandson of the founder of the Chicago department store. As a result of her divorce, Marshall had a trust fund with an annual income of a million dollars. She and Suarez lived in Manhattan and had a large country house in Syosset, Long Island, designed by Suarez in a Georgian Revival style that recalls the work of Delano & Aldrich.

Considering how Paul Chalfin had treated him, it might be said of Suarez that living well is the best revenge. After his fortunate marriage, he did not need to work for a living, although there is a record of his participation in 1946 as "consulting designer" to Edward Durrell Stone on a Brooklyn recreation center, so perhaps he, too, kept his hand in.[19] One of Suarez' hobbies was cataloguing the vast Field family silver collection that his wife had inherited. They were a formal and private couple—she apparently would see her children from her former marriage only by appointment. Although an American citizen, from 1948 to 1952 Suarez served as press

FIGURE 157. Paul Chalfin, 1956.
(Vizcaya Museum and Gardens Archive)

FIGURE 158. Diego Suarez (*left*) and F. Burrall Hoffman, Jr. (*right*), together again at Vizcaya, February 23, 1967. They flank Jefferson T. Warren, director of the museum. (Vizcaya Museum and Gardens Archive)

attaché and consular minister in the Colombian Embassy in Washington, D.C., and at the United Nations. He was a member of several prominent social clubs in the city and served as a trustee of New York University's Institute of Fine Art. He died at eighty-six.

Vizcaya aside, the creative legacy of Chalfin, Hoffman, and Suarez was slight. Nor did their common creation exert an influence on the design of other American country houses; Vizcaya was too unusual in conception, too grand in execution, and too personal in taste. Most of the estates built in the Northeast in the 1920s, such as John Russell Pope's Caumsett (1921–28) on Long Island, or Harrie T. Lindberg's Glencraig (1926) in Newport, were in the decorous Georgian style. Southern California architects, such as George Washington Smith, following in the footsteps of Clinton Mackenzie, built sprawling haciendas in various Hispanic styles—Mission and Spanish Colonial. In Florida, Mizner concocted a picturesque Moorish-Spanish style for Palm Beach and Boca Raton, and the New York architect Dwight James Baum designed Ca' d'Zan (1924–26) in Sarasota for John Ringling in a bumptious style that was modeled on a fourteenth-century Venetian-Gothic palazzo. Most American architects were not drawn to the Italian baroque. An exception was Philip Trammell Shutze, who served his apprenticeship with Hoffman and went on to design several handsome baroque houses, of which the Swan House (1926–28) in Atlanta is the best example.[20] But Shutze's generation closed the chapter on the great country-house era. As Vizcaya was being built, a new kind of architecture was taking shape elsewhere. Adolf Loos was launching the International Style in Vienna, Peter Behrens and Ludwig Mies van der Rohe were designing large abstract-classical country houses for the Kröller-Müllers in Holland, and Frank Lloyd Wright in Los Angeles and the Greene brothers in Pasadena were building residences that owed little to the past. Even that master of traditional domestic architecture, Sir Edwin Lutyens, was moving away from a literal representation of history toward abstraction in his masterful Castle Drogo.

The influence of Vizcaya's garden on contemporary landscape architects was likewise small. There were two Italian-American garden designers who knew as much—or more—than Diego Suarez: Ferruccio Vitale (1875–1933), who began working in America as a landscape architect in 1904, and Umberto Innocenti (1895–1986), who arrived in the United States in 1925 and apprenticed with Vitale.[21] Yet, despite their talent and prominent careers, neither ever had a client as munificent as Deering, nor a project of such scope and scale. The many gardens that Vitale and Innocenti executed on Long Island and elsewhere, while thoughtful and well made—and in many portions lovely—are both simpler than Vizcaya and less encompassing of the great Italian artistic tradition than it was. The work of Fletcher Steele (1885–1971) sometimes included Italianate elements, drawn from a four-month tour of Italy, but these do not owe anything to the work of Suarez and Chalfin. Ellen Biddle Shipman (1870–1950) was one of the best American designers with flowers and herbaceous plants, and Beatrix Jones Farrand (1872–1959) had a great imagination and eye for architectural detail, and produced some of the most thoughtful and restrained institutional plans and garden designs of the period.[22] Yet there is no sign that either was influenced by Vizcaya in any way.

AIR VIEW OF DEERING ESTATE
MIAMI, FLORIDA.

FIGURE 159. Vizcaya, aerial view, c. 1930. Ted Frutkoff captured all the landscape elements of Vizcaya: the formal gardens, the lagoon gardens, the thick jungle of the hammock, and the sparkling waters of Biscayne Bay. (Vizcaya Museum and Gardens Archive)

The stock market crash of 1929 and subsequent worldwide economic depression washed away the fortunes of many potential country-house builders, while for the survivors, caution became the prudent course. The era of the great estate was over. A swath of lawn, with a background of shrubs and trees, was both easier and cheaper to build than the terraces, beds, walls, stairs, arbors, and regular planting of the previous era. Colonnades, pergolas, basins, fountains, parterres, clipped hedges, topiary, and allées disappeared. Flower and shrub borders provided detail and color. These simplified gardens, derived in large part from English landscape parks, were also more appropriate to the casual lifestyle of the rich on both sides of the Atlantic.

There are aspects of Vizcaya's garden that anticipated developments associated with the late 1920s and 1930s: the use of concrete construction, for example, and a shift from Classical and Renaissance revival motifs to a stripped style similar to Art Deco. The quasi-Moorish roof garden of the boathouse, for example, with its tile pool and benches, and the simplified structure and decoration of the Casba with its piazza and its cypress pool, would have looked at home in Hollywood in the late 1930s. Chalfin's ongoing contact with the decorative world in Europe kept him abreast of new developments, and while he clung to Classical inspiration and motifs, he simplified and reworked these forms. For all of his time in Rome, and his references to Renaissance Italy, there is a strong overlay of Paris in much of his garden work.

The house and garden of Vizcaya did have an indirect connection with the most spectacular of American country houses, Casa Grande (1919–25) in San Simeon, California. Shortly after the house at Vizcaya was finished, Deering had as guests an old friend, Rose Douras and her pretty nineteen-year-old daughter, Marion. Marion Davies—her stage name—was a dancer in New York, a Ziegfeld Girl.*[23] The routine at Vizcaya bored her. "After dinner we'd see a picture on the patio; after that we'd go swimming; after that, breakfast in the morning." She also complained that "everybody should be on time."[24] Looking for fun, she escaped to Palm Beach, where she bumped into—literally, she was on a bicycle—an older man who was one of her (many) stage admirers. "It was the first time I really officially met WR," she later recalled.[25] WR was William Randolph Hearst, and within three years, Davies was the newspaper magnate's mistress. There is no record that Hearst ever visited Vizcaya, but Davies surely would have told him about it. In short order, he was making plans to build a splendid Spanish-baroque complex in California, at San Simeon—a Vizcaya-on-the-Pacific. The architect, Julia Morgan, worked hard to integrate her client's huge and varied collection of artifacts, but without the mediating hand of a Chalfin, the house lacked a unifying vision, and while it has some beautiful parts, it remains a flawed work of architecture.

Deering was a sociable man. In addition to his family and many friends, some of the famous visitors at Vizcaya included President Warren Harding, William Jennings Bryan, Thomas

* In her (unreliable) autobiography, Davies writes that her visit to Vizcaya took place in spring of 1916, but that is impossible since the house was still under construction. It was probably in 1918, since she sent Deering a thank-you present that Christmas.

Edison, William K. Vanderbilt, Lillian Gish, and Carl Fisher, the developer of Miami Beach. "It astonishes me some times to learn how intimate I am with some people that I have not seen or heard of for twenty years," he reflected.[26] Of course, people accepted Deering's invitations with alacrity, eager to see the fabulous house and gardens. "Always entertaining, always pretty women," groused Chalfin.[27] "My guests must be as comfortable as I am," Deering used to say, and he provided every sort of entertainment: bowling alley, swimming pool, hidden roulette table and bar, tennis courts, gondola rides, electric boats and canoes, as well as fishing excursions on the *Nepenthe*.[28] In the evenings, there were screenings of rented films in the court. Deering was a movie buff and often invited Hollywood people for lunch. On at least two occasions, he even permitted a movie company to film on the estate grounds.[29]

The heyday of Vizcaya for Deering was 1916–23 (fig. 161). After that, as his health worsened, he entertained less frequently. He spent a large part of his summers visiting European mineral springs and spas. He passed the summer of 1925 in Geneva, at the Hôtel Beau-Rivage, "the best and the most home-like that I know." He seemed to improve. "I am better than I was in Miami," he wrote a friend, "but I am quite willing to be better still."[30] It was not to be. A few months later, he fell into a coma and was taken aboard the SS *City of Paris* to return home. He died while the ship was off the coast of Newfoundland.[31] He was sixty-five. Sargent died the same year, Isabella Gardner the year before, and Charles Deering only two years later. Henry James had long since left the scene, so had Zorn. It was the end of an era.

The estate, which passed to James Deering's nieces and nephews after Charles's death, continued to be used as a winter home, alternating between the Danielsons and the McCormicks.* Unlike many of the Gilded Age country houses, Vizcaya stayed in the family; it never sat derelict, and it never changed uses. During 1934–36, Chauncey McCormick brought Chalfin back to oversee extensive repairs to the gardens and house. Soon after, Vizcaya was opened to the public on an occasional basis. In 1945 the farm property south of the Village and everything south of the Casino were sold. That left the house, the gardens, and the Village—about 50 acres. With time, the estate became more of a burden than a joy. Finally, in 1951–52, Deering's nieces, Marion Deering McCormick and Barbara Deering Danielson, who years earlier had bought out the other heirs, conveyed the house and land to Dade County for $1.4 million. They donated the furnishings and artworks, also valued at $1.4 million.

Like most of the surviving great country houses, Vizcaya has come to rest as a museum. What can one say about the diminution of a highly personal house, as it changes from private to public use? It is not just that some things are different, but how they are different. The life goes out of them. There were many small ways in which a house like Vizcaya was alive when it was occupied: the crunch of gravel in the drive, the clink of china and cutlery from a kitchen window, the smell of fresh-cut flowers, and the sight of a stack of letters on the hall table. The fountain still trickles melodiously in the court, but there are no birds chattering in

---

* In 1914 Charles Deering's daughter, Marion, married Chauncey McCormick (a distant relative of the International Harvester McCormicks). Her family disapproved of the match, and the couple eloped to Europe and were married in Uncle Jim's Paris house.

FIGURE 160. John Singer Sargent, *James Deering*, 1917. The masterful portrait captures Deering's calm willfullness. Watercolor. (Private collection)

FIGURE 161. James Deering with friends on a yachting excursion to Cuba, c. 1920. The helmsman is Deering's friend and neighbor in Coconut Grove, William J. Matheson, a New York industrialist. The woman on the extreme left, beside Deering, is probably Anne Winston. (Vizcaya Museum and Gardens Archive)

their cages, no curtains blowing in the open loggia. When you enter James Deering's library, the books are undisturbed, the chair cushions undented, the air untainted by the smell of a half-smoked cigarette.

Today crowds of noisy schoolchildren traipse over Chalfin's elegant marble floors; Latin girls in white gowns come to be photographed in the garden for their *quinceañera*; there are regular gala evenings that spill out onto the terraces. Occasionally, Vizcaya shows up as a "glamorous" setting in a film. Since 1985, the White Party, a celebrated AIDS fundraiser, takes place annually in the gardens, several thousand gay men descending on the house and turning it into an all-night bacchanal.[32]

But on a cool spring evening, when the crowds have gone, Vizcaya can be a curiously melancholy place. As Henry James wrote of the old Italian villas at the end of the nineteenth century: "About the finest there is something very grave and stately: about two or three of the best there is something even solemn and tragic. Part of the brooding expression of these great houses comes, even when they have not fallen into decay, from their look of having outlived their original use."[33]

FIGURE 162. The Barge, 1934. (Photograph by Frank Bell, Vizcaya Museum and Gardens Archive)

NOTES

Vizcaya Museum and Gardens Archive is abbreviated VMGA in the notes.

CHAPTER 1. AMERICAN RENAISSANCE

1. Bernard Berenson, *The Venetian Painters of the Renaissance*, x.
2. Werner Hegemann and Elbert Peets, *The American Vitruvius*, 7.
3. Harry W. Desmond and Herbert Croly, *Stately Homes in America*, 16.
4. Henry James, *The American Scene*, 224–25.
5. Lewis Mumford, *The Golden Day*, 213.
6. Edith Wharton, *Italian Villas and Their Gardens*, 11–12.
7. James Marston Fitch, *American Building*, 186, 228.
8. For an excellent account of the American country-house period, see Mark Alan Hewitt, *The Architect and the American Country House, 1890–1940*.

CHAPTER 2. DEERING'S TIME

1. *William Deering*, 122–23.
2. John A. Garraty, *Right-Hand Man*, 127.
3. Walter Dill Scott and Robert B. Harshe, *Charles Deering, 1851–1927*, 8.
4. James E. Deering to C. H. Haney, April 4, 1900. Deering Private Letter Book. McCormick–International Harvester Collection, Wisconsin Historical Society.
5. Scott and Harshe, *Charles Deering*, 73.
6. Quoted by Garraty, *Right-Hand Man*, 139.
7. Ibid., 141.
8. Barbara Marsh, *A Corporate Tragedy*, 47.
9. Ernest Samuels, *Bernard Berenson*, 425.
10. James E. Deering to Percy Peixotto, April 8, 1902. Deering Private Letter Book. McCormick–International Harvester Collection, Wisconsin Historical Society.
11. David McCullough, *The Path Between the Seas*, 284.
12. Paul Wolman, *Most Favored Nation*, 21.
13. *New York Times*, Jan. 13, 1897.
14. "It explained to him [Chalfin] why, after so many years of travel, Deering knew so little about the countries he visited or the people who lived there." Paul Chalfin interview with Robert Tyler Davis, May 1956. Robert Tyler Davis Papers, RU 7439, Box 4, Folder 20, Smithsonian Institution Archives.

15. Cyrus H. McCormick, memorandum, April 15, 1902. McCormick–International Harvester Collection, Wisconsin Historical Society.

16. James E. Deering to Percy Peixotto, April 8, 1902. Deering Private Letter Book. McCormick–International Harvester Collection, Wisconsin Historical Society.

17. Gari Melchers to Charles Deering, Sept. 8, 1912. Scott and Harshe, *Charles Deering*, 42–43.

18. Mrs. Cecila Adair (a housekeeper at Vizcaya) interview with Robert Tyler Davis, May 1956. Robert Tyler Davis Papers, RU 7439, Box 4, Folder 20, Smithsonian Institution Archives; Lillian Gish and Nell Dorr quoted by James T. Maher, *The Twilight of Splendor*, 208.

19. Handwritten notes, Paul Chalfin interview with Robert Tyler Davis, May 1956. Robert Tyler Davis Papers, RU 7439, Box 4, Folder 20, Smithsonian Institution Archives.

20. James E. Deering to E. C. Drum, April 15, 1903. Deering Private Letter Book. McCormick–International Harvester Collection, Wisconsin Historical Society.

21. Garraty, *Right-Hand Man*, 146.

22. Marsh, *Corporate Tragedy*, 42.

23. Garraty, *Right-Hand Man*, 189–90.

24. James E. Deering to Percy Peixotto, May 3, 1901. Deering Private Letter Book. McCormick–International Harvester Collection, Wisconsin Historical Society.

25. James E. Deering to Gari Melchers, March 9, 1903. Belmont Archive, Gari Melchers Estate and Memorial Gallery.

26. Scott and Harshe, *Charles Deering*, 62.

27. James E. Deering to Percy Peixotto, May 3, 1901. Deering Private Letter Book. McCormick–International Harvester Collection, Wisconsin Historical Society.

28. James E. Deering to O. M. Coulter, April 10, 1897. Deering Private Letter Book. McCormick–International Harvester Collection, Wisconsin Historical Society.

29. James E. Deering to Percy Peixotto, May 3, 1901. Deering Private Letter Book. McCormick–International Harvester Collection, Wisconsin Historical Society. Chalfin on Deering's "clap": Paul Chalfin interview with Robert Tyler Davis, May 1956. Robert Tyler Davis Papers, RU 7439, Box 4, Folder 20, Smithsonian Institution Archives.

30. Elsie de Wolfe, *After All*, 51.

31. Ibid., 60.

32. Paul Chalfin interview with Robert Tyler Davis, May 1956. Robert Tyler Davis Papers, RU 7439, Box 4, Folder 20, Smithsonian Institution Archives.

33. Ibid.

34. Chauncey B. McCormick, "James Deering, Manufacturer and Philanthropist, 1869–1925," unpublished memo, 3. McCormick–International Harvester Collection, Wisconsin Historical Society.

35. Maher, *Twilight*, 187.

36. I am indebted to Dave Hickey for this aperçu. "Palladio is never impersonating classical architecture, he is performing it, as Glenn Gould performs Bach," he wrote in "A House Undivided," *Harper's Magazine* (April 2003): 69.

37. Henry James, *Henry James Letters*, 346–47.

38. Mariana G. Van Rensselaer, "Recent Architecture in America–V," *Century Magazine* 31 (Feb. 1886): 555.

39. "The Richard Morris Hunt Papers," ed. Alan Burnham, Washington, D.C.: American Institute of Architects, vol. 1, 288.

40. Mac Griswold and Eleanor Weller, *The Golden Age of American Gardens*, 164.

41. Desmond and Croly, *Stately Homes*, 383.

42. Hewitt, *The Architect and the American Country House*, 3.

43. Donald W. Curl, *Mizner's Florida*, 59.

44. James, *American Scene*, 459.

45. Susan R. Braden, *The Architecture of Leisure*, 208–36.

46. Henry M. Flagler to Carrère & Hastings, Feb. 12, 1901. Henry M. Flagler Museum Archive.

47. "Whitehall: The Residence of H. M. Flagler, Palm Beach, Florida," *Architectural Record* 15, no. 4 (April 1904): 385–90.

48. Paul Chalfin to F. Burrall Hoffman, Jr., Feb. 12, 1914, VMGA.

49. James T. Maher, *The Twilight of Splendor*, 178.

50. Gari Melchers to Corinne Melchers, Oct. 24, 1904. Belmont Archive, Gari Melchers Estate and Memorial Gallery.

51. "Current Periodicals," *Architectural Review* 10, no. 9 (Sept. 1903): 139.

52. There are no dates on the Buena Vista sketches, but construction drawings for a gate lodge are dated 1912, which means that the entire project must have started at least a year or two earlier. Janet Snyder Matthews, *Historical Documentation*, 61.

53. Kathryn Chapman Harwood, *Muse News* (Jan. 1972): 353; quoted by Maher, *Twilight*, 178.

54. Handwritten notes, Paul Chalfin interview with Robert Tyler Davis, May 1956. Robert Tyler Davis Papers, RU 7439, Box 4, Folder 20, Smithsonian Institution Archives.

55. Charles A. Platt, *Italian Gardens*, 53, 113. For a full description of the Villa Turicum, see "The Renaissance Villa of Italy Developed into a Complete Residential Type for Use in America," *Architectural Record* 31, no. 3 (March 1912): 200–221.

56. See Neil Levine, *The Architecture of Frank Lloyd Wright*, 61, note 10.

57. James E. Deering to Harold F. McCormick, Aug. 18, 1922. McCormick–International Harvester Collection, Wisconsin Historical Society.

58. Wharton, *Italian Villas*, 211.

59. Quoted by Aline B. Saarinen, *The Proud Possessors*, 30.

60. Henry James, *Letters*, 389.

61. Elizabeth Anne McCauley et al., *Gondola Days*, 224.

62. Morris Carter, *Isabella Stewart Gardner and Fenway Court*, 182–83.

63. See Giovanna de Appolonia, "A Venetian Courtyard in Boston," in McCauley et al., *Gondola Days*, 179.

64. Douglass Shand-Tucci, *The Art of Scandal*, 206–10.

65. James, *Letters*, 389.

66. Martha A. S. Shannon, "The Isabella Stewart Gardner Museum, Fenway Court," *American Magazine of Art* 18, no. 4 (April 1927): 173.

67. See de Appolonia, "A Venetian Courtyard in Boston," 182–84.

68. Saarinen, *Proud Possessors*, 48.

69. Mumford, *Golden Day*, 215.

70. Henry-Russell Hitchcock, *Boston Architecture, 1637–1954*, 22.

71. Shand-Tucci, *Art of Scandal*, 217.

72. Saarinen, *Proud Possessors*, 51.

73. Harold Acton, *Memoirs of an Aesthete*, 244–45.

74. *The Letters of Bernard Berenson and Isabella Stewart Gardner, 1887–1924*, 354–55.

75. Paul Chalfin to Isabella Stewart Gardner, undated, c. 1905. Isabella Stewart Gardner Archives.

CHAPTER 3. HOFFMAN'S PLAN

1. R. Danielson, "Memorandum," March 27, 1953, quoting Barbara Deering Danielson, VMGA.

2. Carter, *Isabella Stewart Gardner and Fenway Court*, 191.

3. Paul Chalfin interview with Robert Tyler Davis, May 1956. Robert Tyler Davis Papers, RU 7439, Box 4, Folder 20, Smithsonian Institution Archives.

4. Ibid.

5. "Westlawn," the C. H. Lee residence. See *Long Island Country Houses and Their Architects, 1860–1940*, ed. Robert Mackay et al., 212–13.

6. Davis, a New York businessman and the author of *Salmon Fishing on the Grand Cascapedia* and *Woodcock Shooting*, died in a mysterious hunting accident in Quebec. Hoffman, too, was an avid sportsman.

7. *Long Island Country Houses*, 213.

8. Ibid.

9. Quoted by Maher, *Twilight*, 180–81.

10. Margo Harakas, "Vizcaya Architect at 97," *Palm Beach Post-Times*, Jan. 21, 1979.

11. James E. Deering to F. Burrall Hoffman, Jr., Sept. 26, Sept. 27, 1913, VMGA.

12. James E. Deering to Harry Creighton Ingalls, Sept. 29, 1913, VMGA.

13. James E. Deering to F. Burrall Hoffman, Jr., Oct. 8, 1913, VMGA.

14. Paul Chalfin to F. Burrall Hoffman, Jr., July 10, 1914, VMGA.

15. Ibid.

16. Paul Chalfin to Harry Creighton Ingalls, July 18, 1913, VMGA.

17. Wharton, *Italian Villas*, 246.

18. Corrado Ricci, *Baroque Architecture and Sculpture in Italy*, 220.

19. James S. Ackerman, *The Villa*, 66.

20. Giuseppe Mazzotti, *Ville Venete*, 82, 289, 317, 371–73.

21. "La villa Rezzonico a Bassano del Grappa," *Architettura cronache e storia* 2, no. 18 (April 1957): 893–99.

22. Handwritten notes, Paul Chalfin interview with Robert Tyler Davis, May 1956. Robert Tyler Davis Papers, RU 7439, Box 4, Folder 20, Smithsonian Institution Archives.

23. George Sitwell, *On the Making of Gardens*, 46.

24. Robin Karson, *The Muses of Gwinn*, 56.

25. Ibid., 4–5.

26. Paul Chalfin to F. Burrall Hoffman, Jr., July 10, 1914, VMGA.

27. The Vizcaya archive contains construction drawings of the house and a very complete record of the building process, but no renderings, drawings, preliminary sketches, or correspondence from the period 1910–13, when the house was being designed. We have been unable to locate a Chalfin archive; Hoffman appears to have destroyed his drawings and office records when he closed his office in 1930.

28. Daniela Mignani, *The Medicean Villas by Giusto Utens*, 92–94, 101.

29. "C. Mackenzie Dies; Yachting Official," *New York Times*, March 11, 1940, 19.

30. John F. Harbeson, *The Study of Architectural Design*, 8.

31. Ibid., 82.

32. Ibid., 75.

33. Ibid., 21.

34. James E. Deering to F. Burrall Hoffman, Jr., April 9, 1913, VMGA.

35. James E. Deering to F. Burrall Hoffman, Jr., Sept. 26, 1913, VMGA.

36. Paul Chalfin to F. Burrall Hoffman, Jr., Feb. 12, 1914, VMGA.

37. James E. Deering to F. Burrall Hoffman, Jr., Dec. 30, 1913, VMGA.

38. McHugh Manufacturing Company to Paul Chalfin, Feb. 1, 1917, VMGA.

39. Paul Chalfin to James E. Deering, Jan. 29, 1915, VMGA.

40. See Paul Chalfin to F. Burrall Hoffman, Jr., Feb. 12, 1914, VMGA.

41. "Heat Drives Paris Crowds to Seaside," *New York Times*, Aug. 20, 1911, C2.

42. James E. Deering to Paul Chalfin, June 30, 1915, VMGA.

43. Paul Chalfin to F. Burrall Hoffman, Jr., April 28, 1916, VMGA.

44. *Long Island Country Houses*, 213.

45. Joe Orr, interview with Robert Tyler Davis, Feb. 17, 1954. Robert Tyler Davis Papers, RU 7439, Box 4, Folder 20, Smithsonian Institution Archives.

46. "Paul Chalfin's 'The Blue Dog' Is an Unique American House-Boat," *Vanity Fair* 8, no. 5 (July 1917): 56; Donald C. Gaby, *The Miami River and Its Tributaries*, 59–60.

47. James E. Deering to F. Burrall Hoffman, Jr., Dec. 30, 1913, VMGA.

48. Handwritten notes, Paul Chalfin interview with Robert Tyler Davis, May 1956. Robert Tyler Davis Papers, RU 7439, Box 4, Folder 20, Smithsonian Institution Archives.

49. Paul Chalfin to James E. Deering, June 8, 1916, VMGA.

50. James E. Deering to F. Burrall Hoffman, Jr., Sept. 26, 1913, VMGA.

51. Vehicle registrations, VMGA.

52. F. Burrall Hoffman, Jr., to James E. Deering, Oct. 1, 1913, VMGA.

53. *Portrait of an Era in Landscape Architecture*, unpaginated.

54. Braden, *Architecture of Leisure,* 155.

55. Joe Orr, interview with Robert Tyler Davis, Feb. 17, 1954. Robert Tyler Davis Papers, RU 7439, Box 4, Folder 20, Smithsonian Institution Archives.

56. James E. Deering to F. Burrall Hoffman, Jr., Nov. 1, 1915, VMGA.

57. James E. Deering to F. Burrall Hoffman, Jr., July 27, 1915, VMGA.

58. James E. Deering to Paul Chalfin, July 29, 1915, VMGA.

59. Paul Chalfin to James E. Deering, Aug. 5, 1915, VMGA.

60. Maher, *Twilight*, 68.

61. James E. Deering to Paul Chalfin, Jan. 14, 1916, VMGA.

62. F. Burrall Hoffman, Jr., to James E. Deering, April 13, 1915, VMGA.

63. Fred T. Ley & Company to Paul Chalfin, July 17, 1916, VMGA.

64. James E. Deering to Paul Chalfin, July 21, 1916, VMGA.

65. James E. Deering to Paul Chalfin, Jan. 23, Jan. 24, Jan. 27, 1917, VMGA.

66. James E. Deering to Paul Chalfin, April 7, 1914, VMGA.

67. Paul Chalfin to James E. Deering, Feb. 13, 1915, VMGA.

68. Maher, *Twilight*, 203.

69. "'Vizcaya,' the Villa and Grounds: A House at Miami, Florida," *Architectural Review* 5, no. 7 (July 1917): 123.

70. Paul Chalfin, "Romance of History in the Language of Art," *Miami Herald*, Dec. 23, 1934.

71. See, for example: Maher, *Twilight*, 198; John B. Bayley, "The Villa Vizcaya," *Classical America* 3 (1973): 72; Hewitt, *The Architect and the American Country House*, 145; and Rogers, *Landscape Design*, 400.

72. "Vizcaya," *Architectural Review*, 143.

73. Ibid., 123.

74. "The Gardens of Vizcaya," *Vogue* (July 1917): 76.

75. Acton, *Memoirs of an Aesthete*, 5.

76. Harold Acton, *Great Houses of Italy*, 140–43.

77. See David Plante, "A Last Fantasy in Florence," *New Yorker* (July 10, 1995): 44.

78. *The Letters of Bernard Berenson and Isabella Stewart Gardner*, 633.

79. Paul Chalfin to Arthur Acton, Feb. 23 [year illegible], VMGA.

80. Robert Hughes, *American Visions*, 216.

81. Charles Moore, *Daniel H. Burnham*, vol. 1, 47.

82. "Gardens," *Vogue*, 36.

83. James E. Deering to Paul Chalfin, May 11, 1917; Paul Chalfin to James E. Deering, Oct. 15, 1917, VMGA.

84. Paul Chalfin to James E. Deering, May 14, 1917, VMGA.

85. Marcus Binney, "Villa Vizcaya, Florida–I," *Country Life* (Jan. 10, 1980): 74.

86. James E. Deering to F. Burrall Hoffman, Jr., Dec. 30, 1913, VMGA. Maher, *Twilight*, 195; for typical house construction costs, see *Architectural Forum* 49, no. 3 (Sept. 1928): 324–400.

87. James E. Deering to Paul Chalfin, July 26, 1916, VMGA.

88. R. Danielson, "Memorandum," March 27, 1953, quoting Barbara Deering Danielson, VMGA.

89. James E. Deering to Paul Chalfin, Jan. 22, 1919, VMGA.

90. "100 in Florida over $10,000," *New York Times*, Sept. 2, 1925, 3.

91. "Last Will and Testament of James Deering," May 18, 1922. McCormick–International Harvester Collection, Wisconsin Historical Society.

92. James E. Deering to F. Burrall Hoffman, Jr., April 9, 1913, VMGA.

93. Brendan Gill, "F. Burrall Hoffman, Jr.," *Architectural Digest* 50, no. 7 (July 1993): 40.

94. Maher, *Twilight*, 188.

95. Geoffrey Scott, *Architecture of Humanism*, 187.

96. "Vizcaya," *Architectural Review*, 123.

97. Ibid., 122. See also Scott and Harshe, *Charles Deering*, 75.

98. See Giuseppe Mazzotti, *Palladio and Other Venetian Villas*, 269.

99. Paul Chalfin, Vizcaya Guidebook, manuscript c. 1935, 13, VMGA. Maher, *Twilight*, 188.

100. Gianfranco Gritelli, *Juvarra*, vol. 1, 323; vol. 2, 238.

101. Travel sketchbook. Hoffman archive, Canadian Centre for Architecture.

102. Paul Chalfin to James E, Deering, Feb. 22, 1915, VMGA.

103. Danielson, "Memorandum."

104. Scott, *Architecture of Humanism*, 185.

105. Horace, *The Odes of Horace*, trans. David Ferry (New York: Farrar, Straus and Giroux, 1997), 187.

CHAPTER 4. CHALFIN'S ROOMS

1. James E. Deering to F. Burrall Hoffman, Jr., June 2, 1914, VMGA.

2. Paul Chalfin to F. Burrall Hoffman, Jr., July 10, 1914, VMGA.

3. "Whitehall," 385–90.

4. James E. Deering to F. L. McGinnis, Oct. 9, 1919, VMGA.

5. Quoted in Bayley, "The Villa Vizcaya," 78.

6. Elsie de Wolfe, *The House in Good Taste*, 319.

7. Paul Chalfin interview with Robert Tyler Davis, May 1956. Robert Tyler Davis Papers, RU 7439, Box 4, Folder 20, Smithsonian Institution Archives.

8. Handwritten notes, Paul Chalfin interview with Robert Tyler Davis, May 1956. Robert Tyler Davis Papers, RU 7439, Box 4, Folder 20, Smithsonian Institution Archives.

9. Edith Wharton and Ogden Codman, Jr., *The Decoration of Houses*, 123.

10. Paul Chalfin to C. Matlock Price, Sept. 28, 1917, VMGA.

11. Quoted in Marcus Binney, "Villa Vizcaya, Florida—II," *Country Life* (Jan. 17, 1980): 156.

12. "Vizcaya," *Architectural Review*, 141.

13. Mario Praz, *The House of Life*, 88.

14. "Vizcaya," *Architectural Review*, 41–42.

15. According to the housekeeper, there was a "great deal of entertaining . . . services always for 30 people." Mrs. Cecilia Adair interview with Robert Tyler Davis, May 1956. Robert Tyler Davis Papers, RU 7439, Box 4, Folder 20, Smithsonian Institution Archives.

16. Quoted in Binney, "Villa Vizcaya, Florida—II," 157.

17. "Vizcaya," *Architectural Review*, 142.

18. Paul Chalfin to Charles E. Deering, Feb. 13, 1915, VMGA.

19. Paul Chalfin, Vizcaya Guidebook, manuscript c. 1935, 20, VMGA.

20. Charles E. Deering to Paul Chalfin, March 21, May 22, May 29, 1916; Paul Chalfin to Charles E. Deering, May 11, 1917, VMGA.

21. "Gardens," *Vogue*, 37.

22. Binney, "Villa Vizcaya, Florida—II," 156.

23. Paul Chalfin to Charles E. Deering, Aug. 4, 1916, VMGA.

24. Handwritten notes, Paul Chalfin interview with Robert Tyler Davis, May 1956. Robert Tyler Davis Papers, RU 7439, Box 4, Folder 20, Smithsonian Institution Archives.

25. "Vizcaya," *Architectural Review*, 143.

26. Paul Chalfin interview with Robert Tyler Davis, May 1956. Robert Tyler Davis Papers, RU 7439, Box 4, Folder 20, Smithsonian Institution Archives. Doris Littlefield, who was a curator at Vizcaya between 1962 and 1996, recalls Eustace Edgecombe, who had been a houseman at Vizcaya, telling her that he had observed Deering's "women" coming to the house "with some regularity." Private communication to author.

27. According to Barbara Danielson, it is common family lore that Deering had a mistress, although she does not recall her name. Private communication to author. According to Chalfin, the mistress was Anne Winston (see Paul Chalfin interview with Robert Tyler Davis, May 1956. Robert Tyler Davis Papers, RU 7439, Box 4, Folder 20, Smithsonian Institution Archives). The Winstons were Deering's very close friends, and they often traveled together, but we have found nothing to substantiate Chalfin's claim.

28. Paul Chalfin interview with Robert Tyler Davis, May 1956. Robert Tyler Davis Papers, RU 7439, Box 4, Folder 20, Smithsonian Institution Archives.

29. Paul Chalfin interview with Robert Tyler Davis, May 1956. Robert Tyler Davis Papers, RU 7439, Box 4, Folder 20, Smithsonian Institution Archives.

30. Mrs. Cecilia Adair interview with Robert Tyler Davis, May 1956. Robert Tyler Davis Papers, RU 7439, Box 4, Folder 20, Smithsonian Institution Archives.

31. Corinne Melchers to her mother, March 1, 1923. Belmont Archive, Gari Melchers Estate and Memorial Gallery.

32. Wharton and Codman, *Decoration of Houses*, 13.

33. De Wolfe, *House in Good Taste*, 25.

34. Maher, *Twilight*, 177.

35. Scott, *Architecture of Humanism*, 36.

36. Ibid., 28.

37. Ibid., 37.

38. Paul Chalfin to James E. Deering, Feb. 24, 1915, VMGA.

39. "Vizcaya," *Architectural Review*, 121.

40. Aline B. Louchheim, "Biscayne Bay's New Showplace," *New York Times*, March 15, 1953, X8.

41. "Vizcaya," *Architectural Review*, 123.

CHAPTER 5. FLORIDA, THE DEERINGS, GARDENS, HORTICULTURE, AND LANDSCAPE

1. I am indebted to an extremely succinct and brief account of this current theory in John McPhee's remarkable work, *Annals of the Former World*, 558–59.

2. See Victor E. Shelford, *The Ecology of North America*, 474–85, for a discussion of this community of plants and animals.

3. Baedeker, *The United States*, 4th rev. edition, 1909, 611.

4. Ibid., 611.

5. The Buena Vista estate was in an area of Miami north of the present urban center which later became an industrial area, only to decline for several decades in the latter part of the twentieth century. Today the area is rapidly developing into a design, interior decorating, and furnishing district with artists and galleries as well. A small park purchased and built by the City of Miami to produce a green buffer between Charles Deering's estate entry drive that extended to Biscayne Bay on the east and development, which he considered offensive, became known as Cow Pasture Park. One can still find it at the intersection of N.E. 2nd Avenue and N.E. 36th Streets.

6. David Fairchild, *The World Was My Garden, Travels of a Plant Explorer*, 401.

7. Ibid., 419.

8. See Rocco J. Ceo and Joanna Lombard, *Historic Landscapes of South Florida*, 28–32.

9. Ibid., 28–30, notes 6, 7, 8, p. 32.

10. Stevens to his wife, April 21, 1916, from Miami, *Letters of Wallace Stevens*, 189, 191–92.

11. Stevens, ibid., to Harriet Monroe, Feb. 3, 1926, p. 227, and to Samuel French Morse, May 27, 1943, p. 449.

12. The plan for Chicago was prepared under the direction of the Commercial Club between 1906 and 1909 by Burnham and Bennett and was edited by Charles Moore. It is an astonishing document, and, with the possible exception of the Greater London Plan prepared between 1944 and 1946 for the Greater London Council (GLC) by Patrick Abercrombie or the Ensance Plan for Barcelona by Idelfonso Cerda, it is hard to think of any document quite comparable, anywhere at any time in the history of city planning. Both Deerings were early subscribers and supporters of this project. See Charles Moore, *Daniel Burnham, Architect, Planner of Cities*, 1:142, 187, 199; 2:45.

CHAPTER 7. A WATERY WORLD

1. Baedeker, *United States*, 622.

2. Interview with Grace W. Bohne, May 28, 1956, VMGA.

3. Ibid.

4. This is an unnumbered large blueprint with Chalfin's office title block dated Dec. 20, 1917, revised Jan. 16, 1918. It shows the entire property, the three small islands resulting from dredging, indicates

the channel as being 70 feet wide, and has been used to annotate areas of grass and groundcover throughout the estate with colored pencils, VMGA.

5. Drawing on Chalfin's title block from November 1916 titled "Pennants and Bargees," VMGA.

CHAPTER 8. IMAGINATION, DESIGN, AND CONSTRUCTION

1. Kenyon Cox, *The Classic Point of View*, 85.

2. Chalfin to Deering, Oct. 7, 1919, VMGA.

3. Chalfin to Sturrock, Western Union Telegram, Dec. 15, 1914, VMGA.

4. Sturrock to Chalfin, handwritten list, Dec. 16, 1914, VMGA.

5. Chalfin to Deering, Aug. 7, 1915, VMGA.

6. Platt, *Italian Gardens*, 13–16.

7. Wharton, *Italian Villas and Their Gardens*, 8.

8. Ibid., 12.

9. Maher, *Twilight*, 190.

10. It is still a touchstone for revival style advocates, most recently having been reprinted by the Classical Society in the United States. It also appears occasionally on reading lists in various curriculums at American universities interested in this period or attempts to produce architectural designs in Neoclassical, Palladian, or other revival styles.

11. Maher, *Twilight*, 191–92.

12. Rice to Deering, 1915, VMGA.

13. Diego Suarez wrote to the *New York Times* in 1952 in response to his outrage at an article written by Aline B. Loucheim (Saarinen) that appeared March 15, 1952, crediting Chalfin with the design of house and gardens of Vizcaya, Vizcaya Archive. His account agrees with the interview he he gave to Maher and with the account of Hoffman's in response to the same article and with voluminous support in the VMGA.

14. Hoffman to Chalfin, Oct. 20, 1913, VMGA.

15. Photos in the Vizcaya Archive show several variations of the house with the laundry wing, an early design for the twin entry gate pavilions, and the later version of each, but no photos have yet been found of the model executed for the garden.

16. From a six-page typescript in the Vizcaya Archive intended for the article written by Suarez and published in the *New York Times* in condensed form May 17, 1952. Excerpts from this text have been frequently quoted in Maher, Bayley, Davidson, and Harwood.

17. Chalfin to Deering, Dec. 11, 1914, VMGA.

18. Chalfin to Deering, Dec. 19, 1914, VMGA.

19. Deering to Chalfin, Dec. 22, 1914, VMGA.

20. Hoffman to Deering, Sep. 29, 1915, VMGA.

21. Sturrock to Chalfin, Oct. 4, 1915, VMGA.

22. Undated letter from Chalfin at the Green Tree Inn, Miami, to Koch in the New York office, followed by telegrams and letters on Dec. 2, 1915, on the topic, and then on Dec. 15, by a wire to Mrs. Suarez stating that they are thankful Suarez is to return to the project, VMGA.

23. Job # 93, set # 1, VMGA.

24. Although a unique undated ozalid paper print (see note 26 below), it is clearly from late 1915 or early 1916 and produced subsequent to Suarez' trip to Italy after his brother's death and visit to the Villa Corsini in Rome where he measured the cascade. It still shows the earlier garden stairs from the south terrace and semicircular basins that were to be built, demolished, and replaced, VMGA.

25. Suarez draft, *New York Times* article, VMGA.

26. This method of reproducing or copying an original drawing made on transparent paper or linen was relatively simple compared with blueprints, which required an elaborate process employing chemical baths, exposure to light, water baths, and hanging out to dry, all of which took considerable time and space. For an ozalid print, one merely exposed the original drawing and a sensitized (chemically coated) paper together to a strong light—either an electric desk lamp under a piece of glass or taped together on a window in the sun for a few minutes—and then one placed the coated paper in a tube with a wad of cotton that had some ammonia on it; within minutes the image of the original would appear on the second piece of paper. Eventually machines employing this method were developed that utilized rollers, lights, and bottled ammonia, that could handle large drawings at fairly high speeds, and came to be used universally in offices and copy houses until the advent of digital copying at the end of the twentieth century.

27. Undated paper print from late 1914/early 1915, "Estate of James Deering, Esq., General Layout of Garden," VMGA.

28. Deering to Chalfin, Jan. 23, 1915, VMGA. Chalfin responded, "misunderstandings with Suarez seem interminable," Feb. 17, 1915, VMGA.

29. Deering to Hoffman, letter from the Hotel Halcyon, Miami, Fla., Dec 1, 1913, VMGA. Even though Deering had engaged Joseph McDonald, an engineer who had helped Flagler get his railroad built and had also been a member of the Miami City Council, to be his overall supervisor and to help with situations such as this, he was reluctant to ask for governmental permission for anything more than was absolutely necessary While McDonald knew everyone, was technically superb, and was the perfect person to get things done in south Florida and would prove invaluable throughout the remaining years, including getting the barge built, the location was wisely set behind the existing shoreline.

30. Chalfin to Hoffman, June 10, 1914, VMGA.

31. Hoffman to Deering, June 9, 1914, VMGA.

32. Deering to Hoffman, June 20, 1914, from rue Spontini, Paris, VMGA.

33. Chalfin to Deering, Feb. 17, 1915, VMGA.

34. Chalfin to Deering, Feb. 22, 1915, VMGA.

35. Deering to Chalfin from Brickell Point, Coconut Grove, March 25, 1915, VMGA.

36. Deering to Chalfin, March 27, 1915, VMGA.

37. Deering to Chalfin, June 15, 1915, VMGA.

38. Deering to Chalfin from Chicago, July 12, 1915, VMGA. The three "sand islands" were created largely from material dredged from the channel created to lead from his dock out to the deeper water. The largest is seen in photos in the Vizcaya Archive to have been heavily planted with palms. Later Deering and the State of Florida argued over ownership of them to his consternation.

39. Calder studied at the Pennsylvania Academy of Fine Arts and for two years in Paris. In 1905 he moved to Pasadena where he lived until 1910. In 1913 he was made Acting Chief of Sculpture for the Panama-Pacific Exposition in San Francisco, executing numerous ambitious works in California between 1913 and 1915. In 1915, partly as a result of the Deering commission, he moved to New York City.

40. Chalfin to Calder at 116 Bake Street, Oakland, Calif., Oct. 5, 1915, VMGA. This and the ensuing quotations are all to be found in letters and telegrams in several separate folders in the archive.

41. Deering to Chalfin, Jan. 8, 1916, VMGA.

42. Deering to Chalfin, Jan. 9, 1916, VMGA.

43. Chalfin to Deering, Jan. 18, 1916, VMGA.

44. Chalfin to Phineas Paist, Jan. 19, 1916, VMGA.

45. Chalfin to Deering, Jan. 22, 1916, VMGA.

46. Deering to Chalfin from Brickell Point, Coconut Grove, Jan. 14, 1916, VMGA.

47. Chalfin to Deering in Florida, Jan. 31, 1916, VMGA. The "regular" is one of several he had hired to work on the site, most likely one of the two Lyons brothers.

48. Deering to Chalfin from Brickell Point, March 23, 1916, VMGA.

49. Chalfin to Deering, March 28, 1916, VMGA.

50. Deering to Chalfin, March 23, 1917, VMGA. A watercolor by Sargent of this state of affairs is now in the Melbourne Museum of Art in Australia.

51. Calder to Chalfin, 22 April 1917, VMGA.

52. Chalfin to Deering, 4 May 1917, VMGA.

53. Deering to Chalfin, May 7, 1917, VMGA.

54. Sturrock to Chalfin, Nov. 9, 1915. VMGA.

55. In a similar manner after months of negotiations, Chalfin's brother Bruce, who lived in Cuba at the time, was able to secure many thousands of antique handmade roof tiles for the project.

56. Deering to Louderback, March 8, 1918, VMGA.

57. Deering to Chalfin, June 20, 1920, VMGA.

58. Deering to Chalfin, Sep. 16, 1919, VMGA.

59. Deering to Chalfin, May 20, 1919, VMGA.

60. Deering to Chalfin, May 22, 1919, VMGA.

61. Chalfin to Deering, May 1918, VMGA.

62. McLean to Chalfin, July 5, 1918, VMGA.

63. Chalfin to McLean, July 8, 1918, VMGA.

64. It is interesting to hear them discussing casuarinas, or Australian pines, as an unknown quantity. As it has developed they thrived and grew remarkably well, so well that they were adopted by commercial growers to act as windbreaks for the citrus groves and to help fight frost problems. As such they were planted in enormous quantities in the Indian River area north of Miami and Palm Beach and elsewhere throughout south Florida, only to escape the world of agriculture and invade the native plant communities, choking out natives, so much so that it is illegal to plant them in Florida today.

65. McLean to Chalfin, July 17, 1918, VMGA.

66. Deering to Chalfin, March 25, 1920, VMGA.

67. Deering to Chalfin, March 12, 1920, VMGA.

68. Deering to Chalfin, March 25, 1920, VMGA.

69. F. L. McGinnis to Chalfin, Jan. 6, 1920, VMGA.

70. McGinnis to Chalfin, April 28, 1920, VMGA.

71. McGinnis to Chalfin, May 4, 1920, VMGA.

72. Author's addition of sums tallied in various correspondence in VMGA.

73. Deering to Chalfin, Sept. 24, 1919, VMGA.

74. I. N. Court diary, VMGA.

75. Construction Drawing G13, April 1, 1916, VMGA.

76. Fairchild Travel Log, Feb. 14, 1914, Fairchild Tropical Botanic Gardens Archive.

77. There were undoubtedly others; the Vizcaya archives, while copious, have been curiously organized so that one must hunt through several dozen areas to piece together such lists or summaries.

78. A peacock appears on the frontispiece of *The Dial* magazine in April 1921, which contained writing by Slater Brown, Marsden Hartley, D. H. Lawrence, Henry McBride, and Paul Rosenfeld. One needs only to think of Aubrey Beardsley, or of Whistler's astonishing Peacock Room for the Frederick Leyland

residence of 1876, now installed in the Freer Museum in Washington, D.C., and the remarkable peacock sconce by Alexander Fisher, now at the Victoria and Albert Museum, or of their use and implication in the work of Gustav Klimt to consider what these bird sculptures may have meant to Chalfin.

79. Samuel Yellin, "Iron in Art," *Encyclopedia Britannica*, 14th ed. (1940), vol. 12; see also H. J. Magaziner, *The Golden Age of Ironwork*, 21–23, and illus. pp. 24–26, 28, 29, 32, 33, 107, 163.

80. Suarez interview with Madeline C. Berry, Dec 13, 1958, VMGA.

81. Chalfin, typed manuscript guide to the property of 1934, 3, VMGA.

82. Ibid., 21.

83. Ibid., 21.

84. See John Dixon Hunt's introduction to the reissue of *On the Art of Making Gardens* by Sir George Sitwell, especially vii–xii.

85. One of Sitwell's principal sources was psychological theory as developed by William James, as well as the philosophy of Herbert Spencer, *On the Art of Garden Making*, 78–81. His allusion at one point to the Law of Relativity (80) is in regard to psychology, not to Einstein's physics of the same era.

86. Sitwell, *On the Art of Making Gardens*, 44.

87. Ibid.

88. Ibid., 46.

89. Ibid., 35.

90. Ibid., 98.

91. Ibid., 106.

92. Ibid., 50.

93. Ibid., 98.

94. Ibid., 104.

CHAPTER 9. FARM VILLAGE AND LOST LAGOON

1. Deering to Chalfin, Dec. 8, 1914, VMGA.

2. Chalfin to Deering, Feb 17, 1915, VMGA.

3. Ibid.

4. Deering to Hoffman, July 12, 1915, VMGA.

5. Hoffman to Chalfin, Nov. 10, 1915, VMGA.

6. Hoffman to Chalfin, Dec. 27, 1915, VMGA.

7. Chalfin to Deering, 12 July 1915, VMGA.

8. Deering to Chalfin, Oct. 17, 1917, VMGA.

9. Deering to Chalfin, Dec. 31, 1918, VMGA.

10. Chalfin to Deering, Dec. 19, 1918, VMGA. A week later he made the remarks qualifying his position as a designer, not a horticulturalist, in a follow-up letter of Dec. 28, 1918, VMGA.

11. See discussion of Pinsent's neo-vernacular work in essays by Benedetta Origo and Laurie Olin in Benedetta Origo et al., *La Foce: A Garden and Landscape in Tuscany*, particularly 204–10, 246–47.

12. Chalfin to Koch, Feb. 9, 1920, VMGA.

13. Signed "Superintendent" during McLean's last month, Dec. 3, 1918, VMGA.

14. I. N. Court Diary, March 5, 1922, VMGA.

15. Letter from McLean (?) to Deering, Dec. 5, 1918, VMGA.

16. Chalfin to Deering, Jan. 21, 1916, VMGA.

17. Chalfin to Deering, Mar. 23, 1916, VMGA.

18. See Charles Moore's biography of Daniel Burnham, 1: 142, 187, 199; 2: 45. Other members of this group of businessmen were also involved with innovative design and architecture; for example, one of the other firms involved in the International Harvester Company merger was that of Warder, Bushnell & Glessner, one of whose principals, J. J. Glessner, had commissioned Olmsted's close friend H. H. Richardson to design a house for him in 1885, now considered a landmark in architectural history.

19. For a discussion of South Park in Chicago with the original plan of its water features and photographs and its successor plans for the Columbian Exposition and Jackson Park, see Beveridge and Rocheleau, *Frederick Law Olmsted*, 84–87.

20. Quoted in both Rybczynski, *A Clearing in the Distance*, 301, and in Sutton, ed., *Civilizing American Cities*, 164. Coincidentally it was James Deering, who had traveled extensively on family business to Latin and South America as well as Asia and Europe, and had seen such sites as Olmsted described, who was instrumental in having the United States take over the construction of the Panama Canal from the French.

21. Ranney, *Olmsted in Chicago*, 25–35.

22. Published originally in a limited edition in 1909, the Burnham and Bennett plan of Chicago was reprinted by Princeton Architectural Press in 1993. Plates XLIX, L, LI, LII, and pp. 50–60 illustrate this proposal.

23. Griswold and Weller, *Golden Age of American Gardens*, 254, 255.

24. Greenleaf was one of the founders of the American Society of Landscape Architects, serving as its president from 1923 to 1927. He was appointed to the Fine Arts Commission in Washington, D.C., succeeding Frederick Law Olmsted, Jr., and played a role in the execution of the Mall. In the period between 1900 and 1920 he was engaged in the design of at least thirty country estates in New York, Connecticut, and New Jersey, among the most prominent being the strikingly Italianate works of Frederick Vanderbilt's estate at Hyde Park and C. Ledyard Blair's residence, Blairsden, in Peapack, N.J. See Birnbaum and Karson, *Pioneers of American Landscape Design*, 146–49, for a brief discussion of his career and works.

25. Chalfin drawing G258, "Revised Development of [South Garden] New South Property," Aug. 8, 1920, revised and reissued Oct. 14, 1920, VMGA.

26. Deering to Chalfin, Jan. 22, 1919, VMGA.

27. Deering to Chalfin, Aug. 16, 1919, VMGA.

28. Deering telegram to Chalfin, Aug. 20, 1919, VMGA.

29. Deering to Chalfin, Aug. 22, 1919, VMGA.

30. Chalfin to Deering, Nov. 24, 1919, VMGA.

31. Deering to Chalfin, Dec. 5, 1919, and Chalfin response to Deering, Dec. 11, 1919, VMGA.

32. Chalfin to Deering, Dec. 11, 1920, VMGA.

33. Chalfin, typed manuscript guide, 1934, p. 26, VMGA.

34. Construction Drawing G285, "Revised Development of [South Garden] New South Property," Aug. 24, 1920, revised Oct. 14, 1920, VMGA.

CHAPTER 10. DISASTER AND ENCORE

1. With the exception of a few drawings in the Vizcaya Archive most of the information documenting this period of work by Chalfin known to exist at this moment resides with the collection of papers of Robert Tyler Davis, the first director of Vizcaya as a public museum, and are located in the Smithsonian Institution Archives in Washington D.C.

2. This is a 28-page typed manuscript now in VMGA.

3. This undated drawing now in the Vizcaya Archive was clearly done by Chalfin on his 1934 visit. A text describing it in detail, now with the Robert Tyler Davis Papers Smithsonian Institution Archives, is dated June 1934.

4. Drawing GR85, and photographs in vols. 12, 23, 24, 26, 1922–1953, VMGA.

5. Undated ozalid paper print annotated by Chalfin, unquestionably described in letter to McCormick, VMGA.

6. Chalfin to McCormick, Feb. 4, 1935, DPSA.

7. See p. 232 for Chalfin's situation at this time and importance of this work.

8. Chalfin to McCormick, March 7, 1936, DPSA. Having got a 30 percent discount off the retail price he then lists bougainvillea, decorative lemons, viburnums, gardenias, carissa, crinum lilies, Dutch irises, climbing roses, strelitzia, euphorbia, azaleas, and tecoma.

9. Chalfin to McCormick from Port Chester, New York, pp. 10–11 of letter May 2, 1936, DPSA.

10. Chalfin to McCormick from Miami, Jan. 23, 1937, DPSA.

11. Ibid.

CHAPTER 11. SARGENT'S INTERLUDE

1. Sargent letter to Thomas Fox, Mar. 11, 1917, now in Boston Atheneum, Herdrich and Weinberg, *American Drawings and Water-colors*, 351.

2. From an interview by Hale, "The Sargent I Knew," 569, quoted in both Olson, *John Singer Sargent, His Portrait*, 254, and Ormond, *John Singer Sargent*, 98.

3. Cited in Herdrich and Weinberg, *American Drawings and Watercolors*, 276, and fn. p. 22, p. 277; although they misattribute this letter to 1918.

4. Deering letter to Chalfin, Mar. 23, 1917, VMGA.

5. Sargent letter to Mary Hunter, April 21, 1917, Olson, *John Singer Sargent, His Portrait*, 254, fn p. 296.

6. Chalfin letter to Deering, May 14, 1917, VMGA.

7. Deering letter to Chalfin, May 12, 1917, VMGA.

8. Maher, *Twilight*, 211.

AFTERMATH

1. "The Gardens of Vizcaya," *Vogue*, July 1917: 36–37; "Villa Vizcaya, Miami, Florida," *Harper's Bazaar*, July 1917: 40–43; "'Vizcaya,' the Villa and Grounds: A House at Miami, Florida," *Architectural Review* 5, no. 7 (July 1917): 121–67.

2. Quoted by Maher, *Twilight*, 204.

3. Paul Chalfin to H. P. Bingham, July 16, 1917. VMGA.

4. Aline B. Louchheim, "Biscayne Bay's New Show Place," *New York Times*, March 15, 1953, X8.

5. Robert A. M. Stern et al., *New York 1930*, 427.

6. *New York Times*, March 1, 1919.

7. Paul Chalfin to Louis A. Koons, Jr., April 5, 1920. VMGA.

8. James F. Donnelly et al., *Miami Architecture: A Guide to the Metropolitan Area* (Miami: unpublished discussion draft, 2003).

9. Alfred A. Gardner, unpublished reminiscences of Paul Chalfin, Oct. 7, 1971. VMGA.

10. Stern et al., *New York 1930*, 297.

11. Gordon Haas Frey, "F. Burrall Hoffman, Jr.: The Architectural Commissions, 1908–1929," table of contents.

12. Brendan Gill, "F. Burrall Hoffman, Jr.," *Architectural Digest* 50, no. 7 (July 1993): 40.

13. Quoted in Frey, "F. Burrall Hoffman, Jr.," 323.

14. Ibid., 417.

15. Ibid., 42.

16. Michael Henry Adams, "House Proud," *New York Times*, May 5, 1994, C10.

17. Diego Suarez, obituary, *New York Times*, Sept. 15, 1974.

18. Mrs. Roberto Suarez, obituary, *New York Times*, Feb. 3, 1949.

19. Betsy Head Playground Recreation Center, Brooklyn, Nov. 1946. Edward Durrell Stone Archive, University of Arkansas.

20. Hewitt, *The Architect and the American Country House*, 231, 282.

21. See R. T. Schnadelbach's *Ferruccio Vitale*; Charles A. Birnbaum and Robin Karson, *Pioneers of American Landscape Design*, 192–95, 417–20; Griswold and Weller, *The Golden Age of American Gardens*.

22. Diana Balmori et al., *Beatrix Farrand's American Landscapes*; Judith B. Tankard, *The Gardens of Ellen Biddle Shipman*.

23. James E. Deering to Paul Chalfin, Jan. 7, 1919. VMGA.

24. Marion Davies, *The Times We Had*, 10.

25. Ibid., 14.

26. James E. Deering to Elbert H. Gary, March 8, 1920. Elbert H. Gary Papers, Northwestern University Archive, Evanston, Ill.

27. Paul Chalfin interview with Robert Tyler Davis, May 1956. Robert Tyler Davis Papers, RU 7439, Box 4, Folder 20, Smithsonian Institution Archives.

28. Ibid.

29. "Our City Now a Libretto," *Washington Post*, Feb. 8, 1920, 44.

30. James E. Deering to Elbert H. Gary, July 21, 1925. Elbert H. Gary Papers, Northwestern University Archive, Evanston, Ill.

31. "James Deering Dies at Sea on Way Home," *New York Times*, Sept. 22, 1925, 25.

32. Bob Morris, "The Gay Party Planet Moves into a Wider Orbit," *New York Times*, Dec. 8, 1996, I: 65.

33. Henry James, *Portraits of Places*, 61.

BIBLIOGRAPHY

Ackerman, James S. *The Villa: Form and Ideology of Country Houses.* Princeton, N.J.: Princeton University Press, 1990.

Acton, Harold. *Great Houses of Italy: The Tuscan Villas.* New York: Viking, 1973.

———. *Memoirs of an Aesthete.* London: Methuen, 1948.

American Traditions in Watercolor: The Worcester Art Museum Collection. Ed. Susan E. Strickler. New York: Abbeville Press, 1987.

An Arcadian Landscape, the California Gardens of A. E. Hanson, 1920–1932. Ed. A. E. Hanson, David Gebhard, and Sheila Lynds. Los Angeles: Hennessey & Ingalls, 1985.

Aslet, Clive. *The American Country House.* New Haven, Conn.: Yale University Press, 1990.

Baedeker, Karl. *The United States,* 4th rev. ed. New York: Scribner's, 1909.

Balmori, Diana, et al. *Beatrix Farrand's American Landscapes: Her Gardens and Landscapes.* Sagaponack, N.Y.: Sagaponack Press, 1985.

Bayley, John B. "The Villa Vizcaya." *Classical America* 3 (1973): 67–93.

Berenson, Bernard. *The Venetian Painters of the Renaissance: With an Index to Their Works.* New York: G. P. Putnam's Sons, 1897.

Beveridge, Charles E., and Robert Rocheleau. *Frederick Law Olmsted: Designing the American Landscape.* New York: Rizzoli, 1999.

Binney, Marcus. "Villa Vizcaya, Florida–I, II." *Country Life* (Jan. 10 and 17, 1980).

Birnbaum, Charles A., and Robin Karson. *Pioneers of American Landscape Design.* New York: McGraw-Hill, 2000.

Braden, Susan R. *The Architecture of Leisure: The Florida Resort Hotels of Henry Flagler and Henry Plant.* Gainesville: University Press of Florida, 2002.

Burnham, Daniel H., and Edward H. Bennett. *Plan of Chicago.* Ed. Charles Moore. Chicago: Commercial Club, 1909; reprint, New York: Princeton Architectural Press, 1993.

Candamo, Luis G. de. "Vizcaya: el sueno de un millonario Americano en Miami." *T.G. Tapicerias Gancedo* 59 (1989): 36–41.

Carter, Morris. *Isabella Stewart Gardner and Fenway Court.* Boston: Houghton Mifflin, 1925.

Ceo, Rocco J., and Joanna Lombard. *Historic Landscapes of South Florida.* Miami: Deering Foundation and University of Miami School of Architecture, 2001.

Cerwinske, Laura. "A Breezy Spectrum: A Florida Garden." *Garden Design* 6. no. 1 (1987): 76–81.

———. "Vizcaya: Regaling the Renaissance in a Private Eden." *Southern Accents* 9, no. 6 (Nov.–Dec. 1986): 96–103.

Chalfin, Paul. "The Decorations of the Avenue of Victory." *Architecture* 39 (1919): 89–91.

"Coconut Grove Rococo." *Art & Antiques* 7 (Oct. 1990): 16–121.

Cox, Kenyon. *The Classic Point of View*. New York: Charles Scribner's Sons, 1911; reprint, New York: W. W. Norton, 1980.

Curl, Donald W. *Mizner's Florida: American Resort Architecture*. New York: Architectural History Foundation, 1984.

Dami, Luigi. *The Italian Garden*. Trans. L. Scapoli. Milan: Casa Editrice d'Arte Bestetti & Tuumminelli, 1925.

Davidson, Rebecca Warren. "Past and Present: Villa Vizcaya and the 'Italian Garden' in the United States." *Journal of Garden History* 12, no. 1 (Jan.–March 1992): 1–28.

Davies, Marion. *The Times We Had: Life with William Randolph Hearst*. Indianapolis: Bobbs-Merrill, 1975.

Desmond, Harry W., and Herbert Croly. *Stately Homes in America: From Colonial Times to the Present Day*. New York: D. Appleton and Company, 1903.

Dunlop, Beth. "Inventing Antiquity: The Art and Craft of Mediterranean Revival Architecture." Florida Theme Issue, *Journal of the Decorative and Propaganda Arts, 1875–1945*, 23 (1998): 190–207.

———. *Florida's Vanishing Architecture*. Englewood, Fla.: Pineapple Press, 1987.

Elliott, Brent. *The Country House Garden: From the Archives of Country Life, 1879–1939*. London: Reed International Books, 1995.

Fairchild, David. *The World Was My Garden: Travels of a Plant Explorer*. New York: Charles Scribner's Sons, 1938; reprint, Miami: Banyan Books, 1982.

Fitch, James Marston. *American Building: The Historical Forces That Shaped It*. New York: Schocken Books, 1973.

Frey, Gordon Haas. "F. Burrall Hoffman, Jr.: The Architectural Commissions, 1908–1929." Master of Arts thesis. New York: SUNY Fashion Institute of Technology, May 1993.

Gaby, Donald C. *The Miami River and Its Tributaries*. Miami: Historical Association of Southern Florida, 1993.

"The Gardens of Vizcaya." *Vogue* (July 1917): 36–37.

Garraty, John A. *Right-Hand Man: The Life of John A. Garraty*. New York: Harper & Brothers, 1957.

Gill, Brendan. "F. Burrall Hoffman, Jr." *Architectural Digest* 50, no. 7 (July 1993).

Griswold, Mac, and Eleanor Weller. *The Golden Age of American Gardens: Proud Owners, Private Estates, 1890–1940*. New York: Harry N. Abrams, 1991.

Gritelli, Gianfranco. *Juvarra: L'Architettura*, 2 vols. Modena: Franco Cosimo Panini, 1992.

Guide to Florida's Historic Architecture. Gainesville: University of Florida Press, 1989.

Hale, Mary. "The Sargent I Knew." *World Today* 50 (Nov. 1927): 569.

Harakas, Margo. "Vizcaya Architect at 97." *Palm Beach Post-Times* (Jan. 21, 1979).

Harbeson, John F. *The Study of Architectural Design: With Special Reference to the Program of the Beaux-Arts Institute of Design*. New York: Pencil Points Press, 1927.

Harwood, Kathryn Chapman. *The Lives of Vizcaya: Annals of a Great House*. Miami: Banyan Books, 1985.

Hegemann, Werner, and Elbert Peets. *The American Vitruvius: An Architects' Handbook of Civic Art*. New York: Architectural Book Publishing Co., 1922; reprint, New York: Princeton Architectural Press, 1988.

Herdrich, Stephanie L., and H. Barbara Weinberg. *American Drawings and Watercolors in the Metropolitan Museum of Art: John Singer Sargent*. New Haven, Conn.: Yale University Press, 2000.

Hewitt, Mark Alan. *The Architect and the American Country House, 1890–1940*. New Haven, Conn.: Yale University Press, 1990.

"Historic Houses: Florida Palazzo 'Vizcaya,' a Dream Realized." *Architectural Digest* 33, no. 3 (Nov.–Dec. 1976): 130–39.

Hitchcock, Henry-Russell. *Boston Architecture, 1637–1954*. New York: Reinhold, 1954.

Hoopes, Donelson F. *Sargent Watercolors*. New York: Watson-Guptill, 1970.

Hughes, Robert. *American Visions: The Epic History of Art in America*. New York: Knopf, 1997.

"J. Clinton Mackenzie Obituary." *Architectural Forum* 72 (May 1940): 68.

James, Henry. *Henry James Letters: Volume IV, 1893–1916*. ed. Leon Edel. Cambridge, Mass.: Belknap Press of Harvard University Press, 1984.

———. *The American Scene*. Bloomington: Indiana University Press, 1968.

———. *Portraits of Places*. Boston: Houghton Mifflin, 1883.

Karson, Robin. *The Muses of Gwinn: Art and Nature in a Garden Designed by Warren H. Manning, Charles A. Platt and Ellen Biddle Shipman*. Sagaponack, N.Y.: Sagapress, 1995.

Lazzaro, Claudia. *The Italian Renaissance Garden*. New Haven, Conn.: Yale University Press, 1990.

The Letters of Bernard Berenson and Isabella Stewart Gardner, 1887–1924. Ed. Rollin Van N. Hadley. Boston: Northeastern University Press, 1987.

Levine, Neil. *The Architecture of Frank Lloyd Wright*. Princeton, N.J.: Princeton University Press, 1996.

Long Island Country Houses and Their Architects, 1860–1940. Ed. Robert Mackay et al. New York: W. W. Norton, 1997.

Louchheim, Aline B. "Biscayne Bay's New Showplace." *New York Times* (March 15, 1953).

McCauley, Elizabeth Anne, et al. *Gondola Days: Isabella Stewart Gardner and the Palazzo Barbaro Circle*. Boston: Isabella Stewart Gardner Museum, 2004.

McCormick, Cyrus. *The Century of the Reaper*. Boston: Houghton Mifflin, 1931.

McCormick, Kathleen. "Vizcaya Verdant: Tropical Vegetation Complements a Celebrated Venetian Villa on Biscayne Bay." *Historic Preservation* 43, no. 1 (Jan.–Feb. 1991): 60–61.

McCullough, David. *The Path Between the Seas: The Creation of the Panama Canal, 1870–1914*. New York: Simon & Schuster, 1977.

McPhee, John. *Annals of the Former World*. New York: Farrar, Straus and Giroux, 1998.

Magaziner, H. J. *The Golden Age of Ironwork*. Ocean Pines, Md.: SkipJack Press, 2000.

Maher, James T. *The Twilight of Splendor: Chronicles of the Age of American Palaces*. Boston: Little, Brown, 1975.

Marmoz, C. "The Building of the École des Beaux-Arts." In *The Beaux-Arts and Nineteenth-Century French Architecture*, ed. Robin Middleton. Cambridge, Mass.: MIT Press, 1982.

Marsh, Barbara. *A Corporate Tragedy: The Agony of International Harvester Company*. Garden City, N.Y.: Doubleday, 1985.

Matthews, Janet Snyder. *Historical Documentation: The Charles Deering Estate at Cutler*. Unpublished report for Metro-Dade County Parks and Recreation Department, May 1992.

Mazzotti, Giuseppe. *Ville Venete*. Treviso: Canova, 2000.

———. *Palladio and Other Venetian Villas*. Trans. Evermont de Scarpis Andreani. Rome: Carlo Bestetti, 1966.

Mignani, Daniela. *The Medicean Villas by Giusto Utens*. Trans. Stephanie Johnson. Florence: Arnaud, 1991.

Moore, Charles. *Daniel H. Burnham, Architect, Planner of Cities*, 2 vols. Boston: Houghton Mifflin, 1921.

Mumford, Lewis. *The Golden Day: A Study in American Experience and Culture*. New York: Boni and Liveright, 1926.

Olson, Stanley. *John Singer Sargent: His Portrait*. New York: St. Martin's Press, 1986.

Origo, Benedetta, et al. *La Foce: A Garden and Landscape in Tuscany.* Philadelphia: University of Pennsylvania Press, 2001.

Ormond, Richard. *John Singer Sargent, Paintings, Drawings, Watercolors.* New York: Harper & Row, 1970.

Parsons, Samuel. "Italian Villas: Their Place and Function in Landscape Architecture." *American Architect* 108 (1915): 49–59.

Patricios, Nicholas. *Building Marvelous Miami.* Gainesville: University of Florida Press, 1994.

Patterson, Augusta Owen. *American Homes Today, Their Architectural Style, Their Environment, Their Characteristics.* New York: Macmillan, 1924.

Patterson, William. "A Florida Echo of the Glory of Old Venice." *Town and Country* (July 20, 1917): 3–30.

"Paul Chalfin's 'The Blue Dog,' Is an Unique American House-Boat." *Vanity Fair* 8, no. 5 (July 1917): 56.

Pennoyer, Peter, and Anne Ealker. *The Architecture of Delano & Aldrich.* New York: W. W. Norton, 2003.

Plante, David. "A Last Fantasy in Florence." *New Yorker* (July 10, 1995): 41–55.

Platt, Charles A. *Italian Gardens.* New York: Harper, 1894; reprint, Portland, Ore.: Sagapress/Timber Press, 1993.

Portrait of an Era in Landscape Architecture: The Photographs of Mattie Edwards Hewitt. New York: Wave Hill, 1983.

Pray, James Sturgess. "The Italian Garden." *American Architect and Building News* 67 (1900): 83–85.

Praz, Mario. *The House of Life.* Trans. Angus Davidson. New York: Oxford University Press, 1964.

Ranney, Victoria Post. *Olmsted in Chicago.* Chicago: R. R. Donnelly & Sons, 1972.

"The Renaissance Villa of Italy Developed into a Complete Residential Type for Use in America." *Architectural Record* 31, no. 3 (March 1912): 200–221.

Ricci, Corrado. *Baroque Architecture and Sculpture in Italy.* New York: E. P. Dutton, 1912.

Rybczynski, Witold. *A Clearing in the Distance: Frederick Law Olmsted and America in the Nineteenth Century.* New York: Scribner, 1999.

Saarinen, Aline B. *The Proud Possessors: The Lives, Times and Tastes of Some Adventurous American Art Collectors.* New York: Random House, 1958.

Samuels, Ernest. *Bernard Berenson: The Making of a Connoisseur.* Cambridge, Mass.: Belknap Press of Harvard University, 1979.

Schnadelbach, R. T. *Ferruccio Vitale: Landscape Architect of the Country Place.* New York: Princeton Architectural Press, 2001.

Schultz, Patricia. "An American Idyll: The Restored Renaissance Garden at Villa La Pietra." *Garden Design* 6, no. 1 (Spring 1987): 46–55.

Scott, Geoffrey. *The Architecture of Humanism: A Study in the History of Taste.* New York: W. W. Norton, 1999.

Scott, Walter Dill, and Robert B. Harshe. *Charles Deering, 1851–1927: An Appreciation Together with His Memoirs of William Deering and James Deering.* Boston: privately published, 1929.

Shand-Tucci, Douglass. *The Art of Scandal: The Life and Times of Isabella Stewart Gardner.* New York: HarperCollins, 1997.

Shannon, Martha A. S. "The Isabella Stewart Gardner Museum, Fenway Court." *American Magazine of Art* 18, no. 4 (April 1927).

Shelford, Victor E. "The Communities of Southern Florida, Cuba, and the Shores of the Mainland." In *The Ecology of North America.* Urbana: University of Illinois Press, 1963, 474–94.

Sitwell, George. *On the Making of Gardens.* Introduction by Sir Osbert Sitwell. Foreword by John Dixon Hunt. Orig. pub. 1909; reprint, Boston: David R. Godine, 2003.

Stephens, Suzanne. "Florida Renaissance: Italianate Splendors Enrich a Villa in Naples." *Architectural Digest* 57, no. 10 (Oct. 2000): 284–88, 298.

Stern, Robert A. M., et al. *New York 1930: Architecture and Urbanism Between the Two World Wars.* New York: Rizzoli, 1987.

Stevens, Wallace. *Letters of Wallace Stevens.* New York: Knopf, 1981.

Sutton, S. B., ed. *Civilizing American Cities.* Cambridge, Mass.: MIT Press, 1971.

Tankard, Judith B. *The Gardens of Ellen Biddle Shipman.* Sagaponack, N.Y.: Sagapress, 1996.

Tucker, A. Richard. *La Pietra: Florence, a Family and a Villa.* Florence: Edizioni Olivas, 2002.

Van Zanten, David. "Le Système des Beaux-Arts." *Architectural Design* 48, nos. 11–12 (1978).

"A Venetian Palace in Miami/Decorations by Paul Chalfin." *Vogue* 50 (1917): 42–45.

"La villa Rezzonico a Bassano del Grappa." *Architettura cronache e storia* 2, no. 18 (April 1957): 893–99.

"Villa Vizcaya, Miami, Florida." *Harper's Bazaar* (July 1917): 40–43.

"Vizcaya: James Deering's Italian Villa in Miami." *Connoisseur* 155 (March 1964): 140–45.

"'Vizcaya,' the Villa and Grounds: A House at Miami, Florida." *Architectural Review* 5, no. 7 (July 1917): 120–67.

Weinhardt, Carl J. "Vizcaya, Miami, Florida." *Antiques* 121, no. 1 (Jan. 1982): 312–21.

Wharton, Edith. *Italian Villas and Their Gardens.* New York: Century Company, 1904; reprint, New York: Da Capo Press, 1988.

Wharton, Edith, and Ogden Codman, Jr. *The Decoration of Houses.* New York: Charles Scribner's Sons, 1897; reprint, New York: W. W. Norton, 1997.

"Whitehall: The Residence of H. M. Flagler, Palm Beach, Florida." *Architectural Record* 15, no. 4 (April 1904): 385–90.

William Deering: Born in Maine, 1826. Died in Florida, 1913. Chicago: privately printed, 1913.

Wolf, Reinhart, Peter Lauritzen, and Harold Acton. *Villas of the Veneto.* New York: Abrams, 1987.

de Wolfe, Elsie. *After All.* London: William Heinemann, 1935.

———. *The House in Good Taste.* New York: Century Company, 1916.

Wolman, Paul. *Most Favored Nation: The Republican Revisionists and U.S. Tariff Policy, 1897–1912.* Chapel Hill: University of North Carolina Press, 1992.

Yellin, Samuel. "Iron in Art." *Encyclopedia Britannica,* 14th ed. 1940, vol. 12.

INDEX

ACKNOWLEDGMENTS

We would like to thank a number of people associated with Vizcaya Museum and Gardens for their help during the researching and writing of this book. Richard Farwell, previous executive director of Vizcaya, and Joel Hoffman, the current executive director, were unfailingly helpful and extended every courtesy during our several visits. Laurie Ossman, deputy director for collections and curatorial affairs, reviewed the manuscript with a penetrating eye. Our general thanks to the Vizcaya staff, especially to Remko Jansonius, Collections and Archives Manager, and Lea Nickless Verrechia. Doris Littlefield, a long-time curator at Vizcaya, kindly shared her recollections. Our appreciation, too, to Max Blumberg and The Vizcayans, for their most generous support at several critical junctures during the writing and production of this book. We are greatly indebted to the indefatigable Lynn M. Summers, who discovered important research materials, provided archival assistance, and arranged an unforgettable evening sail on Biscayne Bay. Steven Brooke patiently listened to our requests and created beautiful photographs.

Brooks McCormick, James Deering's grand-nephew, and Barbara Danielson, his great-grand-niece, were generous with their time, and cast an interesting light on family life at Vizcaya. Thanks also to the Deering heirs for allowing us to reproduce the Sargent watercolors of Vizcaya, and the Zorn portrait of James Deering, which have not been previously published in color. Lindley Hoffman provided useful reminiscences of his uncle. Our appreciation to James T. Maher, for sharing his thoughts about Hoffman and Chalfin, and for his pioneering research into Vizcaya. Thanks also to John Blatteau, Mark Alan Hewitt, Joanna Lombard, and Elizabeth Plater-Zyberk, for their architectural advice and assistance.

Our gratitude to the following librarians, archivists, and curators, who provided assistance during our research: Amy Berman and Carissa Kowalski, Art Institute of Chicago; Michelle Boxley, Librarian, AIA Library, Washington, D.C.; Joanna Catron, Curator, Belmont, The Gari Melchers Estate & Memorial Gallery, Fredericksburg, Virginia; Alan Chong, Curator of the Collection, Isabella Stewart Gardner Museum, Boston; Daniel Hartwig, Archival Assistant, McCormick IH Collection, Wisconsin Historical Society, Madison, Wisconsin; Andrea L. Kuchembuck, Collections Reference Assistant, Canadian Centre for Architecture; Ted O'Reilly, Manuscript Department, Library, New-York Historical Society; Janet Parks, Curator of Drawings & Archives, Avery Architectural & Fine Arts Library, New York City; John D.

Stinson, Manuscripts Specialist, Manuscripts and Archives Division, The New York Public Library; Mike M. Thornton, Art & Architecture Department, The New York Public Library; Annie Tully, the Chicago Humanities Festival; Jordan Walker, Research Assistant, Chicago Historical Society; N. Adam Watson, archivist, Florida State Archives; Wim DeWit, Special Collections & Curator of Architectural Drawings, Getty Center.

Julia Moore Converse originally suggested that we should guide a group of Members of the Academy of the University of Pennsylvania through Vizcaya in March 2002, which began our relationship with this remarkable place. Our friend, John Dixon Hunt, conceived this book as part of the University of Pennsylvania Press landscape architecture series. His erudite editorial direction and advice were greatly appreciated. Our colleague, Frank Matero, shared information about the conservation survey of the Vizcaya gardens. Our thanks to Jo Joslyn and Noreen O'Connor-Abel, our editors at the Press, and to Andrew Wylie, our agent. Thanks to Jen Mui for drawing the map of the Vizcaya estate. Finally, our appreciation to our capable research assistants, Acalya Kiyak, Fernando Moreira, and Anne Lutun.